# Women and Revolution in Nicaragua

## Edited by Helen Collinson

Lucinda Broadbent, Helen Collinson, Daphne Davies,
Elaine Ginsburg, Clare Nuttall, Jean Somers

**Zed Books Ltd**
London and New Jersey

*Women and Revolution in Nicaragua* was first published by
Zed Books Ltd, 57 Caledonian Road, London N1 9BU, UK, and
171 First Avenue, Atlantic Highlands, New Jersery 07716, USA,
in 1990

Copyright © Lucinda Broadbent, Helen Collinson, Daphne
Davies, Elaine Ginsburg, Clare Nuttall, Jean Somers, 1990.
Editorial copyright © Helen Collinson, 1990.

Cover designed by Sophie Buchet.
Cover photograph by Jenny Matthews/Format
Typeset by CentraCet, Cambridge.
Printed and bound in the United Kingdom
by Biddles Ltd, Guildford and King's Lynn.

**British Library Cataloguing in Publication Data**

Women and revolution in Nicaragua.
 1. Nicaragua. Women. Social conditions
 I. Collinson, Helen II. Broadbent, Lucinda
 305.42097285

 ISBN 0-86232-934-5
 ISBN 0-86232-935-3 pbk

**US CIP is available from the Library of Congress**

# Contents

# Acknowledgements

The authors wish to thank: Maria Boniface, Amalia Chamorro, Christian Aid, Ros Cooper, Annabel Crowe, Jane Dibblin, Heliette Ehlers, Carole Grimshaw, Hermione Harris, Frances Hollis, Stella Lewis, Fiona Macintosh, Jenny Matthews, Maxine Molyneux, Rosario Mora, Nicaragua Health Fund, NSC Womens Network, Oxfam (Scotland), Scottish Medical Aid to Nicaragua, Rachel Sieder, Mary Stead, Linzi Stonebridge, Rachel Stringfellow, Maggie Walker, Jenny Watson, Beth Woroniuk, Helen Yuill, and Sharon and Melba in Nicaragua.

Special thanks go to Veronica Campanile and Stephanie Williamson.

# Glossary

## Spanish Terms

| | |
|---|---|
| *barrio* | urban district, usually working class |
| *brigadista* | participant in popular 'brigades' for health, literacy, coffee-picking etc. |
| *cabildo* | open meeting |
| *de cara al pueblo* | 'Face the People' meeting |
| *campesina/o* | peasant, worker on land which s/he owns or rents, either individually or as part of a co-operative |
| *compañera/o* | comrade, friend, partner |
| *contra* | US-backed counter-revolutionary forces |
| *costeños* | popular name for people living on Nicaragua's Atlantic Coast |
| *fresco* | cold drink |
| *manzana* | land measure — 2.5 acres |
| *mercado* | market |
| *mestizo* | term used to describe people of 'mixed' Spanish/Indian descent |
| *mujer* | woman |
| *obrero/a agricola* | waged agricultural worker employed on a farm |
| *partera* | midwife; often means traditional midwife in Nicaragua |
| *Proclama* | Proclamation by the FSLN on Women and the Sandinista Revolution published on 8th March 1987 |
| *promotora* | instigator |
| *Sandinista* | supporter of the FSLN |
| *Somocista* | supporter of Somoza |
| *tortilla* | pancake made with corn flour and water |

# Organisations

| | |
|---|---|
| AMNLAE | – *Asociación de Mujeres Nicaragüenses 'Luisa Amanda Espinosa'* <br> Association of Nicaraguan Women 'Luisa Amanda Espinosa' |
| AMPRONAC | – *Asociación de Mujeres Ante la Problemática Nacional* <br> Association of Women Confronting the National Problem |
| ANDEN | – *Asociación Nacional de Educadores Nicaragüenses* <br> National Association of Nicaraguan Teachers |
| ATC | – *Asociación de Trabajadores del Campo* <br> Rural Workers Association |
| CAS | – *Cooperativa Agrícola Sandinista* <br> Sandinista Agricultural Cooperative |
| CCS | – *Cooperativa de Crédito y Servicios* <br> Credit and Service Cooperative |
| CDI | – *Centro de Desarrollo Infantil* <br> Child Development Centre |
| CDS | – *Comité de Defensa Sandinista* <br> Sandinista Defence Committee |
| CEB | – *Comunidad Eclesial de Base* <br> Basic Christian Community |
| CEP | – *Colectivo de Educación Popular* <br> People's Education Collective |
| CEPAD | – *Centro Ecuménico para el Desarrollo* <br> Ecumenical Centre for Development |
| CIDCA | – *Centro de Investigaciones y Documentación de la Costa Atlántica* <br> Atlantic Coast Documentation and Research Centre |
| CIERA | – *Centro de Investigación y Estudios de la Reforma Agraria* <br> Centre for Research and Study of Agrarian Reform |
| CIIR | – *Catholic Institute for International Relations (UK)* |
| CONAPRO | – *Confederación Nacional de Profesionales* <br> National Confederation of Professionals |
| CST | – *Central Sandinista de Trabajadores* <br> Sandinista Workers' Federation |
| EPS | – *Ejército Popular Sandinista* <br> Sandinista People's Army |
| FDN | – *Fuerzas Democráticas Nicaragüenses* <br> Nicaraguan Democratic Forces |
| FETSALUD | – *Federación de Trabajadores de Salud* <br> Health Workers' Federation |
| FSLN | – *Frente Sandinista de Liberación Nacional* <br> Sandinista National Liberation Front |

INIES      – *Instituto Nicaragüense de Investigaciones Económi-cas y Sociales*
Nicaraguan Institute of Economic and Social Research

INIM      – *Instituto Nicaragüense de Investigaciones de la Mujer*
Nicaraguan Institute of Research on Women

JS      – *Juventud Sandinista*
Sandinista Youth

MIDINRA      – *Ministerio de Desarrollo Agropecuario y Reforma Agraria*
Ministry of Agricultural Development and Agrarian Reform

MINSA      – *Ministerio de Salud*
Health Ministry

MINT      – *Ministerio del Interior*
Ministry of the Interior

MIREN      – *Mujeres Internacionalistas Residentes en Nicaragua*
Internationalist Women Living in Nicaragua

MISATAN      – *Organisation of Miskitos of Nicaragua*

MISURA      – *Organisation of Miskitos, Sumus & Ramas*

MISURASATA      – *Organisation of United Sandinista Miskitos, Sumus & Ramas*

NSC      – *Nicaragua Solidarity Campaign (UK)*

OGM      – *Oficina Gubernamental de la Mujer*
Women's Governmental Office

SMP      – *Servicio Militar Patriótico*
Patriotic Military Service

SSTV      – *Sistema Sandinista de Televisión*
Sandinista Television Service

UNAG      – *Unión Nacional de Agricultores y Ganaderos*
National Union of Agricultural and Livestock Producers

UNO      – *Unión Nacional de Oposición*
National Opposition Union

# Authors' Note

Since our study was written, the Sandinista Front for National Liberation has been defeated by the US-backed UNO coalition[1] in a general
election which international observers widely proclaimed to be free and
democratic. The news came as a great shock to all those who had
worked with the FSLN since 1979 to bring about change in Nicaragua.
US military and economic destabilization had finally driven some (but
not all) Nicaraguans to cast a 'hunger vote' which would lift the US
trade embargo and bring an end to the Contra war. Nicaragua is likely
to revert to becoming a vassal of Washington and many of the positive
changes of the past ten years will be reversed. But the authors of this
study do not believe that the developments we have recorded in the
following pages can be washed away by one general election. We
predict that many of the processes which have altered women's lives so
fundamentally over the past ten years will survive this setback and that
Nicaraguan women will continue to find new forms for their struggle.
As a result of their participation in the revolution's mass organizations
and in paid employment and literacy programmes, most Nicaraguan
women have acquired much independence and self-confidence over the
past ten years. Not only in society at large, but also in their personal
relationships with men, for these women there is no going back to the
invisibility and servitude of the Somoza era.

[1] UNO is a coalition of 14 parties, the majority of which are right-wing. The coalition is
backed by the US administration and received from the US $6m in election campaign
funds.

La Sorpresa state coffee farm in Matagalpa soon after a contra attack.

A woman and her children collect water in Managua. The city centre was destroyed by an earthquake in 1972. (Jenny Matthews)

Martina Rodriguez (at the wheel) and Victoria Torres driving a tractor in Jalapa, 1984. They were replacing men mobilized in the war.

# 1. Introduction

## Frontiers

> I've learnt something from this struggle — still not enough I should add — but I feel my eyes are opening. I'm learning that this revolution is what we make it . . . and the serious problems we face, they get harder every day. . . . Some changes came easy, some with blood, sweat and tears, but I've found freedom working for this revolution and no one can take that away. Once I never dared raise my hand and question what was going on. Now we question everything.[1]

With the 1979 victory of the Sandinista revolution, the door was opened to a completely new social order in Nicaragua, and one in which the Sandinista Front for National Liberation (FSLN) promised to make women's emancipation a major feature. But years of foreign domination and tyrannical rule by the Somoza family have left their mark and change has not come overnight. Indeed, it has often been a painful process, punctuated by the continuing military aggression and economic hardship of the US-backed Contra war and by reactionary attitudes towards women's role in society lingering on from the Somoza era, attitudes that are still held by large sectors of the population. The road has been rough but ten years on there is no turning back; Nicaraguan women now assert their needs and demands more confidently than ever before.

Throughout Central America, women are actively mobilizing for their rights; the crucial difference in Nicaragua is that the new government has a commitment to support them. The challenges they face are similar to those faced by each of the neighbouring republics — but only in Nicaragua have concrete opportunities for change arisen.

In this account of Nicaraguan women's lives, we are looking at frontiers. Not so much the war-torn frontier between Nicaragua and Honduras where the US-funded counter-revolutionary military camps face *campesino* communities; but the more intimate frontier between men and women inside Nicaragua and between women's specific demands and those of the nation's fight for survival. We look at the struggle for women's liberation in the midst of a revolutionary process under savage attack from the US administration and at the extent of women's participation in this process. We also examine the impact of the revolution on women's daily lives.

It would be easy for women in other countries to misunderstand or misinterpret the directions Nicaraguan women have chosen. Accurate news about events in Nicaragua is not easy to come by. In the murky atmosphere of claims and counter-claims, and with the poverty of news coverage of Latin America, the truth about women is always the hardest to dig out. For this reason we have tried to pull together the scattered information on women's place in the Nicaraguan revolution.

We are aware that Nicaraguan women, like women elsewhere, are not an undifferentiated category. Through their distinct — and some-times conflicting — interests and experiences, women have formed a variety of allegiances and identities. For this reason we have eschewed generalization as much as possible. Apart from class differences, the contrast in experience between women in the countryside and women in the towns, older and younger women, and women of different ethnic groups and cultural backgrounds (particularly the Atlantic/Pacific Coast divide, and within different ethnic groups on the Atlantic coast itself), are especially significant.

We are also aware that not all Nicaraguan women support the FSLN or indeed the revolution. Out of 85% of the population who took part in the last national elections in 1984, 67% voted for the FSLN, reflecting massive majority support for the Sandinista experiment but by no means unanimous approval. Inevitably, our study focuses on those women who are active in the revolutionary process, but we have attempted a much wider analysis of women's experience *in general* over the past ten years.

Thorny issues inevitably arise for a group of women based in Britain, when writing from a solidarity perspective about women who live in a country with a long history of foreign domination. As citizens of an imperialist power, are we in a position to comment on the actions of those fighting against imperialism? And is it really possible for Western women to interpret events in a culture so different from their own? These questions are not easily answered. But what became clear to us when writing this book was how much women (and men) in the West can learn from the experience of our sisters in this Central American country. The tactics they have adopted in order to raise their demands within the wider movement for social change, the opposition they have faced from some quarters of the revolution, the methods they have used to involve women from the most marginalized sections of society, the obstacles arising in their personal lives and the conflicts between motherhood and participation in the revolution — all these can bring new insights to women's struggles in the West.

Moreover, there is a dialogue in progress, an interchange of experiences, initiated by the Nicaraguan women's organizations themselves. They set great store by international solidarity with their revolution, and are keen to learn of the experiences of women in other countries.

As part of this interchange, we have attempted a 'warts and all' portrayal of the revolutionary process because we believe that solidarity can be truly effective only if it is founded on accurate information, rather than an unrealistic, idealized picture. This approach in no way diminishes the inspiration we have derived from learning about Nicaragua, inspiration that we sorely need as over the last ten years conditions in Britain have been in such sharp contrast. At times, understanding the Nicaraguan experience since 1979 is like turning our own experience inside out. They have won political power for the mass of the people yet often lack the resources to make it real, whereas our government with its huge resources is fast depriving us of many of our hard-won political gains.

## The historical context: invasion, insurrection, low-intensity warfare

Nicaragua's history of colonial domination began in the 16th century with the Spanish *conquistadores'* invasion of Central America. Under Spanish rule, vast tracts of land on the Pacific Coast were turned into plantations, for the maintenance of which the colonial authorities created a system of slavery. In common with other parts of Latin America, Spanish occupation was marked by ruthless exploitation of the local people, resulting in a large proportion of the indigenous population being wiped out. Today only 4% of modern Nicaraguans are pure-blooded Indians; three-quarters of the population are *'mestizo'* — of mixed Spanish and Indian blood. Nicaragua's Indians were renowned for their militancy and, throughout the Spanish colonial period, they remained intractable to colonial rule. Local revolts were commonplace throughout the 17th and 18th centuries. There is evidence to suggest that women took part in this resistance.[2] Legend has it, for example, that a group of Indian women, raped by Spanish colonists, killed themselves rather than bear children into slavery.

Spanish rule was confined to the Pacific Coast. From the early 17th to the late 19th century, the Atlantic Coast was subject to British domination (although never fully integrated into the British Empire) and remained separate from the rest of Nicaragua until 1894. With the eastern part of Honduras and what is now Belize, the British established the 'Mosquito Kingdom' ruled by kings chosen from the local Indian population. But there was no Spanish-style plantation system or colonial infrastructure on the Atlantic Coast as there was on the Pacific Coast.

With the break-up of the Spanish empire, Nicaragua achieved independence as a republic in 1821. Before long, however, a new imperialist power made itself felt. The first military expedition into Nicaragua from the USA took place as early as 1856 when the adventurer, William Walker, invaded the country, reinstated slavery, and was recognized as President by the US government. The local population ousted Walker within a couple of years, but US hunger for Nicaragua's natural riches had been awakened, and soon afterwards a string of US-based commercial companies moved in, amongst which fruit, mining, and timber concerns figured most prominently. In order to keep Nicaragua safe for US exploitation, and maintain dominance over what Washington liked to see as its 'backyard', the US brought in its Marine Corps, who occupied the country almost continuously from 1909 to 1934.

While the traditional parties of the Nicaraguan ruling classes accepted US control, one leading political figure — Augusto Cesar Sandino — refused to compromise on Nicaraguan sovereignty. 'The liberty and sovereignty of a people are not matters for discussion', he declared. 'They are to be defended with arms',[3] and he organized a peasant army to fight US occupation. Despite the use of aerial bombardment on a totally world-wide unprecedented scale, the Marines were unable to defeat Sandino's 'crazy little army', as the Americans called it. In 1934 they returned to the US, but not before they had established the National Guard: a sort of private army of Nicaraguans loyal to US interests, whose remit was to clean up Sandino's peasant army once and for all. At its head the Americans appointed their own puppet leader, Anastasio Somoza, whose first act was to murder Sandino, and then declare himself President and set up a corrupt oligarchic government that was to rule the country for nearly half a century in the interests of the Somoza family and their US allies. This regime came to an abrupt end in July 1979, when Anastasio's son and successor, Tacho, fled the country, having lost all control in the face of mass popular resistance. His last act before abandoning power was to bomb his own cities from planes supplied by the USA.

The fall of the Somoza dictatorship was the fruit of a long campaign by the FSLN, the national liberation organization founded in 1961 with the aim of reviving Sandino's bid for sovereignty free of US domination. The FSLN's efforts culminated in a massive popular insurrection, with women and men of all classes taking up arms against Somoza and his hated henchmen of the National Guard, at the cost of thousands of lives. On 19 July 1979, the Sandinistas marched triumphant into Managua, and began the programmes of social and political transformation that are explored in this book.

But the Nicaraguan people were not to be allowed to reconstruct their shattered country. An independent nation in Latin America successfully managing its own economy without foreign interference, was too great a threat for the incoming US Reagan Administration. The CIA was instructed to mount a secret war against the Sandinistas, using the tattered and discredited remnants of Somoza's National Guard.

The 'Contra' army operated mainly from military camps in neighbouring Honduras, mounting a destabilization campaign known as 'low intensity warfare'. The idea was to stifle the revolution's progress by concentrating attacks on 'soft' targets, such as schools, health posts and co-operative farms. This was combined with a well-orchestrated propaganda offensive and secret political interventions designed to strengthen artificially the civilian opposition; simultaneously, Nicaragua was to be squeezed dry economically. Moves to cut, illegally, Nicaragua's quota of sugar exports to the US were escalated to a full-scale trade embargo in 1985, which strangled Nicaragua's fragile and dependent economy.

Nicaragua has, therefore, been forced to fight desperately for its very existence. Precious human and material resources have been leached from essential social programmes to support the heavy defence costs. Nicaragua has been reduced to economic ruin, and many gains in the early years of the revolution have been reversed.

## The road to peace

Despite massive funding from the CIA and US Congress, the Contras were unable to overthrow the Sandinista revolution. By 1987, defeated militarily and diplomatically, the Contras' choice was limited to negotiating with the Sandinista government or resettling in the USA.

The effective defeat of the Contras was largely attributable to the Sandinistas' military mobilization within Nicaragua, but various neighbouring South and Central American countries also played their part in promoting peace, despite strong pressure from the US to isolate Nicaragua. Initially, a group of five countries (Mexico, Venezuela, Colombia, Panama, and Costa Rica) — the Contadora Group — later reinforced by the Contadora Support Group, consisting of most of the democracies in South America, attempted to devise a peace plan. This initiative floundered, owing to US opposition and divisions among the Central American countries. But it was a hopeful sign, a sort of second declaration of independence and autonomy, and a challenge to US hegemony in the area.

Real progress was only achieved when all five Central American presidents signed the Esquipulas Peace Accord in August 1987. Esquipulas established a timetable and a structure for an end to Contra aid, a cease-fire in countries where armed conflict was going on, a national dialogue within each country, and various measures to protect civil liberties and human rights. The Accord recognized that all conflicts in the region were contributing to destabilization, and not only the Contra war in Nicaragua.

The Sandinistas took immediate steps to comply with the agreement, declaring a unilateral cease-fire in a number of areas, lifting press and media censorship and appointing their arch-critic, Cardinal Obando y Bravo, as President of the National Reconciliation Commission. This represented a new stage in the search for peace rather than an end to the war; Contra attacks continued. Negotiations were then opened with the Contras, culminating in the signing of the Sapoa Accord between Contra leaders and government representatives in March 1988. This agreement covered: a 60-day truce; the concentration of Contras in specially designated zones; the release of most National Guard prisoners, and their incorporation into the country's political life.

Implementing the Esquipulas and Sapoa Accords has proved very difficult because of the US State Department's continued efforts to increase pressure on Nicaragua. Summits of the Central American Presidents were delayed pending the outcome of the US presidential election in November 1988, and again until the new administration was inaugurated, clearly demonstrating the limits of autonomous action in the region. In February 1989 the Presidents finally met and agreed to disband and relocate the Contras. In return, Nicaragua agreed to release almost all its National Guard prisoners. This summit also brought forward Nicaragua's second general election (the first was in 1984) to February 1990 and laid down certain conditions for the electoral process, such as lifting restrictions on foreign funding of election campaigns. While many concessions had to be made, ending the war was seen as vital to allow Nicaragua a chance to begin to recover from the destruction of its economy and infrastructure.

At the time of writing it remains to be seen whether Nicaragua will really be allowed to manage its own affairs in peace. Despite claims that the Contra war was over, in March 1989 the Contras received a new aid package from US Congress in the form of US $4.5 million a month until February 1990. This aid was supposed to be non-military and, to placate the more liberal-minded congressmen, it was agreed that Congress could halt payments if it could be proved that the Contras were still actively engaging in military action. Needless to say, Contra attacks have continued in Nicaragua (albeit more sporadically and on a smaller scale) but when evidence of these attacks has been brought to the attention of congressmen on Capitol Hill, the response has been almost nil. Meanwhile, political destabilization and the funding of right-wing opposition parties in the run-up to the elections in 1990 have been stepped up by the US. Finally, the economic blockade, arguably the US Administration's most effective weapon, is still solidly in place with ever more dire consequences for Nicaragua's survival. In this continuing climate of foreign domination, peace has yet to be established in Nicaragua.

Reading the pages that follow, it must never be forgotten that the advances made by Nicaraguan women take place against this grim backdrop of a tiny nation pitted against the wrath of the US, the world's most powerful country. In October 1988, Hurricane Joan hit Nica. gua's Atlantic Coast and swept across the country, leaving 187,000 homeless and incalculable damage in its wake; Bluefields, the major town on the Atlantic Coast, was flattened. With indomitable patience and endurance, Nicaraguans simply started to pick up the pieces that remained, and began again. A sense of their perseverance is captured by the Nicaraguan woman poet, Vidaluz Meneses:

> Pain has been our challenge
> and the future our hope.
> We build as though composing a poem:
> writing, erasing, and creating anew.[4]

Clearly if nothing else, Nicarguan women can teach us the values of resistance in adversity, of hope against hope.

## Notes

1. Alicia Andino, tobacco worker, quoted in Angel & Macintosh, 1987, p. 123.
2. See Black, 1981, p. 15.
3. Quoted by Chris Taylor in the *Big Red Diary*, Pluto Press, 1986.
4. Vidaluz Meneses, 'In the New Country' in Hopkinson (ed.), 1989, p. 134.

# 2. The Home Front: Family Life and Sexuality

## The Nicaraguan family

If the Western stereotype of the stable nuclear family consisting of husband, wife, and children was ever appropriate to sum up British home life, it is certainly far from the Nicaraguan reality. The family group in Nicargua, while the centre of most women's personal lives, is more like an extended web, much more fluid and variable than the British 'cornflake packet' ideal. In Nicaragua, not all women get married, but few remain childless. Many, especially in the countryside, start bearing children at fourteen or fifteen, and have a large number, often by different men. About half of all heads of family are women, bringing up their children without a male partner and with sole economic responsibility. When women go out to work, children are often cared for by relatives, or left to care for one another. A woman's relations with her sisters, brothers and mother (who frequently provides a crucial support system) are often more important than those with her male partner, who may provide no support.[1] As discussed in the chapter on urban women, the family unit is essential for economic survival, but the worsening economic crisis has put great strains on family ties.

The fact that the family might not feature any male head of household was reflected in Nicaragua's 1987 Constitution. In the draft version, the family was given the status of 'fundamental nucleus of society' and defined as a married or unmarried couple plus children. This led to protests from those women who felt that they and their children or other relatives also constituted families and were equally legitimate nuclei of society, even though they were not in a couple relationship with a man. In the final version of the constitution, this definition was withdrawn, with the result that nowhere is this 'fundamental nucleus' defined.

## Machismo

*Machismo*, which is deeply engrained in Nicaraguan society (particularly on the Pacific Coast), demands that, in order to prove his virility to other men, a man must father many children. Men therefore often expect 'their' women to bear many children, while they are free simply to abandon their family. This is what is meant by 'irresponsible paternity'. As Otilia Casco Cruz, a health worker in El Regadío farming community in northern Nicaragua, put it:

> Men have children with as many women as they can fool . . . But what's happened? Poor Mother ends up looking after all my sister's children, four of them. She could go mad. It's not right. It's her time to rest. A family should have more consideration for its elders.[2]

The lack of a stable monogamous family life can be partly explained by the legacy of a seasonal migrant labour system which was exploited in the past by Somocista landowners to maintain a cash crop economy. In the words of psychologist Vilma Castillo:

> Many agricultural jobs are seasonal . . . men moved around, spent 4 months in one place, got a woman pregnant, then moved on somewhere else and got another woman pregnant . . . Men never took responsibility for their actions.[3]

This irresponsible attitude was not only a rural phenomenon; landless agricultural labourers also usually drifted to the town in the 'dead' seasons between harvests. Families in the countryside with land of their own tend to be more stable than urban families because there is no pressing economic reason for the men to leave the household.

On the other hand, if men do remain with the same woman, their presence can often be more oppressive than their absence. 'Machismo means reducing the woman to an object', says Comandante Carlos Núñez. 'The man acts as head of the family, directs everything, takes command, imposes his will without taking into account what I would call the exercise of democracy in the home'.[4] This sort of *machismo* is particularly apparent in the countryside where — partly for geographical reasons — women are more isolated from each other. Here the community does not interfere with 'family' matters and consequently it is very difficult for women to forge alliances outside the home. They are left to deal with their men's *machismo* single-handed.

The wandering *machista* abandons his woman like a disposable object, while the more rooted male head of household treats his woman like a possession over which he has complete power. Frequently he will deny her the freedom even to go out of the house unaccompanied. Gladys Martinez, a Sandinista Defence Committee co-ordinator who has worked in rural areas around Leon, describes the lengths to which this can sometimes be taken: 'If a child was sick a man wouldn't let his wife go unaccompanied to the hospital — better the child should die!'[5]

It would have been utopian to have expected *machismo* to die with the Revolution. Nevertheless, its continuing virulence in a new revolutionary society provokes some challenging questions: how are the *machista* attitudes perpetuated? Are women partly responsible for them? Many Nicaraguans — both men *and* women — claim that had women struggled as hard against *machismo* as the Sandinistas did against Somoza, they would be free from male oppression today. This has given rise to the popular idea that women are partly, if not largely, to blame for their subordinate position. A man writing to *Barricada* in August 1988 complained:

> It always happens that males receive all the blame for machismo, and in many cases it is the mothers, the women themselves, who are conscious or unconscious accomplices in perpetuating the inequalities.

But this fails to take into account the way in which men's power over women often makes resistance impossible. A British social worker based in the remote Quilali region of northern Nicaragua in the mid-1980s observed that because men so habitually ditched their women or left them to bring up the children single-handed, it was something of a status symbol merely to have a man about the house, especially if he contributed economically to the family unit. Women would, therefore, put up with any manner of abuse from their partners just to keep them in the house. Rather than fighting against *machismo*, the women were thus passively accepting it.[6]

Replying to the man quoted above, Gioconda Belli, prominent poet and feminist, commented:

> Effectively, as the compañero says, it is we women — as reproducers of the ideology in the home — who pass on the machista patterns of society to our children. We cannot, however, shift all the blame onto women, because we would be wrong to affirm that women are responsible for our own repression . . . women suffer a condition of subordination which, for thousands of years, has been sold to her as an inherent part of being a woman. It is not strange but natural that women reproduce that pattern of society . . . She doesn't create the ideology, she reproduces it. What we have to state is not that men should liberate women, but how do we liberate ourselves from this unjust situation, which affects *everybody* [author's emphasis] but whose most painful effects are suffered by women?[7]

The psychologist, Auxiliadora Marenco, in her *Barricada* agony column emphasizes that women have the power to choose not to be victims of *machismo*. But she also urges *men* to liberate themselves from *machismo*. She once responded sympathetically, for example, to a letter from a married man bewailing the fact that he felt compelled (by *machista* ideology) to have sex with every woman who asked him.

## Making the break

The state of affairs described for Quilali may still be quite common, but clearly there are thousands of women in the new Nicaragua who have refused to tolerate *machista* behaviour. Indeed, participation in the general revolutionary struggle has given many a new view on the family, as Arlen Siu, an FSLN activist killed by the National Guard at the age of 19, wrote:

> Regarding the role of wife, mother, she is limited to the living conditions imposed in her home, that offer only a restricted space. In practice, her participation is passive . . . She is obliged to give what she has to give and receive what others want to give and this happens at all levels, even the sexual.[8]

Women who have tried to find an identity beyond the 'restricted space' of the home have generally had to wage quite a struggle with their menfolk, as verified by Mailene Rugama Hernández, a co-ordinator of adult education in León:

> I must say it was only the enthusiastic support of my mother who looked after my 5 children while I was doing the course [to be an auxiliary nurse] that enabled me to complete it. I received very little support from my husband. In fact he was very against it at first and we used to have a lot of rows . . . It's partly sexual jealousy: they think the successful woman is only out to sleep around with other men . . . I made my position quite plain: nothing was going to stop me getting this formal training which was above all for the sake of my children's future. So he left. Eventually he came back when he realised that I was not only determined but doing very well! He started giving me some support but basically he is not a progressive man.[9]

Since the Revolution, the growth in women's confidence and activity outside the home has caused many couples to separate. Printworker, Maria Lopez Calero, is one example:

> In the end I told him to choose between me and the booze. Perhaps I'm a little harder up but at least I feel calmer and the children are more secure. I've moved on. We fought over politics, his vices, bad behaviour and character. I said 'We'll never understand each other but let it be clear, I'm no little woman, and if you don't want to understand me it's because you don't love me.' He said 'That's fine.

It's your decision.' But now he's sorry. The mates at work have told me he misses the children.[10]

For many women, separation from oppressive husbands has made life a lot easier. Maria Calero says: 'Now that I've just separated from my man it's much easier to go to meetings.' Maria Calero has benefited directly from the Law of Nurturing (see p. 14) which means that 'despite being separated, my man still has to contribute financially to the family.'[11]

## The new man in Nicaragua

It would be wrong to suggest that only women have changed as a result of the Revolution. As part of the general exposure to new ideologies brought about the Revolution and by changing attitudes amongst women, many men are also beginning to re-examine their position in relation to women. Comandante Carlos Núñez, President of the National Assembly, reflects on the impact of the Nicaraguan women's movement on his own thinking:

> It's not easy to be machista; if a man's brought up that way, he can't show his feelings, he can't cry, he can't love in such a way that he gives himself up to the relationship and achieves equality there, he can't make concessions because he has to be tough, he has to be brave . . . machismo can exist in revolutionaries . . . I can't say categorically that I don't have machista traits, but . . . In 1971 when I joined the FSLN, I was more machista than I am now. I have tried to shed the defensive mechanisms that can mean denying women's rights.[12]

Significantly, Nunez is married to Milu Vargas, an active member of AMNLAE National Executive and a vocal campaigner on women's issues.

Tacho Cruz, President of El Regadío co-op, FSLN activist, and husband of Otilia (quoted p. 9), is another Nicaraguan man who has obviously taken these issues seriously:

> . . . this new work of mine [travelling round agricultural co-ops doing political work] has upset Otilia's plans to do regional health training as she doesn't want to burden her mother with the children . . . It's not even a matter of sharing out the housework, as I'm away for days on end . . . I don't think a woman's place is in the home, but plenty of Sandinistas do. What's needed are more children's centres which would free Otilia. It's a real problem.[13]

Mailene Hernández from León adds a sense of hope for the future:

I'm hopeful that the new generation of boys will be better than their fathers . . . at school my son learnt from his teacher that housework is shared . . . one evening I came home and found him cooking because his grandmother hadn't been able to do it.[14]

Women's increasing independence has created new anxieties for Nicaraguan men. In August 1987, *Barricada* published a discussion between Roberto Larios, a *Barricada* reporter, and Vilma Castillo. Larios stated that though he had become accustomed to many changes in the male-female relationship — for example, the division of labour in the home, having a female boss — he had problems of accepting sexual equality:

Just the idea of women's sexual emancipation . . . is difficult to swallow. I believe that this is where we most resist the feminine offensive. One cannot avoid feeling jealous, insecure, possessive and choked like a good machista when some provocateur launches the million dollar question: if a man can go to bed with whatever woman, why can't a woman do the same?

Castillo replied that Larios's anguish centred around an unstated but related fear — that a woman will stop having sex with the man she is living with, that she will develop sexual and emotional independence. She argued that women were not demanding the right to sleep with every man who came along, but rather more equal relations sexually, emotionally and regarding responsibilities in the home and for children.[15]

## Motherhood revered

In the context of families headed by women and absent fathers, the mother/child relationship (particularly mother/son) assumes far greater emotional and economic significance. Maternal sacrifice and women's daily struggle for their children's survival are acknowledged and revered. Gloria Margarita Martínez Largaespada, who lost two sons in the fight against Somoza, spoke at the Managua women's open meeting on 10 June 1986 in favour of the inclusion of the veneration of heroes and martyrs in the Constitution:

As working class Nicaraguan women, we gave our children for the struggle to overthrow the oppressive Somoza dynasty. If our wombs are left empty and our hearts are broken because our fruits have been torn away, why are we asking permission to have our children venerated? [Applause] We were freed with the blood of our working class children . . .[16]

Many women first become politically aware through their children's involvement as activists in the struggle against the dictatorship. The 'Mothers of Heroes and Martyrs' organization grew from a nucleus of women who met in the gruesome circumstances of searching for their children among the crushed and tortured corpses dumped by the National Guard at the *Questa de los Martires* on the outskirts of Managua. Since 1979 women have continued to organize specifically as mothers of sons killed in the war and of mothers of mobilized combatants. These organizations give a political meaning to women's experience of loss; over 11,000 women in Managua alone are mothers of soldiers who have died in the war.

Their prominence illustrates the fact that mothers are a force to be reckoned with in Nicaragua. As well as offering mutual support and political mobilization, the mothers' organizations have been known to stand up for women's rights in the community: *El Nuevo Diario* reported that the Mothers of Heroes and Martyrs in Santa Rosa Barrio in Managua publicly denounced the release of a local man who had raped his own daughter.[17]

## Families and the new laws

In the wake of the chaos and destruction of the war against the Somoza dictatorship, it was FSLN (and AMNLAE) policy to support the traditional Christian idea of the family as a nucleus, symbolizing stability and reconstruction, whilst simultaneously promoting the idea that women should participate equally with men both as productive workers and political activists. (See chapters 3 and 8.)

Early measures such as the Law Regulating Relations Between Mothers, Fathers and Children (*padres* [Spanish] means 'fathers' or 'parents') (1981), which created equal rights over children for both parents; and the Law of Nurturing (1982), which obliged all men to contribute to their children's upkeep and to do their share of household tasks, were designed to strengthen nuclear family bonds. In practice, the Law of Nurturing was intended to make men take more responsibility for children, so as to enable women to participate equally outside the home (as well as protecting children from economic exploitation). It is difficult to enforce on men a legal duty for childcare and housework, but this measure at least gave women support in insisting that men do their share, and stimulated discussion at all levels. The passage of both laws through the Council of State was highly controversial; AMNLAE representatives had to fight hard for *mothers* to be specifically mentioned in the title of the Law Regulating Relations . . . and to fight again to have 'mothers' put first. In the end the measure was passed with a slender majority of one vote. A new divorce law passed in 1988 might seem to undermine the FSLN's efforts to strengthen the family; but on the contrary, without recourse to divorce, marriage tended to be devalued, as couples who felt unable to continue their relationship would part company even though they were still married.

This enabled a marriage to be dissolved by mutual consent or by the will of *either* party. Previously, only men had had the right to divorce their wives, unless the woman could prove that her husband had been adulterous in a public or scandalous manner. One contentious provision of the divorce law was that, in addition to wages, work in the home should be recognized when the couple's goods were divided. Thus the economic value of housework was recognized.

## Women's role as carers

Under Somoza, in the absence of state provision for the support of children, old people, the sick or the disabled, women were society's unpaid carers. During the early years of the Revolution, some limited state provision was introduced, despite the government's economic difficulties. State pensions are now available for the elderly, disabled, victims of accidents at work and war widows; there is a limited network of state childcare provision and women are entitled to three months paid maternity leave. If they work in the state sector, they are allowed paid time off to care for sick children. But in the face of worsening economic crisis, the government has since had to make severe cuts in its social welfare provision. At the same time, the war has accentuated women's role as carers, partly because they are excluded from male conscription and are therefore expected to 'keep the home fires burning' and partly because many men have returned from the front with disabilities.

## Childcare and nursery provision

Since 1979 childcare provision for pre-school children has taken three forms: crèches for working mothers, nurseries run by the Ministry of Education, and 'popular' nurseries founded by local communities. In 1983 66,800 children were in state nurseries — only a small proportion of the pre-school population.

Whilst the need for more women to join the productive sector has stimulated demands for more childcare provision, the strain on the economy has put the limited state nursery provision introduced in the early years after the Triumph under great pressure. By early 1989 mothers were fighting for the survival of nurseries and workplace crèches. Two possible strategies were encouraged by the government in the absence of state resources. Firstly, employers were urged to take over running already established nurseries and to set up new ones. For example, in January 1989 there was a drive to get private coffee farms to provide a total of 25 new crèches in Region VI during the harvest, with union and government representatives arguing that such provision would guarantee employers increased production. Secondly, parents of children in state nurseries were asked to fund-raise or to provide the children's midday meal themselves.

Local communities have also been encouraged to set up their own nurseries. In May 1988 Barrio Santa Rosa in Managua, for example, announced the formation of a committee to raise 140 million cordobas to build a pre-school centre for 120 children aged 4 and 5. The residents had been resourceful in persuading Tomás Borge to donate part of the building materials as a celebration gift for the ninth anniversary of the Revolution. This project was cited by *El Nuevo Diario*, as an example to other barrios of how 'to develop their areas and defend the revolution'.[18]

But until comprehensive pre-school childcare is available to all, most women will still have to depend on informal family networks for support. Children are usually cared for by their grandmothers, as in the case of printworker, Maria Lopez Calero:

> The children were left on their own [during the day] so for their sake I decided to do the night shift while my husband worked the day one. But I fell ill from only having four hours sleep and with all the washing and cooking as well. So after a year I sent the two girls to Mother and the boy stayed here, and I went back on the day shift. At weekends I visit the girls with the boy.[19]

Many women actually prefer their mothers and relatives to care for their children. In the opinion of psychologist, Vilma Castillo:

> Women don't have a social conception of children. [They] are their personal responsibility, not society's. And that has always been true. Under Somoza there was one public nursery in the whole of Managua. But many women won't let their kids go to the nursery or even stay with their father — they feel they have to do it themselves or they ask their sister or aunt or mother to look after them — never a man or an institution. They say that childminders only do it for the wages and won't look after them properly. It's all part of this idea that the children are the private property of the woman. It was worse at first. When they created the CDIs [day nurseries for working mothers], there were rumours that the state wanted to steal women's children and send them to Cuba![20]

## Domestic violence, rape and child abuse

### Breaking the silence

During the early years of the revolution, male violence against women in the home was rarely publicly discussed. But since 1985, it has been recognized as a serious problem. This recognition stemmed from a study conducted by the Women's Legal Office (OLM) and the INSSBI Office on Family Orientation and Protection (OPF), in response to the disturbingly high numbers of battered women coming into their offices. In 1985, for example, 10,500 women sought help for problems of a domestic nature from the Women's Legal Office. The study showed that violence against women was widespread in all social sectors and not confined to poorly educated, lower-class men. It revealed that 44% of a random sample group of women aged 25–34 were victims of beating. Some of the women interviewed had suffered for as long as ten years before daring to report the problem to the authorities. Inability to support children alone, difficulty in finding housing, guilt feelings and fear of reprisal were the most common reasons for women failing to seek help.

The OLM report defined abuse as a social problemn, not a problem of individual women. They argued that it was rooted in an unequal relationship between men and women, and for the situation to change, this inequality had to be addressed and the 'privateness' of the home had to be challenged. Work was needed to change images of women, the definition of roles, and the division of labour within the family.

## FSLN *Proclama* breaks new ground

Article 36 of the new 1987 Constitution laid the basis for laws to be passed that aimed to prevent violence against women. It guarantees every citizen the right to physical, psychological and moral integrity; it states that cruel, inhuman or degrading behaviour is a crime punishable by law. The specific problem of male violence against women was officially recognized for the first time in the policy statement on Women and the Sandinista Revolution issued by the FSLN National Directorate on 8 March 1987. This document (known as the *Proclama*) included a commitment to struggle against: 'the physical and moral abuse of women and children, by promoting, on a social and institutional level, ever stronger responses against those guilty of such conduct.'

Practical strategies for reducing male violence against women have followed a two-pronged approach. On one level, there have been attempts to tighten up laws against such violence and to introduce stiffer penalties against the perpetrators. For example, in August 1988 a Women and Law conference organized by the professional workers' association, CONAPRO, recommended that domestic violence be treated as a crime with punishment equal to that administered for any act of violence committed outside the family; the conference also proposed that if a man battered a woman he should be denied active participation in a political project.

On another level, the focus has been on education and propaganda, with the aim of bringing to bear the weight of public disapproval on potential abusers. To this end, the OLM published a simplified version of their research findings for wider distribution, and offered training workshops for women in which their right under the Constitution to be free of violence was the starting point. Following the *Proclama*, a campaign of mass education against domestic violence or *maltrato* was also taken up by AMNLAE during 1987 and 1988.

In addition, the change in government policy as laid down in the *Proclama* has meant that the police are now supposed to regard domestic violence as a social problem, not a private family dispute. They can arrest a battering man and keep him in custody for 24 hours, then bring him before a tribunal if the woman wishes to proceed further. That the Chief of Police is a woman (Doris Tijerino) who has made strong personal statements against male violence has also encouraged social attitudes to domestic violence to change.

According to Gladys Martínez, a CDA co-ordinator in León:

> There used to be enormous amounts of wife battering. Of course men still do this but I think less than before if a woman complains she is protected by the law . . . [and] men know that it is punished by the law, with gaol for three months or more depending on the level of violence.[21]

## Speaking out in Region VI

In July 1988 a comprehensive paper on domestic violence published by the Matagalpa CONAPRO Regional Womens' Commission, contained a detailed campaigning plan. This included outlines for educational workshops; proposals for a specific crime of maltreatment to be punishable by three months to two years imprisonment for a first offence and double that for subsequent offences; a project to give legal and psychological help to battered women in Matagalpa and to organize popular education against domestic violence. As an example of their consciousness-raising work, the paper also included the script of a play on domestic violence by the Matagalpa women's theatre group, Cihuatlampa, which was performed all over Nicaragua.

The Matagalpa CONAPRO women also produce a quarterly magazine: *Arante*. Martha Valle (co-ordinator of the regional Women's Section of UNAG — the association of rural co-operatives and small farmers) is interviewed in the October 1988 edition and describes the sensitive approach the UNAG Women's Section adopts for educational work on domestic violence:

> When we give talks one of the things we discuss is that a woman is a subject not an object, not 'the shoe that I pick up, take off and throw away'. We can't talk directly about violence because the woman is still dependent on whether the man will let her come to our meeting . . . if the man suspects something we won't see that woman again. If we approach the subject by saying you must do this and that then the man feels we're threatening his power . . . that would destroy years of work.

In 1988 the same group of women in Matagalpa produced a series of radio programmes broadcast twice weekly on the local station 'Radio Insurrection', one of which took a radical perspective on domestic violence.

### A woman destroyed

In August 1988, in the midst of this refreshing blast of publicity and activity, the Diria case hit the headlines, revealing another aspect of marital violence. Margarita, aged 15, was shot dead in the classroom by the wife of the man with whom she was having an affair. Unreconstructed *machista* attitudes dominated the reporting of this case — and the news — for more than a month. The wife was universally vilified and characterized as a neurotic who had driven her husband to be unfaithful, whilst Margarita was cast as the helpless innocent victim. The fact that this interpretation was hardly commented upon shows that much remains to be done to change popular attitudes. *Barricada* published a letter from a man appalled by the macho nature of the reporting; but it was Auxiliadora Marenco (psychologist and *Barricada* agony columnist) who made the strongest intervention.[22] She focused on the double standard, asking why there was no such media outrage when a man committed murder in similar circumstances. She placed the blame in the Diria case on the husband for his infidelity, and expressed pity for the wife who had now been 'liquidated by society'. More boldly still, she asked why AMNLAE had not protested about the press handling of the case in the same way that they had protested about the pornographic content of the satirical magazine, *Semana Comica*, a few weeks earlier. (See pp. 168–7.)

### Rape and child abuse

Under the Somocista system, women were particularly vulnerable to sexual abuse. Mailene Rugama Hernández remembers:

> The landlords were the worst. If a woman was working for such a man and he decided that he wanted to sleep with her, she had the choice of either complying or losing her job. Necessity forced lots of women to comply.[23]

Rape and sexual assault are still private offences: a woman must take out her own prosecution rather than the state prosecuting on her behalf. And as Silvia Isabel Rosales Bolanos, a lawyer working for the Sandinista Police, put it:

> The conservative ideology of society makes many rape victims prefer to keep the rape to themselves rather than report it, however great the dishonour and the wrongdoing.[24]

Once domestic violence became the subject of public attention, rape also began to be more openly discussed. From 1988 onwards, reports of rape and child abuse appeared frequently in the Nicaraguan press. In the same year, AMNLAE presented a petition to the Supreme Court condemning violence against women and children. An AMNLAE advertisement appeared in *Barricada*: 'Rape is a Criminal Offence — Report it!', together with an announcement reminding the public that AMNLAE had already demanded of the national Assembly that all cases of violence against women and children be treated as a crime rather than simply a civil wrong, and calling for the strengthening of the campaign for legal and ideological change.[25]

### Sexual abuse in the home

From the start, press reports and articles emphasized the incidence of rape inside the family as much as outside it. In an interview, psychologist Damaris Enríquez[26] pointed out that the most common form of rape is that of a wife by her husband, and that this causes the same trauma as any other rape, although it is more easily disguised because of the persistent idea that a woman is a man's private property. The prevalence of father/daughter rape was also highlighted in the wave of publicity about child abuse, causing many people to speak up for the first time. A Managuan housewife, Silvia Toruna, for example, told a British worker in 1988 that her next-door neighbour, Cony, had left her husband because he tried to rape their 13-year-old daughter. She did not prosecute him because she did not want to traumatize her daughter, but now she wishes she had pressed charges. There are no statistics about the true incidence of incest, but for many mothers it is a constant source of anxiety. Silvia Toruna herself (who had her husband put in gaol for four days for beating her) said that one reason she stayed with her husband was that at least she could ensure that he would not rape her daughters.[27]

The lawyer, Silvia Bolanos,[28] recorded in 1988 that the clear-up rate for reported rapes from 1979 to mid-1988 was 204 out of 227 and noted that most reported rapes occurred in Region III (Managua). She cited as causal factors little or no sex education, alcoholism, pornographic films and overcrowded living conditions. Bolanos stressed that the maximum sentence for rape (12 years) is relatively minor considering that the maximum penalty in Nicaragua is 30 years, and considering the psychological damage a victim — especially a young girl — can suffer.

### Women express their anger

The CONAPRO conference on women and law proposed stiffer penalties for rape and child abuse, suggesting that a maximum of 30 years would be more appropriate. This, it was argued, should be adopted with a policy of flexible sentencing to take account of the victim's age and circumstances. The conference laid great emphasis on the need for sex education and state promotion of a responsible attitude towards sexuality. Hard on the heels of the CONAPRO conference, AMNLAE and other womens' organizations called a mass meeting outside the National Assembly building to demand that rape and child abuse be treated as major, not minor, crimes.

The latest horror stories of child-battering and/or child sexual abuse now figure quite frequently on the front pages of the national newspapers. In the publicized cases the emphasis is on the brutality of the perpetrators and on children's rights, and there is (as yet) apparently little backlash against state intervention in 'family life'.[29] For example, one father's savage sexual attack on his baby daughter and another father's beatings of his nine-year-old son who fled to a reservists' battalion for refuge, were reported in horrific detail. When *El Nuevo Diario* ran a front page story in which (unusually) a mother had beaten her children brutally,[30] there was a quick response both from AMNLAE and from the director of an INSSBI children's home, emphasizing the need for basic education on childcare as well as the responsibility of the whole community for children and for parents.[31] Recognizing the sudden torrent of concern about child abuse in 1988, the government set up a National Campaign for the Defence of the Life of the Child in which all relevant institutions aim to work together on a preventive strategy. At the Latin American conference on Women and the Law, which followed the CONAPRO conference, the Nicaraguan delegation suggested that the Campaign should pay attention to the mother's situation (and particularly her own vulnerability to abuse) in approaching the problem of child abuse.

## Sexuality

Women are embarrassed to talk about the sex act. I call it the Virgin Mary complex. The majority have no social shame about bearing children but it would make them ashamed to talk of having made love. They talk as if it was the Holy Ghost that produced children, not sex. In one class we were talking about orgasms. Not one woman had heard the word. Some of the 45–50 year-olds talked: women have no participation sexually with their men. They tend to regard sex as just another burden to bear in marriage. They used the term 'my husband occupies me', 'abuses me once a month' . . . In no way is sex synonymous with pleasure. It's just another obligation . . . The traditional idea is that everything to do with reproduction stems from a man. The woman is a vessel for him and raises his children.

This is how Susana Veraguas, who runs training workshops for midwives in northern Nicaragua, described the views of the rural women with whom she worked.[32]

Maria de Zuniga, founder of the self-help health care organization CISAS, which has specialized in work with women, reports similar attitudes.[33] Many women lack even basic knowledge about their own bodies: out of 200 women from all classes and levels of education participating in one of her workshops, only ten knew that women are most fertile on the 15th day of their menstrual cycle.

Widespread ignorance and *machista* assumptions about sexual life clearly limit Nicaraguan women's control over their own bodies and their freedom to explore and enjoy their own sexuality. Housing conditions offer little privacy for sex; and the Church plays its part in promoting what Veraguas calls the 'Virgin Mary complex'. It would, however, be wrong to give the impression that Nicaragua suffers from hopeless sexual repression and strict Catholic morality. The culture allows more physical closeness between people than does, for instance, British culture. The fact that most couples never officially marry shows that Nicaraguan Catholicism is less restrictive over people's personal lives than its reputation might suggest.

Moreover, the Revolution had led many women to question traditionally held views about sex. Some women argue that they have the right to sexual pleasure as well as the right to control the number of children and the interval between them. Auxiliadora Marenco writes:

> A woman should know her body, not only its functions and reproductive anatomy, but its pleasure as well. Many old beliefs still exist, including that which says her body is something given to another to enjoy.[34]

### Sex education

Mailene Rugama Hernández remembers how before the revolution 'we had none of the opportunities there are now. I think girls suffered particularly badly. We had no sex education so puberty was a frightening mystery. When I had my first period I thought I was going to die.'[35]

In the first years of the Sandinista revolution sex education was not seen as a priority. But the Ministry of Education and the Sandinista Youth have now recognized that to have omitted this from their programmes, when thousands of young men and women were mobilized in the Literacy Crusade and on coffee brigades, was irresponsible. These young people, many of them teenagers released from the home for the first time, were given guidance and training about their work and what to expect from the *campesino* communities — but no advice on contraception or sexual relations. Predictably, the result was many unwanted pregnancies.

More recently, sex education has been enshrined as a right in the Constitution, and taken up as a central demand by AMNLAE, the Sandinista Youth, and some Trade Unions. In 1985, a UN-funded National Commission on Sex Education was set up, with representatives from the Ministries of Health, Education, and Social Welfare. A national programme was created for students in primary and secondary education, and teachers went out to organize workshops for harvest brigade volunteers.

The Commission was also responsible for 'Sex and Youth', a bi-weekly series screened on Sandinista television (SSTV) in 1986. The 18 programmes, directed by sexologist Auxiladora Marenco, covered such subjects as: male and female reproductive systems; birth control; sexually transmitted diseases; masturbation; and homosexuality. Such open discussion of taboo issues generated some heated debate — much of it aired on Voz de Nicaragua's popular radio phone-in 'Contacto 6–20' — with outraged viewers voicing their complaints. Presentation of female masturbation was seen as particularly shocking. The Ministry of Education and SSTV began to scrutinize the programmes more closely after these protests. The week after 'Sex and Youth' had dealt with homosexuality — setting out to show that homosexuals are not suffering from an illness but from unjustified discrimination against them — SSTV presented a studio discussion of 'experts' repudiating much of what Marenco's programme had said. The series stopped appearing at about this time.

Taking the lid off issues of sexuality is clearly bound to dismay and perplex as much as it enlightens and reassures. But at least possibilities are emerging for these matters to be more openly explored.

## Lesbians

Lesbian liberation has never been part of the Sandinista strategy. In a revolution where it seems that every possible aspect of private and public life has become politicized, issues relating to sexual orientation and homophobia remain submerged. Speeches and documents from AMNLAE freely recognize sexuality as a concern for the women's movement; but, so far, this is limited to birth control and heterosexual sex education.

The Nicaraguan women's movement is haunted by a fear common to all largely heterosexual feminist groups: that their credibility with men would be at risk if they were suspected of harbouring a lesbian tendency. An example of the perception of 'lesbian' is an *El Nuevo Diario* editorial, in which the male author asks AMNLAE: 'You claim to be intelligent, conscious and revolutionary. When will you stop imitating this lesbian song of European women and let the voice of Nicaraguan women be heard?'[36] He also betrays a common assumption that sex between women is something that happens only in other countries.

Obviously, there are lesbians in Nicaragua, as there are anywhere else in the world. It may be imagined how many of them suffer from isolation, oppression and self-hatred — like anywhere else — compounded, perhaps, by their position in a Catholic-dominated *machista* society, and the lack of an organized lesbian movement or 'scene'.

There are no lesbian bars or clubs in Managua; prejudice is rife; and most people's social life is largely based around the family. Very few Nicaraguan lesbians regard their sexual practice as a political issue.

> I am a working class Nicaraguan. Although my family is very religious, they have accepted me as the lesbian I am. My first love was a classmate in my 4th year at school. We were studying together, and one night . . . we fell on to the bed, and found we were kissing each other. We spent the whole year together . . . her parents realized what was going on, and banned our friendship; but she saw me in secret and our love grew every day. That was in 1977. At that time my country was governed by Somoza, one of imperialism's worst creatures. There was terrible repression and discrimination against homosexuals, there was strong psychological oppression, which kept us isolated. We couldn't go out to a party — people condemned us as low, dirty, and barbaric; they said we were abnormal, and didn't want anything to do with us. To begin with I felt bad, but since love doesn't allow any barriers to happiness, and I loved my girlfriend, I didn't care about people's prejudices.[37]

In revolutionary Cuba in the mid-1960s, a vicious purge took place against homosexuals, apparently on the grounds that their sexuality was a symptom of bourgeois decadence.[38] Nicaragua has no such policy. The Sandinista government, while not providing any positive support for lesbian and gay activities, has not engaged in any deliberate repression of homosexuality.

On the contrary, the Revolution has broken new ground in which there is now the chance for social transformations to take root. A few small-scale and fragmentary indications show that lesbians are beginning to find a small space in the Revolution.

**Politicizing lesbianism**

In October 1987 in Mexico, the first Latin American Lesbian Gathering was held. This was an offshoot of the Latin American Feminist Conference held biennially since 1978, and attracted delegates from Chile to the Caribbean. Five Nicaraguan lesbians attended (with financial support from British solidarity, among others) — a breakthrough in terms of Nicaraguans making contact with organized lesbian movements from their own continent. Rita Arauz's openness about her lesbian sexuality, plus the high profile of lesbians from other countries in the workshops and discussions, forcefully introduced the issues of lesbian politics for the first time to a wide range of activists and leaders in the Nicaraguan women's movement.

Perhaps it was the impact of this exposure that was responsible for the attitude expressed by Lea Guido, then General Secretary of AMNLAE, never previously known for liberal attitudes to lesbian sexuality, at a workshop organised by MIREN in May 1988. When questioned about the position of lesbians in the women's movement, she said that although the lesbian struggle was not identical with women's struggle in general, 'lesbians march under their own banner'. Later, when asked if AMNLAE's sex education referred only to sex with men, she replied, 'I'm sure there will be a space for lesbians too, for everybody'.

At the Women and Law Conference in Managua in September of the same year, a spontaneous workshop on lesbians and the law took place. President Ortega, who attended the 'Face the People' meeting which rounded off the event, when asked about lesbians in Nicaragua by a Costa Rican delegate confirmed publicly that no policy of discrimination or denial of homosexuals' human rights was practised in the country.

## Lesbians and gays organize against AIDS

The most positive developments for lesbians in Nicaragua arose from a project on AIDS. Medically, lesbians have less reason than any other sexually active group to concern themselves with AIDS prevention; but the issue here is politics rather than medicine. Motivated by their solidarity with gay men, some lesbians in Managua began in 1986–87 participating in an informal grouping of lesbians and gays discussing how to educate themselves about safer sex, and the danger of AIDS. They were spurred on by the efforts of lesbian and gay health *brigadistas* from San Francisco, who were keen to involve themselves in grassroots education work in Managua. Naturally their health-based discussions evolved into slightly wider-ranging 'coming-out' sessions — laying the basis perhaps for an indigenous gay liberation movement.

At this time there were no known cases of AIDS or HIV infection in Nicaragua (by January 1989, three deaths and 16 cases of HIV were recorded); nevertheless the Health Ministry MINSA was actively setting up an AIDS prevention programme.

Their campaign was relatively frank and helpful, and apparently without overtones of an anti-gay panic. The crucial point from a lesbian perspective was MINSA's attempt to apply its tried and tested techniques of community-based preventative health care to the case of AIDS. Aware that in North America the disease had spread first among gay men, the Ministry realized that they must mobilize the gay community. Thus Health Minister Dora Maria Tellez invited the informal discussion group members in Managua to a meeting, and proposed that they form the basis of a new sex education project in conjunction with MINSA. Lesbians and gay men would become health *brigadistas* taking the message of safer sex to the whole gay community and beyond.

The AIDS work is an extraordinary example of co-operation between the state and grassroots lesbian and gay activists. From this point, it is hoped that the work of these *brigadistas* leads not only to a reduction

in the spread of disease, but also to the flowering of a new consciousness
and pride among Nicaraguan lesbians and gay men.


## Hope for the new generation

The Revolution has given women the hope that their daughters will
break out of the straitjacket of childrearing and *machista* abuse that
circumscribed their own life in the past. The printworker, Maria Calero,
says:

> I hope [my eldest girl] can be independent and eventually get a grant
> to go to university. I'm gentle with the children, to let them come
> into their own. When I was young we were always getting a
> flogging.[39]

In 1987 a young woman at school in Estelí wrote, perhaps rather
optimistically:

> *Machismo* exists in Nicaragua but mostly amongst older people who
> still have the idea that a woman's place is in the home doing the
> housework whereas men work outside the home. But young couples
> aren't like this — they do the housework together.[40]

Nevertheless, Gladys Martínez of León stresses that women have to
keep up the pressure on men to change:

> On a personal level, the fact that I was mobilized last year and left
> my children with my husband for several months is an important
> advance. As for getting men involved in domestic tasks, well . . .
> one works at it slowly. Men can't be changed by passing laws, it's up
> to us to work at creating the new man . . . I never let my eldest
> daughter act like a slave to the younger boys. They must learn how
> to look after themselves and help in the house. If we were to bring
> up our children in the same way that we were brought up we'd never
> get anywhere. We women, have got to teach the new generations
> how to be new men.[41]

And Alicia Andino (a single parent, worker and shop steward in the
Jalapa tobacco factory, and local reporter for the ATC) says:

> You know what I think we need? To sit these men down so that their
> women can tell them we're not just born to be slaves and bring up
> the kids alone. It's the men who have to change. Even the revolution-
> ary men.[42]

# Notes

1. Deighton et al, 1983, pp. 124–5.
2. Angel & Macintosh, 1987, pp. 103–4.
3. Vilma Castillo, interview, 1986, unpublished.
4. Carlos Núñez, interview, *El Nuevo Diario*, 24 September 1988.
5. Gladys Martínez, interviewed by Rachel Stringfellow, 7 September 1987, unpublished.
6. Hilary Brakewell, speaking to Nicaragua Solidarity Campaign (NSC) Women's Network, July 1987.
7. Gioconda Belli, quoted in *Outwrite* 51, October 1986.
8. Arlen Siu, 'La Mujer y su Liberación', no original date given, reprinted in *Barricada*, 10 August 1983.
9. Mailene Rugama Hernández, interviewed by Rachel Stringfellow, 21 August 1987, unpublished.
10. Angel & Macintosh, 1987, p. 113–14.
11. Ibid., pp. 112–13.
12. Carlos Núñez, interview, op. cit.
13. Angel & Macintosh, 1987, pp. 100–101.
14. Mailene Rugama Hernández, interview, op. cit.
15. *Barricada*, 18 August 1987.
16. Gloria Margarita Martínez Largaespada, quoted in *Intercontinental Press*, 28 July 1986.
17. *El Nuevo Diario*, 4 January 1989.
18. *El Nuevo Diario*, 2 May 1988.
19. Angel & Macintosh, 1987, p. 112.
20. Vilma Castillo, interview, op. cit.
21. Gladys Margarita Martínez Largaespada, interview, op. cit.
22. *Barricada*, 24 August 1988.
23. Mailene Rugama Hernández, interview, op. cit.
24. Silvia Isabel Rosales Bolanos, 'Information on Rape', paper for Nora Astorga Conference on Women and Law, organized by CONAPRO, August 1988.
25. *Barricada*, 20 May 1988.
26. Damaris Enríquez, interview, *El Nuevo Diario*, 16 June 1988.
27. Silvia Toruna, interviewed by Rachel Sieder, 1988, unpublished.
28. Silvia Isabel Rosales Bolanos, paper, op. cit.
29. *El Nuevo Diario*, 8 January 1989.
30. *El Nuevo Diario*, 17 November 1988.
31. *El Nuevo Diario*, 19 November 1988.
32. Susanna Veraguas, quoted in Deighton et al, 1983, p. 156.
33. Kovel, 1988, p. 94.
34. *El Nuevo Diario*, 10 October 1987.
35. Mailene Rugama Hernández, interview, op. cit.
36. Carlos Ivan Torres Meza, *El Nuevo Diario*, 15 January 1987.
37. Esther Bojorge, testimony, *Square Peg*, Summer 1988.
38. See Young, 1981.
39. Angel & Macintosh, 1987, p. 114.
40. Secondary school pupil, Estelí, interviewed by Stephanie Williamson, 1988, unpublished.
41. Gladys Martínez, interview, op. cit.
42. Angel & Macintosh, 1987, pp. 119–20.

# 3. Work: Key to Liberation?

## Introduction

In line with socialist tradition, the FSLN has always promoted the idea that getting women out of the home and into the productive sphere is the key to their liberation. Waged work, it is argued, gives women economic independence and thus brings them close to equality with men. It also brings them into the 'public', and hence, the political arena. As Comandante Tomás Borge told a crowd in 1980: 'the destiny of women is not making *tortillas*. They are going to work in industry, in factories, in the development of agriculture. This will be a form of ending the exploitation of women.'[1] Maria Duarte, a market seller from Managua, holds a similar view to the National Directorate:

> I think that a woman should work [outside the home] because then she has more to think about and doesn't think so much about things like quarrels with her husband. Women have the same right as men to get out of such situations . . . but when the woman can say: 'I earn and you earn', what's the problem? I think that when the woman works, it takes away some of the man's *machismo*.[2]

Of course, thousands of working-class and peasant women were already earning a living well before the Triumph. Indeed, as the principal income-earner for their family, many had no choice; men come and go in Nicaraguan society and cannot be relied upon. Before 1979, an estimated 85% of single mothers worked, but almost solely in areas that were extensions of their domestic chores: by taking in laundry, selling homemade food and so on. Given this concentration of women in the informal sector, their economic participation was always under-estimated in offical statistics. Many worked as maids and domestics in private houses away from the public eye — barely acknowledged as 'workers'. In the country the names of women working at the peak harvest times did not even appear on farm payrolls. Thus, before 1979, women's paid work outside the home — at least officially — was invisible and totally undervalued.

It was the *productivity* of women's paid work that the FSLN was keen to improve, in order to reactivate the country's productive forces after the destruction from the war against Somoza.

> Forty-eight per cent of the labour force in the country, that is 183,448 women, work outside the home [declared Borge in 1982]. At first glance this might look like a pretty high figure, and might lead us to think that women have a really significant role in production. But if we analyse the kind of work women are doing, we see that a high percentage of them are underemployed and that another large group is employed in domestic service — work that is not productive.[3]

## Labour legislation affecting women

With the aim of encouraging women's entry into the mainstream workforce, several new laws were introduced, the most fundamental of which was equal pay for equal work. Equal pay had been a legal right before 1979, but this had been largely ignored by employers. A statute passed immediately after the Triumph stated that:

> Everybody has the right to enjoy equitable and satisfactory working conditions, ensuring in particular:
> 1. Remuneration which provides workers, as a minimum: a) equal salary or wage for equal work in identical conditions of efficiency and adequate for their social responsibility, without sexual discrimination; b) dignified existence both for workers and their families.
> 2. Health and safety at work.
> 3. Equal opportunities for promotion without limitation, while dependent upon length of service and capability.
> 4. Rest, enjoyment of free time and reasonable hours of work. Payment for public holidays.

The Constitution, ratified in 1986, established an eight-hour working day and paid maternity leave. Other labour laws passed that directly concerned women included: two half-hour breaks each day for breast-feeding; a guarantee of no loss of pay when sick children cause women to be absent; in places with more than 30 women workers, the employer is obliged to provide a space where they can feed their children; it is illegal for employers to dismiss or turn away women because they are pregnant or on maternity leave. This latter provision is particularly important as many employers used to insist that prospective female employees take a pregnancy test before being employed. When the law is violated, women may seek the support of their trade union which, if there is a valid case, will take the matter to a labour tribunal.

Nevertheless, for many women workers, the new labour laws remain hypothetical. In the absence of major changes in the sexual division of labour, both in the labour market and at home, women's place in the workforce as casual, part-time and self-employed worker has kept many outside the boundaries of this legislation. Market sellers, domestic workers in private houses and temporary agricultural workers are amongst the thousands of women not protected by laws.

Even those women in regular and stable paid employment have not yet won all the rights listed above. The equal pay for equal work clause in the Constitution is virtually inoperable, as women rarely do the same jobs as men, and work in completely different sectors. Service sectors, such as domestic work, health and education, for example, are almost entirely female and are traditionally badly paid. Even in the sectors where both sexes supposedly work alongside each other, research has revealed that, here too, women are relegated to different jobs from those undertaken by their male colleagues. Significantly, the 'female' jobs are undervalued and less well-paid (see 'Women as industrial workers', pp. 77–81).

Employers maintain that they lack the material means with which to implement the labour laws, while the government lacks the personnel or infrastructure to enforce them. Thus, the length of maternity leave, the working day, and holidays usually have to be negotiated between the management and trade union within each workplace. In places where union representation is weak, the laws are often ignored altogether. In 1989, for example, there were reports in the press of women being dismissed from their jobs because of pregnancy. *El Nuevo Diario* focussed on the case of Elba Cuadra Prado who because she was pregnant was dismissed from the OCALSA company, with a stream of verbal abuse from the general manager. Elba appealed to the Ministry of Labour and an inspector was sent to investigate the case. On arrival, the inspector was mocked and ridiculed by the management and Elba was refused entry into the workplace.[4] This episode is typical of the Ministry's ineffectiveness.

Despite the impediments obstructing the implementation of these laws, however, their mere existence has given women a firm basis from which to fight against discrimination. Elba Cuadra may not be reinstated without a struggle but the Revolution has at least given her the legal authority with which to fight her case publicly. 'I want justice' she declared in the newspaper report and *El Nuevo Diario* responded with the hope that, 'the Ministry of Labour, the trade unions and the women's organizations would support Elba and put in their place those people who think they are still living in Somocista society'.[5]

## Impact of war

Obviously, the effectiveness of labour laws affecting women may vary in accordance with general ebbs and flows in the Nicaraguan economy and the overall significance of women's position in the workforce at any given time. When the war against the US-backed Contra forces escalated in 1983, women were desperately needed to fill positions left vacant by mobilized men, particularly at the height of the fighting from 1984–86. Information from the Ministry of Employment indicates that in 1985 at least half the workforce involved in state sector production of food and beverages, cloth and clothing, paper and plastic, and pharmaceuticals was female. In the same year, the Agricultural Workers' Union (ATC) estimated that 70% of coffee pickers were women, compared to 42% in 1983–84. Women also comprised 70% of textile factory workers. Visitors to Nicaragua between 1985 and 1987 observed entire government ministries run entirely by women. In the absence of men, women were trained to do jobs never before assigned to them, such as tractor-driving, fire-fighting, and crop fumigation.

It could be argued that women's predominance in the war economy gave them more bargaining power. For one thing, the country's decision-makers started to listen more carefully to the demands of women workers. The FSLN *Proclama* of 1987 on women's liberation can be seen as a response to women's growing importance in the economy. It recognized that Nicaragua's economic survival *depended* on the solution of some of the specific problems that prevented women from participating more fully in production: 'The struggle to wipe out discrimination against women cannot be separated from the struggle to defend the Revolution . . .'

Prior to the FSLN *Proclama*, the Sandinista trade unions had already responded to the increase in their female membership by initiating discussions on issues such as childcare, housework, and paternal irresponsibility — issues that had never before been raised in a trade union context. In this respect the Agricultural Workers' Union led the way; its women members work in the vital export cash-crop sector. By the end of 1987, each of the trade unions representing industrial workers, agricultural workers, small producers, teachers, health workers, and professionals had started to hold special meetings to discuss the interests of their women members.

## Double work day

As women's entry into the mainsteam workforce placed the issue of women's oppression firmly on to the public agenda, attention was directed towards their 'double work day': of both productive work in the field or factory plus housework and childcare, for which women still take prime responsibility. It is estimated that the average *campesina* woman still spends 9–12 hours a day on household chores (preparing food, washing dishes, hauling water etc.) and her daughters a total of six hours on similar tasks. By comparison her husband and sons together devote a total of 50 minutes to domestic tasks.[6] For most women, moving into the formal workforce has thus meant working longer hours and harder than ever before.

Working through AMNLAE and the trade unions, women have pushed hard to alleviate some of the pressures of their double day. In the period 1984–87, for example, a number of workplace crèches and children's canteens were set up. From three crèches in the whole country in 1979, by 1988, there were 182 urban crèches and 69 on state farms. But the economic crisis promoted by the war has effectively put a brake on such material improvements to women's workload; the establishment of many more crèches while the economic crisis continues is unlikely.

In the absence of adequate resources, a more personal solution has been sought to the double day problem within the family itself. The domestic workload, it is now recognized, needs to be shared equally amongst all its members and particularly between men and women. Hence the emphasis in the late 1980s on getting men to take more responsibility for children's upbringing and for domestic chores. In 1987 a TV programme on the family, for example, showed the model husband and father washing clothes, a task that normally is considered quite outrageous for a man to perform.[7] In a government TV commercial, small boys were shown tidying their bedroom. The FSLN *Proclama* of 1987 states: 'We will promote an effective solidarity within the couple with respect to domestic chores and family responsibilities.'

## And when the men come home?

Behind the enthusiasm for women's newly-found role in the workforce lurks a familiar question; what happens when the war finishes? Will the men not want their better-paid and better-skilled jobs back again? Is women's entry into the more secure areas of the workforce merely a temporary symptom of war or a permanent change in the economic landscape? Clearly there is a contradiction facing any country at war. Women's labour is desperately needed while the war continues but once it is over, the men will expect to be justly rewarded for their service and perhaps to be granted an even better place in the workforce than they had before. Indeed, the military service law guarantees all demobilized soldiers the right to regain their jobs.

This issue has created something of a dilemma amongst the country's policymakers. Lea Guido, General Secretary of AMNLAE 1987–89, told a group of British women in 1987 that, 'while we really want women to work, the returned combatants are fundamental to the revolution . We can't just say it would discriminate against women to give men the job.'[8] At AMNLAE's 10th Anniversary meeting in 1987, a factory worker complained that opportunities for technical training were always given to returned combatants. Clearly, training is an important factor in deciding whether or not women will maintain their position in the workforce when the men return.

Until the late 1980s, AMNLAE and the trade unions generally tried to put people's minds at rest by pointing out that the contradictions were at least being confronted. Unlike mobilizations in the First and Second World Wars, it was argued, soldiers in the Sandinista armed forces fought for only a few months at a time (once they had completed an initial two years of military service). This meant that there was a constant wave of men leaving and returning from the war front to challenge their women's new positions: not after some future ceasefire but here and now. On the whole, there was an optimistic feeling that the problems could be solved. 'We women are getting on,' declared a tractor driver from Jalapa in 1986. 'When the men come back from the fighting we'll all work together.'[9]

## Compactación

In the face of economic recession and national cost-cutting measures, however, women's security in the workplace has suffered. In 1988 and again in January 1989, thousands of state workers (mainly urban) were made redundant in a process known as '*compactación*'. The first round of cuts in 1988 was mainly intended to contain what was regarded as an oversized revolutionary bureaucracy; office workers in the various government ministries were therefore particularly badly affected and there were complaints that many more women than men had been dismissed (according to Stephanie Williamson in conversation with clerical workers in 1988). In 1989 the second round of *compactación* was not only more widespread but, in some cases, appeared to be *targeted* at women (although still confined primarily to the towns). In this respect there seemed to be a connection with the diminishing intensity of the military Contra war and the demobilization of large numbers of soldiers.

\* \* \*

*Women banana workers — a case-study of* Compactación
*During the 1980s, the female workforce in the banana plantations rose to over 50% of the 4,000 workers, as more and more men were mobilized. After decades of sporadic temporary work on the plantations, women were given permanent jobs, entering traditionally 'male' areas of work such as packing, cutting back the plants and applying fertilizers and pesticides.*

*Nationalized in 1983, banana production is the least profitable area within the agro-export sector. Moreover, the sector lost its closest and most logical market, the United States, when President Reagan imposed a trade embargo in 1986. Not surprisingly, therefore, the managements of the state plantations want to reduce or 'compact' their workforce.*

*'Compactación' has coincided with the virtual cessation of Contra*

*attacks, giving rise to other tensions. Since the military service law guaranteed soldiers the right to return to their jobs, the management felt obliged to dismiss the 'substitute' women workers in classic post-war style. The women were to be used only as packers for no more than two out of every 15 days, thereby making it impossible for them to earn a living wage. 'They used us as a way out [of the labour problem] and now they want to abandon us,' banana worker Carlota Caceres complained at a national union meeting. In her view, the management was removing women because of their supposed low productivity. Women caused more problems because many of them got pregnant and their children got sick.*

*Only by vociferous protests did these women succeed in saving at least some of their jobs. Having publicized their plight nationally at various trade union and women's meetings and having gained the full backing of the national ATC union, the 'bananeras' were in a strong position to negotiate. In April 1989 they persuaded the management to ensure that any workers made redundant should be comprised of equal numbers of men and women.*

\*   \*   \*

## Women in trade unions

The moral of the *bananeras*' story is that organization and trade union participation are crucial if women are to defend their position in the workforce. 'We're finding that where women are not very strong in their union, they are being dismissed,' comments Heliette Ehlers of the ATC Women's Secretariat and propaganda worker at AMNLAE 1988–89.[10]

Nevertheless, trade union involvement is not straightforward for large numbers of women. Invariably, it means working a triple day and for many women, union meetings on top of paid work and domestic chores are just too much. Those with husbands may also have to contend with outright opposition to their participation in the union, especially if it means attending evening meetings where most of those present are likely to be other men. A lack of confidence in the face of male-dominated structures is another hindrance to women's trade union activity. In 1987, the Sandinista newspaper, *Barricada*, cited the case of Ana Julia Velazquez, a metal worker and one of the few female union activists in her workplace. 'She's the first woman we would propose for a place on the committee, because she has all the requirements for trade union leadership,' states the branch secretary. But Ana Julia is apparently too shy to put herself forward for trade union elections and is quoted as saying, 'It's because of my educational level which is very low . . .'[11]

A recent study conducted by the ATC revealed that 81% of female agricultural workers were nominal members of a union or mass organization but only a third actively participated in the assemblies and meetings.[12] Similarly the secretary of a union branch representing industrial workers admitted in 1987 that even though women were now 10% of the total workforce, 'we realize self-critically that not one woman has any position of responsibility in the directive committees of the union, a situation we must change.'[13]

Despite the continuing predominance of men in trade union structures, however, women are proving themselves a force to be reckoned with. Indeed, with the stress and commitments that women have to withstand in other areas of their lives, it is a wonder that so *many* women are involved in the trade union movement. The creation of Women's Sections inside some of the major unions and the established practice over the past few years of holding separate national, regional and local meetings for female members in addition to the general mixed meetings, has given women a space in which to formulate their demands and build up their confidence.

This was clearly demonstrated on International Women's Day in March 1989 at a meeting of women trade union representatives from all the various sectors or 'fundamental forces', ranging from landless agricultural workers to teachers and professionals. In the months leading up to this day, women workers had held local meetings in workplaces and regions throughout the country. Around 25,000 women were directly involved in the discussions, and the final meeting in Managua was attended by around 1,370 — double the number expected. The main aim of the women's discussions was to review their respective achievements as women over the ten years of the Revolution and to assess the effects of *concertación*. Translated as 'harmonization', *concertación* was a new government policy introduced at the beginning of 1989 to improve co-operation between the country's producers (both large and small) and the government. Under this new social contract, various concessions were granted to private employers and landowners, by way of reactivating production.

The women representatives' response to *concertación* at the 'Fundamental Forces' meeting was luke-warm. Those present expressed their concern that some employers were treating *concertación* and *compactación* as one and the same thing. Large producers and employers, having gained new commercial liberties from the Sandinista government, now seemed to think they had a *carte blanche* to break whatever labour laws they pleased without provoking state interference. Dismissal of pregnant women was an issue in women's contributions. 'Some people want to take advantage of the opening [provided by *concertación*] to dismiss pregnant women and make redundant female staff,' complained one delegate.[14] All delegates insisted that *compactación* must not discriminate against women. The essence of the message conveyed by the meeting was that women were not be forced from their hard-won place in the workforce without a struggle.

As the military war against the Contra draws to a close, it may be that women workers feel more confident about asserting their needs.

Before the war, many willingly accepted that the country simply did not have the resources to service such needs. Now they may see less reason for withholding their demands. In addition to grumbles about cuts and *concertación* the Fundamental Forces meeting also made a number of material demands. One woman proposed the establishment of four months' paid maternity leave as a right for all women; another argued that 20% of union funds should be devoted to social projects. The final document drawn up by the meeting demanded that workplace crèches should be a financial priority in both state and private companies and not merely a 'social perk'.

### A key to liberation?

Revolution and war have enabled women to gain a strong foothold in the Nicaraguan workforce. Yet their involvement in productive work clearly has not been a ticket to instant emancipation. Women have entered the workforce on an unequal footing with men. They have suffered from a lack of confidence and of training, from the prejudices of male colleagues and, most importantly, from the continuing burden of childcare and domestic work, which remains their responsibility, whether or not they have paid work. These factors have put them at a disadvantage when defending their jobs in the face of redundancies and military demobilizations. On the positive side, however, the Revolution and the Sandinista trade unions have at least provided women workers with a space in which to develop and assert their demands, many of which have been taken on board by the Sandinista government and by employers. In the process they have been able to challenge attempts to push them back into the home or into the sporadic, temporary, and marginalized employment of the past.

### Notes

    1. *Barricada*, 24 April 1980.
    2. Maria Duarte, quoted in 'Mujeres en los Mercados', *Cuadernos de Investigación*, INIES.
    3. Tomás Borge, quoted at AMNLAE's fifth anniversary celebrations.
    4. *El Nuevo Diario*, 4 March 1989.
    5. Ibid.
    6. Figures from *La mujer en las co-operativas agropecuarias en Nicaragua*, CIERA, Managua, 1984.
    7. *Sexo y Juventud*, STV programme on sex education, Managua, 1987.
    8. Nicaragua Solidarity Campaign women's study tour, September 1987.
    9. Angel & Macintosh, 1987, p. 124.
    10. Heliette Ehlers, interviewed by Helen Collinson, London, May 1987, unpublished.
    11. Trade unionist, quoted in *Barricada*, 31 July 1987.
    12. *Barricada Internacional*, April 1988.
    13. *Barricada*, 31 July 1987.
    14. *Barricada*, 9 March 1989.

# 4. Rural Women

## Assessing the changes

In the absence of a developed industrial base, Nicaragua's national income (and hence its ability to fight the costly Contra war) is dependent on the export of a handful of cash crops, particularly coffee. The agricultural sector is therefore of vital importance to the revolution and it is here that some of the most far-reaching changes have been felt, both economically and ideologically. For women, the changes in the countryside have been uneven. While revolution and war have opened up new opportunities (particularly in employment) the extreme poverty of Nicaraguan rural life cannot be swept away overnight. Because of their continuing isolation, many rural communities remain virtually untouched by the revolution. Meanwhile eight years of war have all but cancelled out the material improvements initiated in the early stages of the revolution.

### Rural women's daily lives

Hard work dominates the lives of most rural women. Traditionally, women have taken prime responsibility for family subsistence plots and livestock, combining the business of production with that of reproduction. Activities such as weeding and picking the crops (mainly beans and corn), husking the corn, sowing the seed, preparing the ground, obtaining water and fuel, and looking after the household's pigs or cows are all squeezed in around domestic tasks such as clothes washing, childcare, and cooking. These daily chores are not only tiring but intensely time-consuming. Making the traditional maize pancakes, 'tortillas', for example, a staple of the Nicaraguan diet, is a laborious process occupying several hours each day. In the towns tortillas (though still made by women) can be bought from street sellers, but women in the country have no access to ready-made food; grinding the corn to make tortilla dough often takes two hours; creeping deforestation means that an increasing amount of time is spent hauling water and collecting wood. Daily walks of between five and eight kilometres in search of these resources are not uncommon nowadays. To make ends meet, many peasant women also work on local cash crop farms, particularly as seasonal labourers. For most peasant women, all this adds up to an 18-hour working day.

\*     \*     \*

### Doña Antonia — A day in the life of a 'campesina'[1]

*Doña Antonia's day starts at 4.00 a.m. Living in a house with no electricity, she rises in the dark and rekindles the stove with dry firewood . . . then starts to grind boiled maize for the morning* tortillas. *The maize is ground once (either with a pestle and mortar or in a hand-operated mill), then mixed with water and ground again to give a fine paste [which] is rolled into small balls and patted out into pancakes. By the time the* tortillas *are ready to cook (on a metal plate over the fire), beans and rice (if there are any) will be reheating. (For most of 1988 many people were living on nothing but* tortillas, *salt and unsweetened coffee, because the crops had failed.)*

*While Doña Antonia prepares breakfast, the oldest child helps the younger children to get up and then goes to collect the first water of the day. Fetching water is a major part of the day's work, the spring being half a mile away down a hill the height of a 10-storey building. Doña Antonia and her children make this journey constantly, carrying a gallon container on their heads, hips or shoulders. Daily, she and the children carry clothes down to the spring and scrub them on stones. Then they wash themselves and carry the wet clothes back to the house to hang them out on the barbed wire fence to dry.*

*The older child goes to school at 8.45, leaving Doña Antonia to care for the other two and to look after the animals. The family has a cow and a calf which Antonia perpetually has to chase or drag around on the end of a rope. The cows and a few chickens buffer them a little from the effects of crop failures, enabling them to eat a little cheese or an egg with their* tortilla.

*Antonia makes* tortillas *three times a day and this, together with fetching water, washing clothes, cleaning, caring for the children and animals, takes up nearly all her time. But she also works in an agriculture co-operative of which she is a member and goes to literacy classes when she can. She is in bed by 8.00 p.m., the sun having set at 6.00 p.m.*

\*     \*     \*

Rural life is still arduous, but the revolution has at least tried to ensure that rural people are supported, valued, and treated as human beings, which was not the case before 1979. Over the decades of Somoza dictatorship, more and more land was appropriated to create huge private farming estates or *haciendas* for cash crops such as cotton, tobacco, coffee, and sugar-cane. Plantations of cotton, introduced in the 1950s, expanded 120-fold between 1949 and 1955. To make way for these cash crops, thousands of peasant families were thrown off their land and forced to join the growing army of landless labourers drifting from one *hacienda* to another in search of paid work. Accommodation on the *haciendas* consisted of windowless barracks full of wooden 'drawers' stacked up to five deep in which workers were expected to sleep. There was no light, water, or sanitation and families were segregated by sex. Piecework wage rates were based on the amount picked by the fastest pickers. Nearly all the wages went on food, which had to be bought at inflated prices from the landowner's store. By the end of the picking season many workers were in debt.

With the exception of a small minority of permanent workers, employment on the estates was for only a few months, as the different crops are all harvested at roughly the same time of year. For the rest of the year, peasants either grew subsistence crops on meagre plots (often as tenant farmers or sharecroppers) or, if totally dispossessed of land (as were 30%), migrated to the towns and even to neighbouring countries to look for work. On top of the economic problems was the savage repression inflicted by Somoza's National Guard, which kept peasant populations in a state of almost constant fear and subjugation. Against this backdrop, conditions in the countryside deteriorated to the extent that between 1960 and 1977 the rural population declined from 60% to 48% of the total, with thousands settling permanently in the urban *barrios*.

## Conditions for rural women: before and after Somoza

Under Somoza, peasant women were at the bottom of the social pile, oppressed not only by the general rural conditions of that time but also by the norms of a *machista* society and by their own menfolk.

In landed peasant families, women undertook the lighter agricultural work, but they rarely owned the land, and took no decisions nor had any control over what they earned. Women from landless families were even more marginalized. Most paid work in the countryside was for men, but women were called upon as a source of cheap labour during peak harvest times when there was a shortage of workers. Single women were sometimes barred from employment on the *haciendas* altogether but married women often worked alongside their husbands. Some 40% of coffee pickers before 1979 were women, yet their contribution to the rural economy was invisible: female workers' labour was not included in *hacienda* payrolls as it was assumed that men as 'heads of households' received a wage for the whole family group. Payment to male workers for the estimated labour put in by their womenfolk was calculated at half the piece rates paid to men.

The constant pressure to make ends meet placed a great strain on the peasant family unit and on women in particular. Many husbands who left home to find work never returned, or disappeared for months or years at a time, leaving the women to bring up the children entirely alone, as in the case of Adela Cruz, a peasant woman from a village in northern Nicaragua. 'My husband worked sharecropping for Briones [local landowner] which meant he got back half my husband's harvests,' she recounts. 'Later he threw my husband off the land when he brought in the cattle. It was then that my husband started drinking, morning, noon and night. In the end he left for Jalapa . . . I kept going by making and selling bread.'[2]

Added to the economic burden of peasant women's lives was the insecurity caused by their vulnerable legal position. Somocista society recognized only men as property owners, therefore single women rarely held land titles or tenants' rights and could be evicted and exploited at their landlords' whim. Such was the experience of Adela Cruz; once her husband had left, the landlord, Briones, tried to evict her once and for all. But Adela was not easily beaten; when Briones had her roof pulled down, she simply replaced it with a sheet.

Adela's experience graphically illustrates the lack of respect for peasant women that characterized Somocista society. After decades of subhuman treatment, only with the revolution are these women rebuilding a sense of dignity and self-confidence. The contrast between the experience of Adela and of her daughter, Otilia, bears witness to some of the changes precipitated by the Revolution. Whereas in her childhood under Somoza Otilia remembers 'working like oxen for the landlords' and living in a 'stinking house made of cardboard', she now lives happily on a co-operative farm with her husband and five children, teaching literacy and undertaking training in herbal medicine. In 1986 she was sent on a medical course in Mexico where she was asked to speak to representatives of the Contadora Group of Latin American countries.

To counteract the extreme deprivation of rural life under Somoza, the new government made it a priority to improve social conditions in the countryside. Women were the main beneficiaries of these social improvements, amongst which new housing, health posts, schools, electricity and safer water supplies were the most significant. The vaccination campaigns (which rural women themselves helped to organize and carry out), the reduction in diarrhoea-related infant mortality and the eradication of polio also greatly alleviated the anguish and suffering of peasant mothers. The distribution of basic foodstuffs and provisions through government channels and state farm shops also reduced women's housekeeping problems. Items such as sugar and salt, once regarded as luxuries beyond reach, can now be purchased relatively easily.

Adequate transport was another major change affecting peasant women. For the first time in their lives they could now travel to nearby towns, thanks to the creation of a skeleton rural bus service. In the past, many peasant women would go to the nearest market town only once a year and to Managua perhaps once in a lifetime. Nowadays, such trips are fairly regular occurrences.

War and economic crisis, however, have almost totally occluded the improvements described above. Many of the social programmes initiated in the early 1980s have had to be abandoned. Since 1985, a large proportion of rural schools and health posts have not been staffed owing to Contra attacks and cuts in social budgets. The vaccination campaigns are erratic and polio is reappearing, as is malnutrition amongst children in some areas.

Soon after the Revolution, various measures were introduced to facilitate women's participation in the rural labour force. Most importantly, women could at last receive their own pay packets, thus greatly reducing their dependence on men. A dramatic increase in rural minimum wages was another significant advance, particularly in view of the high proportion of minimum wages paid out to female workers. But again, war and economic crisis have devalued these gains: the rise in wages was rapidly cancelled out in the late 1980s by the spiralling inflation that spread from the towns to the countryside. In Matagalpa towards the end of 1988, agricultural co-operative workers were receiving a daily wage of 40 *córdobas*, while the cost of one cabbage in the local market was 50–100 *córdobas*.

## Agrarian reform: its impact on women

The distribution of land brought about by the revolution is arguably the most solid gain for the thousands of rural people who, before 1979, were landless. Under the process of agrarian reform some 20% of all cultivable land — which belonged previously to Somoza and his closest allies — has become state farmland. The idle or misused land that remained has been divided into co-operative farms and small individual plots for previously landless farmers.

At a legal level, the Agrarian Reform and Co-operative laws of 1981 were the first in Latin America to recognize women's equal rights with men in relation to wages, access to land, and co-operative organization. They were also the first laws to define women as co-operative members and landowners in their own right, regardless of whether or not they were heads of households or had adult male children to reap the benefits of agrarian reform.

There has, however, been a considerable time lapse between theory and practice. While on paper the legal position of rural women is praiseworthy, implementation of the law has proved to be another matter. A report published by the pro-Sandinista agricultural workers' union (ATC) in 1985 was very critical of the shortcomings in the agrarian reform laws relating to women. 'Rural women still don't know what their rights are and without working out any measures for ensuring that the law is carried out, its effectiveness has been reduced to a mere declaration of intentions.'[3] The report pointed to the lack of directives either to state farm managers, co-operative members or the instigators of the co-operative movement in relation to women's participation. Once the law had been passed, no attempt was made to identify factors such as childcare, domestic responsibilities, or *machismo*, which might prevent women from taking advantage of agrarian reform. During the grassroots *cabildos* (meeting) discussions on the new Constitution in 1985, one of the main demands put forward by women peasants was that they should be granted land titles. The fact that women had already gained this right on paper had clearly made little impression.

The conclusion of the ATC report is that the Agrarian Reform Law was, in itself, an insufficient guarantee of equality between the sexes in the country. Hence, few women were incorporated into the direction of agricultural co-operatives or managerial positions on state farms. Women were found to be doing routine jobs of secondary importance with little opportunity for advancement or training. Apart from a few women tractor drivers in the northern tobacco region, there were virtually no women employed on mechanical or technical tasks either on co-operatives or state farms. This was very marked in the cotton belt where cultivation was becoming increasingly mechanized. Here, women workers had been relegated to manual labour which is more arduous and less well paid than the mechanized work carried out by the men.

According to the ATC report, part of the problem was that women still seemed to be primarily seasonal workers, both on the big farms and in the co-operatives. Despite the legal obligation for employers to enter female workers individually on their payrolls, managers on the private farms have been slow to change and many women still work as unpaid appendages to their husbands. As seasonal workers, women do not have equal access to the improved working conditions now available to men, such as job security, occupational hygiene, social security, and less intensive working days.

But two factors have been instrumental in changing this unequal state of affairs; the war (ironically) and the recent policies of the ATC and UNAG, the rural trade unions.

## War and the rural labour force

While on the one hand the war has eroded rural women's material gains, on the other hand it has opened up employment opportunities previously closed to them. As more and more men from the rural workforce were mobilized in the defence effort, women moved in to fill the gap, not simply as seasonal harvesters, but also as permanent workers. In the absence of their male counterparts, many women have learnt to do jobs never before assigned to them, such as fumigating crops, ploughing, and so on.

This has given them confidence and determination to realize their full potential in the rural workforce, as was vividly portrayed in the Nicaraguan feature film, *Women of the Frontier* (1986). Based on fact, this film focuses on a newly-formed co-operative in the war zone whose women members learn to drive tractors while their men are at the war front. When the men return, trouble breaks out. In a fit of rage, one man demands that his wife alight from her tractor and hand over the ignition keys. But she refuses and, with the firm support of her female colleagues, succeeds in out-facing her husband.

Some male agricultural workers have admitted that women do the more skilled jobs better than men. In 1987 a cattle farmer from Boaco commented: 'In this farm, we've got 75% women workers . . . Really women are almost 100% effective because they're not like us men, who go out on the streets, to live it up, perhaps end up with a hangover or get wiped out. The woman is a top achiever.'[4]

As more and more peasant women move into skilled, permanent jobs outside the home, the division of labour inside the home is also beginning to change. 'Before 1979 men occasionally went out and collected firewood,' says Ana Criquillon of the ATC. 'Now that's more usual. Some men now carry the water from the well or the river — you never saw that before. Inside the house, if the man lives there all the year round, he's more likely to help look after the children.'[5]

## The Agricultural Workers Union: a forum for women

When it comes to defending women's newly-found role in the rural workforce, the Agricultural Workers' Union (ATC) is particularly important. Heliette Ehlers of the ATC Women's Secretariat recounts:

> We [the union] looked particularly at the situation of women in Canada after the war when women had to go back into the home and give up the jobs they'd been doing. We noticed that although Canadian women were involved in trades unions at that time, there hadn't been any organisation strong enough to put its foot down and prevent their return to the home. So, in contrast, we women are aiming to be represented in all the different power structures.[6]

Established by the FSLN in 1978, the ATC is the main representative body of salaried agricultural workers on the cash crop farms, both state and private. In common with other Sandinista trade unions, the ATC maintains close links with the government, and government and waged rural workers' objectives receive equal priority. Rural workers are not compelled to join the ATC but a majority of permanent employees and a large number of temporary workers are members.

Despite the government's establishment of legal minimum wages and other new labour laws, conditions on most private farms remain poor and the ATC has had to press hard to get improvements for workers in this sector. The situation on state farms differs slightly: here, the government is, in effect, the employer and, due to the close links between the ATC and government, union and employer may at times appear to be one and the same. Wages and conditions of employment, for example, are fixed jointly by the ATC and MIDINRA, the government agricultural ministry which administers state farms. In Nicaragua, both parties' interests tend to coincide: there is a common understanding, for example, that cash crop production has to be maintained and increased if the revolution is to survive and that workers' demands must be taken into account if production is to be raised. Because ATC members tend to be Sandinista supporters, major clashes between the ATC and the government are unusual. Nevertheless, this does not preclude lively and open discussion, nor does it prevent the ATC from lobbying state farm managements or MIDINRA on behalf of workers. Above all, the ATC provides its members with a voice for making known its demands to the Sandinista leadership and also with a forum for developing political ideas. These functions have been particularly important in promoting the specific interests of rural women.

With more and more men leaving home to fight the Contra, and with the resulting influx of women into the cash crop sector, the number of female affiliates to the ATC increased rapidly in the early 1980s. By 1983, women comprised 40% of total ATC membership, sparking off the first major dicussion inside a Sandinista trade union about the specific problems facing women workers.

At first the growing numbers of women entering the ranks of the ATC caused some anxiety amongst the union leaders, of whom 99% were men. Their priority (in line with Sandinista policy) was to boost production in order to counteract the effects of economic crisis and a costly war. With so many men away fighting, ATC leaders were therefore concerned to raise rural women's productivity levels, especially as these were widely accepted to be lower than those of male workers. Yet how exactly was women's productivity to be raised? What was preventing women from achieving high productivity levels or indeed from participating in agricultural work at all? It was then that the ATC realized how little was known about the situation confronting rural women.

The first step out of this dilemma was to organize a meeting of women working in agriculture. The 1983 National Assembly of Rural Women Workers was attended by 100 delegates representing women in all the main areas of agricultural production. While exposing some of the inequalities that women face in their work, the meeting brought to light the acute lack of information about rural working women. For this reason, the delegates decided that a thorough investigation into rural women's working conditions should be carried out by the newly formed ATC Women's Secretariat.

## Women discuss their reality

The investigation, undertaken by ten researchers, themselves rural women workers, lasted a year and a half and achieved mass grassroots participation. The findings of this investigation formed the basis of the report on women and agrarian reform quoted in the previous chapter. Going beyond the question of agrarian reform, the investigation gave women the opportunity to discuss subjects never before considered to lie within the scope of the union's work, such as pregnancy, childcare, abortion, and many other issues concerning the home and family. 'For these women it was the first time they'd ever had the chance to think about their own reality,' says Heliette Ehlers of the ATC Women's Secretariat.[7] These discussions made it clear to the union that the successful integration of women into the rural workforce could not be accomplished without taking into consideration women's traditional responsibilities and their daily routine.

In the light of this research, the Women's Secretariat decided to concentrate their efforts on women's fulfilment of the 'work norm', the amount of work every employee must do each day in order to receive the basic wage. The maintenance of the work norm is of central importance to the goal of increasing production and is therefore a major issue inside the ATC. Focusing on the problem in this way, the Women's Secretariat could count on the full support of the union in their work. Such an issue could neither be considered marginal nor be dismissed as merely a 'woman's matter', as perhaps some men might have done if the women had begun by demanding childcare. This does not mean that other issues were considered unimportant. On the contrary, it was hoped that discussions about work would inevitably raise all the other specific issues relating to women. This approach also helped to establish the principle within the union that every labour issue should be considered from a woman's point of view.

In order to assess women's attitudes to the work norm, the Women's Secretariat returned to the grassroots, organizing a series of workshops at both local and regional level. To facilitate discussion and encourage mass participation, the Secretariat produced a pamphlet in photo-story form with a brief text, explaining what the work norm meant and relating this to the experience of women workers. For example, one photo sequence addressed the problems of women as childbearers: Rosa comments that she is too tired to work as she has got up very early to see to the children; she also has to leave work early to go and look after her son who has had an accident. Taking into account the low literacy level of rural women, the pamphlet was designed in a way that was easy to read, with a large type face and minimum text.

The discussion groups were a great success and culminated in the second national assembly of rural women workers in September 1986. This time, literally hundreds of delegates reported on the conclusions of the grassroots meetings. All agreed that they should accept the same work norm as men, in recognition of the need to raise production. But at the same time, they emphasized that this would be possible only if women's domestic work was reduced. To this end they passed resolutions calling for more childcare centres, more paid maternity leave, paid days off to tend sick children, the installation of drinking water where it was not yet available, communal washing places, and mills for grinding corn. The Assembly called on the ATC to incorporate these demands into the mainstream collective agreements drawn up with state farm managements and MIDINRA. One resolution also demanded that the union encourage male members to help with domestic tasks. Delegates them returned to their different regions like seeds to the earth, taking their resolutions back to their fellow branch members and persuading local and regional union leaders to negotiate with farm managers on the women's demands. Gradually such issues as childcare and housework became a daily theme in most of the regional trade unions.

Women's work is always more intensive during the major crop harvests. In the 1986–87 season, some notable improvements resulted from the resolutions passed at the Second National Assembly, particularly in the field of childcare. As already noted, in 1985 there were only 30 farm crèches in the whole country; during the 1986–87 harvest 500 were operating (though most of them were temporary). On some state farms, 72 new public sinks for washing clothes, as well as collective maize mills, helped considerably to lighten the domestic workload. 'Amongst other things,' commented one woman worker, 'we struggle through the union to have our maize ground for us. Before we used to get up at two in the morning to do the grinding. Now we only have to get up to make the *tortillas*.'[8]

## Communicating with ATC women

Following the 1986 assembly, the ATC Women's Secretariat established the practice of devoting a double page of the ATC national newspaper to women's issues. Most of the articles on these pages are written by women agricultural workers who serve as voluntary local reporters for the Union. The boost this job has given many women is demonstrated by Alicia Andino from Jalapa:

The union asked me to work as one of their local reporters and I began to appreciate much more the common problems that we tobacco workers face — all the housework, children and husbands who stop us getting involved in outside activities. . . . Now I'm teaching other workers to become local reporters. Being local, people tell me their worries. Some of the important news gets national coverage. We have regular meetings where reporters from the union farms pool their information. It's a real encouragement for people to hear themselves over the radio, and especially for the women when they hear about things involving them. This never happened before.[9]

In 1987 the ATC Women's Secretariat also made a video programme on the participation of rural women in production. The message the programme tried to put across was that production and reproduction cannot be separated. One issue raised in the programme that had been given little attention in the past was sexual harassment. One of the women who speaks frankly about her experiences in this regard is tractor driver, Melba:

> I've had a lot of problems with the other tractor drivers who keep saying to me, 'If you let me have you, I'll teach you. If not, I won't teach you' . . . Then our boss sent us to a seminar in the Cacao School. We were there for six months and the same happened with some of the tutors. One said, 'Look, Melba, you can get a good mark from me but I want you to give yourself to me'.[10]

## The Third ATC Women's Assembly
Unfortunately the level of debate that had taken place before the Second Women's Assembly was not repeated in the period before the Third National Assembly in September 1987. Heliette Ehlers of the Women's Secretariat admitted that, 'The women workers have not been able to get together to evaluate the progress of the resolutions taken at the Second Assembly or to reflect over the quality of their participation in the life of the union or to speak about thesmelves, their changes, their worries, their advances.'[11]

The worsening war situation and the growing economic crisis may have put a dampener on the women's discussions but in some areas the lingering resistance of men members of the ATC to women meeting together was just as much an obstacle as was the war. One regional secretary claimed: 'Because of the various tasks and mobilizations, the women have not been able to meet regionally. Moreover, we haven't got a budget for this type of expense.' The response from the women of the Secretariat to this assertion was stern. In *Machete*, the ATC newspaper, they wrote: 'Men must value and respect women's own way of going about things within the life of our trade union instead of fearing that the women might dominate things with their specific problems. This will enable us to strengthen the unity of the working class.'[12]

Clearly the reaction of men in the union to the developments of recent years is varied and there is still a long way to go. Nevertheless, the overall change in the men's attitude is very noticeable. At the beginning especially at the lower levels, there was widespread scepticism about the issues even being raised. Men were being forced to think about problems they had never before considered. Some reactionaries asserted that the so-called 'women's issues' had nothing to do with the tasks of the union. Yet what convinced a lot of men in 1986 was the obvious increase in production following the meetings held to discuss the work norm. Since then, the importance of incorporating women's demands into the official, mainstream work guidelines is at least partially recognized.

In fact it is precisely because of a shift in attitudes amongst men in the ATC that real change has been able to take place. This is why extreme care was taken by the ATC's Women's Secretariat not to ghettoize 'women's issues' by creating a separate, subordinate structure to deal with them which by-passed the men. Women meet together to discuss as women but always come back to the mainstream of the union with their demands and their strategies.

One example of this is the way that the ATC Women's Secretariat organized itself in the national ATC office. The five women who service the Secretariat all work alongside men doing regular work for the ATC. But significantly, each of the five is stationed in a different department. Once a week, the five women come together to assess how the various areas of the ATC's work are developing and then to relate this to the demands of women in the union; the same approach is mirrored at regional and local level. Every branch committee and most committees on the state farms now have representatives (themselves women) to deal with women's issues. This has helped to increase women's participation in the running of the union. Women now hold 28% of union posts compared to 1% in 1983.[13]

### The Fourth ATC Women's Assembly
Although many women agricultural workers still have problems meeting with each other to discuss their situation on a regular basis, the demands put forward at the Fourth ATC Women's Assembly in 1988 showed just how far they had come since the First Assembly in 1983. Here, calls for union involvement in the fight against sexual harassment and for access to low-cost contraception were particularly prominent. In the past, such demands would have been unheard of or, at best, dismissed as marginal in the union context. To the applause of delegates, Olga Maria Espinosa, head of the ATC Women's Secretariat, read out the proposal that the 'unions incorporate into the contract [with farm managements] sanctions against sexual blackmail at work, rape attempts, and any act that violates our dignity.'[14] The conference also approved the demand that 20% of the dollars earned by state and private enterprise for export crops be used for social projects such as childcare centres, communal laundries, and health care.

\*

By opening up a unique space for rural women to discuss their problems and assert their demands, the ATC has been a trail-blazer for the Nicaraguan women's movement. Its new and creative approaches to women's participation in the economy and in the Revolution have proved so successful that they are thought to have been a major force behind the FSLN's *Proclama* on women's emancipation in 1987. Similar strategies have since been attempted by other unions — namely UNAG (rural co-operatives and small producers union), the CST (Confederation of Sandinista Workers, primarily representing the urban sector), and Fetsalud (union of health workers).

But the ultimate success of the ATC's work rests on more fundamental social changes. In the words of Ana Criquillon from the ATC Women's Secretariat: 'If we don't change the situation in the home, we will never be able to meet women's demands and we'll never raise production.'[15] As long as the possibilities for the socialization of rural women's domestic burden (through more statutory material improvements, like crèches, canteens, and laundries) are limited by the deteriorating economic situation, the solution to the unequal division of labour within the family will continue to be an issue for women in the ATC.

## Women in rural co-operatives

The co-operative movement, is at the heart of Sandinista ideology; its history goes back to the 1930s when Sandino himself organized his peasant fighters into co-operative farms. As already noted, under the process of agrarian reform, some of the land abandoned by members or supporters of the Somoza family has been turned over to co-operative farming.

Most of those now working on co-operative farms were landless seasonal workers who, before the Revolution, endured long periods of unemployment for most of the year and rarely had any secure form of income. Soon after the Triumph, landless workers' families started to organize themselves into Seasonal Workers' Committees with the support and supervision of the ATC. These committees reported idle lands to MIDINRA (Ministry of Agrarian Reform) and in most cases received permission to work such lands co-operatively, using government credit to purchase the necessary agricultural equipment, seed and fertilizer.

There are two types of agricultural co-operative in Nicaragua: the CAS (Sandinista Agricultural Co-operative), a totally co-operative venture where land is farmed collectively by all the families involved: and the more individualized CCS (Credit Service Co-operative), in which families continue to farm their own plots and only share resources and credits; this latter type is much more popular.

**Where women are in control**

Scattered around Nicaragua are a handful of agricultural co-operatives which are either exclusively female or have a majority of female members, indicating the considerable enthusiasm amongst women *campesinas* for collective work as well as the shortage of male labour at a time of war. In October 1984, the AMNLAE magazine, *Somos*, printed a profile of the Rigoberto López Peres co-operative in Chichigalpa, consisting of six women and three men. Significantly the co-operative works as a CAS because the women felt that the CCS structure would lead to individualism. The women appear to be in control on this co-operative: one male member admits that he used to beat women but nowadays would not dare even to look at his women colleagues in a sexist way.

The Rigoberto Peres co-op remains quite exceptional, as the membership of most agricultural co-operatives is predominantly male. Yet on co-operatives with a minority of female members, women speak just as positively of the changes co-operative farming has brought to their lives. Many gauge the improvements in terms of the co-operative's progress as a whole without reference to their own individual fortunes. Nubia Boniche, for example, emphasizes the importance of controlling land, a right her community has gained through their co-operative farm: 'The future is ours now,' she says, 'and it looks good, this is our chance.'

Controlling land is a recurring theme amongst women in co-operatives. In 1987, when a group of British women visiting the José Díaz co-operative farm in Matagalpa asked the women members what improvements they would like to see in their lives, they met with the following responses: 'One woman said that she was really happy here: she had her own land and this was much better than living on rented land. The people on the co-op seemed very poor: some of the children looked undernourished, but, for them, controlling their own land was a real achievement.'[16] For women who worked as seasonal labourers on Somoza's feudalistic *fincas*, land represents the economic and financial security they have dreamed of for years. 'I worked on various *fincas* [before the revolution],' says Modesta Martínez from a co-operative in León. 'At that time, we never made any money . . . Now we can save up and we do earn something.' Modesta also feels that co-operative farming is more accommodating to women's heavy domestic responsibilities: 'There's more flexibility. If for example I need to go and do some personal business, I ask permission and the *compañeros* give it to me. Before they never used to give us permission. Now there is understanding.'[17]

**Low participation**

But the benefits to women of co-operative farming have been less than might be imagined, because on the whole their participation has been quite limited, despite the encouraging exceptions. Legally, women are entitled to equal rights with their male colleagues, but only 6% of full co-operative members are women and only 50% of co-operatives contain women members. This is despite the fact that women make up the majority of the workforce on many co-operatives. Most women continue to work as seasonal labourers. Although they now receive the same pay as men for the work they do, they lose the benefits of full membership: they cannot take part in the decision-making process nor receive a share of the profits; they also lose out on technical training opportunities.

A number of factors contribute to this low participation. Top of the list are the eternal problems associated with women's traditional role as mother and housekeeper. Consuelo Talavera, now a member of a co-operative in Miraflor, was for a long time reluctant to join because 'I felt I couldn't leave my eight children alone.' Anita Casco, one of the few women to become president of a co-operative, admits that, 'The double burden of work and childcare means that women participate less.'

Significantly, several of the women who have taken up leadership positions in their co-operatives talk positively of the support they have received from their *compañeros* at home. Modesta Martínez, for example, also president of her co-operative, has seven children. Because of illness, her husband cannot work but instead cares for the children and has learnt to cook.[18] This arrangement, however, remains rare in rural Nicaragua; women at the José Díaz co-operative in Matagalpa laughed when asked if their men helped at home.

Men's attitudes in fact add to women's burden. Women have traditionally been regarded as docile, conservative and unwilling participants who would be incapable of making decisions about production. Because their contribution to productive work has been so undervalued in the past, many men have still not even considered the possibility of women becoming full co-operative members. Others profess to feelings of jealousy that would be aroused if their *compañeros* were to work so closely alongside other men. Anita Casco recounts that, 'my relationship with my husband was affected a bit as it was difficult for him, on account of his own *machismo*, to understand my work in the co-operative, since most of the members were men.' She says that this changed only when he himself, as a co-operative member, started to value her work as president.[19]

Linked to the feelings of jealousy is the fear that women's great involvement in the co-operative will lead to their increased independence from men's control. When a woman becomes a member of a co-operative and is able to share in the profits of the co-operative (however small), she is no longer financially dependent on her man. In the words of Consuelo Talavera, 'We're going to become independent of our husbands. We don't always have to be asking for pennies from his pocket. We're going to have the freedom to buy what a woman really needs.'[20]

## UNAG pushes for more women co-operative members

Until 1986, AMNLAE had tried to raise the issue of women's participation in agricultural co-operatives at national meetings and through its magazine, *Somos*. Some local and regional AMNLAE offices followed this up by visiting co-operatives in their areas. But only in 1986 did UNAG, the representative organization of landed peasants, begin to look more closely at the issue; this was largely in response to the concern expressed by women themselves. At the 1986 UNAG conference one woman delegate complained that: 'Very few women have participated as delegates, despite the fact that many women are working in co-operatives. In the conference, UNAG is much more willing to recognize the participation of men.'[21] In recognition of the seriousness of the situation, delegates passed a motion stating that co-operatives 'will promote the full integration of women in the productive tasks of the co-operative, incorporating them as members in the same conditions as men.'

To give added weight to this policy, a UNAG Women's Section was formed in 1986, which now works in close collaboration with AMNLAE in most regions. Following the path of the ATC, the strategy has been to start with the grassroots, visiting individual co-operatives and encouraging co-operative committees to organize discussion meetings on the issue. Initial 'training' has involved men and women, partly to avoid alienating the men and partly to make the point that the participation of women is an issue that everyone should tackle — men especially. To this end, a booklet has been produced containing structured workshop activities intended to take place in both individual co-operatives and at local UNAG meetings over a number of weeks.[22]

Using interviews and quotes from co-operative members themselves, this booklet focuses on why it is so important for women to play a larger role in the co-operatives, stressing that Nicaragua is a poor country with immense problems posed by imperialism and that to overcome this crisis, 'we must all pull together — men and women.' The economic benefits to the family of women's increased participation are also emphasized. One co-operative member quoted by UNAG said: 'It's nice that the woman works alongside her husband because for her family she increases the production of the co-operative. If with one member we make two litres of milk, with two members we make four litres for us and our children.' Another male co-operative worker insists that women workers are more reliable than men: 'You'll find her here every day, whereas us men you'll find here sporadically, perhaps we'll go off with a friend or move off to another place.' The closing activity in the booklet asks the group to evaluate the involvement of women in their own co-operatives and to discuss practical measures for improving the situation.

In 1987, after these initial discussions involving both men and women, women-only meetings began, so as to give women more space in which to identify their problems and gain great confidence. In May 1988, for example, 600 women from co-operatives and peasant farms throughout the Chinandega region got together to review their current position. The role of meetings like these in enabling *campesinas* to speak about their general problems as women — often for the first time — is illustrated by the scope of the discussion at Chinandega. Some of the issues were directly related to the work environment: the need for more technical training was emphasized; women must learn to drive tractors, insisted one delegate, because when the men drink, they wreck the machines which costs the whole co-operative a lot of money; anger was also expressed at those men who still placed obstacles in the way of women becoming full co-operative members. But work did not set the parameters for this meeting. Many of those present called for political courses while others lamented the fact that most of those who are illiterate are women.[23]

In February 1989 the first National Assembly of UNAG women was held, attended by around 100 delegates. The mood of the meeting appears to have been quite militant with a whole range of demands put forward. There were complaints, for example, that some co-operatives still paid women less than men. Delegates also called for land titles granted to collective farms to be written in the names of families and not simply the male heads of households, 'because men always leave women, not the reverse, [and] the woman and children are thrown out on the street.' 'And what about the rights of widows?' added another delegate. According to current law, the widow of a member of a collective farm has no right to inherit her husband's share in the farm.[24] But many demands related to the general state of co-operatives, indicating that women in the rural co-op movement are as keen to contribute to the sort of 'mainstream' discussions held by their male colleagues as they are to raise 'women's' issues. During a session attended by President Ortega, Martha Vialle from the Matagalpa UNAG Women's Section asserted that the state department, MIDINRA, was too slow in granting land titles and did not give struggling co-operatives enough support.

\*     \*     \*

## Matagalpa women's coffee brigade

'*Watch out! Watch out! We're warning you: we're so much more than we were before,*' chanted the first-ever Nicaraguan women's coffee brigade as they picked coffee on the steep, wet mountainsides of Matagalpa, from

*November 1987 to February 1988. This brigade had been organized by Matagalpa UNAG specifically to boost the participation of women in the region's co-operatives.*

Those involved were from all over Nicaragua and all walks of life. There were ATC activists from Granada, secretaries and factory workers from Managua and a number of women from co-operatives in the Matagalpa region. 'We are showing what women are capable of doing, and letting women from different areas share their experiences,' said Marta Valle (brigade co-ordinator). 'It is a big step', she emphasized. 'The idea that a peasant woman would leave her home and husband and go miles away to pick coffee was unheard of. . . Many men said: "Who'll cook my food? Who'll wash my clothes?" Or they became angry and jealous just thinking of their wives off on their own.' Yet despite all the obstacles, 75 women, nearly twice the initial goal of 45, participated in the brigade.

For many of them the most rewarding aspect of the experience was working with other women. This was particularly important for the campesinas, *several of whom were quite isolated in their co-operatives. 'I live on a co-operative, but I didn't even know how they work,'* said Efautina Lopez. 'I wanted to learn more. This was all my decision,' she stressed. 'My husband doesn't know I came. He mobilized with another UNAG harvest brigade and then I came here. We'll see what happens when he gets back . . .' At each of the co-operative farms the brigade visited the women held meetings with the co-operative families, and acted out scenes of women discussing their decision to join the brigade. There were also practical classes on farm organization, chairing meetings, giving reports and other skills.

The experience of this first-ever Nicaraguan women's coffee brigade reverberated throughout the Matagalpa region. A second brigade was held in 1988–89 in which many more women participated, as those who could not leave their homes were able to take part in mini-brigades organized inside each co-operative coffee farm. In total, around 600 women were involved.

\*     \*     \*

## Conclusion

It will be several years before the overall success of UNAG's new policies can be gauged. Yet even within the space of a year, a small increase in women's participation in co-operatives was noted. In early 1987, there were only 819 women members in the co-operatives of Region VI (central northern part of the country) — fewer than 5% of the total but by the end of the year, there were 1,249 women co-operative members in the region.[25] As far as participation in the union was concerned, by February 1989, 18,000 of UNAGs 125,000 members were women and of these 900 were on local UNAG leadership bodies and two were members of UNAG's national executive committee.[26]

The full participation of women in all the country's rural co-operatives may still be far off, but through the UNAG Women's Section, *campesina* women are at least beginning to find a space in which to develop their strategies and gain confidence for the challenge presented to them in their individual co-operatives.

## Notes

1. Frances Hollis, account of a day in the life of Dona Antonia, 1988, *Nicaragua Today*, February 1989.

2. Angel & Macintosh, 1987, pp. 82–3.

3. See *Revolución y mujeres del campo. El Impacto de la Reforma Agraria Sandinista sobre la subordinación de la mujer rural*, ATC, September 1985.

4. Cattle farmer from Boaco, interviewed in ATC documentary video on women agricultural workers, 1987.

5. Ana Criquillon, interviewed during Nicaragua Solidarity Campaign (NSC) women's study tour, 1987.

6. Heliette Ehlers, speaking in London, May 1987.

7. Ibid.

8. Juana Córdoba, quoted in *NSC Women's Network Newsletter*, Summer 1987.

9. Alicia Andino, quoted in Angel & Macintosh, 1987, pp. 116, 122, 123.

10. Melba, interviewed in ATC video, op. cit.

11. Heliette Ehlers, quoted in *Machete*, ATC, September 1987.

12. Ibid.

13. Figure given by Olga Maria Espinosa, head of ATC Women's Secretariat, quoted in *The Militant* (USA), 16 December 1988.

14. Ibid.

15. Ana Criquillon, quoted in a workshop organized by British Residents in Nicaragua Women, Managua 1987.

16. NSC women's study tour report, 1987.

17. Modesta Reyes Martínez, quoted in *Barricada*, 9 May 1988.

18. Ibid.

19. Anita Casco, quoted in *Somos*, AMNLAE, No. 28, 1986.

20. Consuela Talavera, quoted in *Barricada*, 25 October 1987.

21. *Somos*, 1986.

22. See *La participación de la mujer campesina en la producción*, UNAG, 1987.

23. *Barricada*, 28 May 1988.

24. *The Militant* (USA), 31 March 1989.

25. *The Militant* (USA), 19 February 1988.

26. *The Militant* (USA), 31 March 1989.

# 5. Urban Women

## Surviving economic crisis

Conditions for Nicaragua's urban women differ significantly from those facing women in the country. Urban living standards are generally regarded as being higher than those in the countryside. In revolutionary Nicaragua, however, the picture is not quite so simple. From one angle, the two groups remain very distinct, from another, revolution and war have acted as a leveller between town and country.

Much existing research on this issue relates to the capital city, Managua, but the conditions described below were to be found in most other Nicaraguan cities during the mid to late 1980s.

### Managua — migration lake

Throughout Latin America, deteriorating conditions in the countryside have caused peasant communities to migrate in their thousands to the cities; Nicaragua is no exception. Between 1940 and 1975 the population of Managua grew from 62,500 to 400,000. Ten years later it was home to nearly a million people, approximately one third of the entire Nicaraguan population. In proportion to the total population, Managua is more populous than Mexico City.

Revolution has not curbed the influx of rural immigrants to urban centres; on the contrary, some changes initiated since 1979 have actually stimulated urban migration. 'The abolition of semi-feudal relationships in the countryside freed people from longstanding ties to particular landowners,' writes researcher Doreen Massey.[1] At the same time the revolution heightened expectations and encouraged people to seek out new opportunities further afield. Better transport facilities and communications also made it easier for rural populations to reach urban centres. Despite improvements in the rural areas, migration therefore remained an attractive option, and became even more attractive with the implementation of an Urban Reform Programme in the early 1980s. At that time a number of state-funded housing complexes were built in poor urban *barrios*. In Managua, some of the empty, disused land was distributed amongst individual households, and illegal 'squatter' settlements were legalized. Meanwhile a materials bank was established to provide resources for self-build housing developments. To rural people, the grass still looked greener in the city.

During the mid-1980s, war accelerated immigration; as fighting intensified in the rural war zones, peasant families fled to the relative safety of nearby towns, before moving on to Managua.

Despite the valiant attempts of the new government in the early 1980s, Managua has been unable to absorb its growing numbers. In 1972 the city was devastated by an earthquake, which not only killed 20,000 people but destroyed half the city's housing and 90% of its commercial buildings. Managua never recovered from the disaster, not least because Somoza and his close circle squandered most of the international aid money. The empty wasteland that constitutes the centre of Managua is an eery reminder of this episode. Vast distances still separate one part of the city from another; pavements and street lighting are almost non-existent and urban communications remain a nightmare.

Meanwhile, war has rapidly eliminated most of the improvements of the early 1980s. With 45% of the national budget diverted to the defence effort, the government can no longer meet the needs of its sprawling urban population, and shanty towns without running water, sanitation or electricity have become commonplace. Even in neighbourhoods already equipped with facilities, the water and electricity is routinely turned off for many hours, if not days, at a time. The severe shortage of imported goods, fuel and spare parts as a result of the US economic blockade has also taken its toll in urban centres: the scarcity of building materials has sent house prices rocketing and forced extended families to live cramped together under the same roof; public transport has become depleted and dangerously overcrowded as buses awaiting parts have been left to rust; vital pieces of machinery, such as water pumps, are often left unrepaired for months.

In addition, Managua has experienced serious food shortages in the face of continuing war and, more recently, drought. This has been aggravated by extreme difficulties in maintaining efficient state distribution channels. On several occasions, the capital has been drained of even basic foodstuffs such as rice, oil, and beans, all staples of the Nicaraguan diet. Amidst this climate of scarcity, a parallel market for goods in short supply (often referred to as the 'black market') has flourished, which in turn has fuelled galloping inflation. Between January and September 1988, prices rose by 4,508%,[2] while average wages rose by less than half this amount.

In July 1988 the government took measures that temporarily weakened the unofficial market, but at the same time removed price controls. Even basic consumer goods are now subject to the whims of the free market with the result that by the end of 1988, much food on sale was beyond the pockets of ordinary people. The average salary was 30,000 *córdobas* (£15) a month, and in the markets, 1lb of potatoes cost the equivalent of 25p and four onions 70p.[3] In the absence of food subsidies, employees working in production centres such as factories and farms must now rely on small productivity bonuses to supplement their inadequate wages. After the changes of July 1988, state employees in the health and education sectors were provided with monthly food parcels of beans, rice and sugar, but these only helped cushion the effects of price rises.

Life for the majority of Nicaraguans has thus become a constant struggle for survival. The pinch has been felt particularly in Managua because, in 1979, the capital's inhabitants were economically the most privileged in Nicaragua. Since then, average living standards have plummeted. Meanwhile, living standards in the countryside, traditionally lower than those of the towns, have fallen much less dramatically. In the mid-1980s the government specifically prioritized the countryside, both to boost agricultural production and to quell the tide of migration to the cities: during the coffee harvest of 1987–88, for example, state farm stores stocked items such as sanitary towels and wellington boots, which in Managua were regarded as luxury goods available only on the unnofficial market. This shows that, at an economic level, urban, as well as rural people have suffered equally from the crisis of war, despite being further removed from the battlefield.

### Women coping with crisis

The women of Managua's working classes have borne the brunt of this crisis. 'As women we feel the economic crisis much more than the men because we have the responsibility for feeding and clothing the children,' says Gladys Martínez from the town of León.[4] Women must spend hours each day searching for the cheapest food, standing in queues, walking long distances, and battling with crowded buses. At home, the extra workload is endless: cloth is now so scarce and expensive that a family's small selection of clothes — many children possess only one set of clothing — must be repaired and washed almost daily. Washing clothes is no easy task when the water is turned off most days and may come on for only a few hours in the dead of night; photos in the press of mountains of dirty washing in urban *barrios* bear witness to the problem. The lack of water has also increased the incidence of hygiene-related illnesses such as diarrhoea, particularly amongst children; the burden of caring for sick children falls inevitably on the women.

Apart from these domestic tasks, most women must also support their children financially. The concept of the male breadwinner supporting a wife and children is fairly alien to most Nicaraguans. As explained elsewhere in this study, men come and go in Nicaragua and women can rarely depend on a man's income. An estimated 60% of households in Managua are headed solely by women.[5] It is therefore not surprising that by 1983 urban women comprised 42% of the economically active population.[6] This figure probably increased in the mid-1980s at the peak of the war when a large proportion of the urban male population was away fighting the Contra. According to a study conducted by the University of Central America in 1986, women in Managua now work at least twice as many hours as men, and around 90% of women's time is absorbed in paid or remunerated work, the search for essential food supplies, and domestic tasks.[7]

## Survival strategies

But women are great adaptors. Against all odds, they have managed to keep going by devising a complex array of survival strategies. To cope with inflation, for example, those earning a monthly wage tend to spend all their money in the first week to prevent it from becoming devalued. In the second half of the month, when there is no money left, they themselves may go without food so that their children can eat. In times of extreme scarcity, women with relatives in the countryside often devise ways of securing their own private supplies of beans or rice direct from source. Some women are prepared to break the law to help make ends meet. A minor scandal erupted in the press in June 1988 when it was revealed that women textile workers were smugglling needles and cotton out of a factory in sanitary towels between their legs.[8] Almost exclusively, the perpetrators of the increasing number of urban robberies and muggings are men, yet in desperation, some women may also be turning to crime. In May 1988 a young girl in the northern town of Chinandega was reported to have been robbed by two women while on her way to college.[9]

But the commonest survival strategy is based on the 'let's all pull together' philosophy. The image of the single mother struggling on her own is relatively rare in Nicaragua: in working-class *barrios* all members of a family unit — children, grandchildren, sisters and mothers — contribute collectively to the survival strategy. Generally, each person performs a different role: one may be a salaried worker in the state sector where there is a possibility of subsidized provisions; another may spend the day searching for food, while a teenage daughter might do most of the housework. Increasingly, at least one teenage or adult son will leave to work (usually illegally) in the United States, and will send home a few dollars from time to time. Dollars go a long way in Nicaragua. If a grandmother lives with the family, she will usually look after the smallest children; but children in the 7–12 age range are expected to work, often spending at least some of the day selling *tortillas* or other consumer goods prepared by older members of the family.

The study compiled by the University of Central America concluded that the larger the economic unit, the better off its members. Small units consisting of a single or abandoned mother and her children fare the worst, producing barely enough on which to survive.

The so-called 'women's collective' is one of the most successful survival models. Instead of living in poverty and loneliness, groups of women strengthen their position by uniting in one single home and creating a circle of cottage production. In these situations there are very few men who help maintain the family. Generally, the circle is composed of close relatives: sisters, daughters-in-law and sisters-in-law, as in the following case-study.

In 1986, Rosario, 36, her daughter, Claudia, 16, and her sister, Isabel, 29, were working together in a collective making *fresco* (fruit drinks) and sweet *atol* (a corn and milk drink). Rosario also had two younger daughters who helped prepare the drinks and accompanied her to sell them or to buy more ingredients. Claudia helped in this process but studied at the same time. Isabel, who had three small children, took the major responsibility for the care of the house. Outside this production circle, but helping the group, was Rosario's niece, Roxana, 22, who cleaned the floors in the Ministry of Agrarian Reform and contributed to the group with her CAT card (abolished in 1988) which gave her and other public employees the right to buy certain products at very favourable prices.[10]

In this economic strategy, it is difficult to distinguish between paid work and housework. The making and selling of *atol* and *fresco* is intimately linked to the process of feeding the family as these products are an essential part of the family's diet.

The work of the Sandinista Defence Committees (CDS) in urban working-class *barrios* can be seen as an extension of women's collective survival strategy. Women comprise 67% of the membership of these local street and *barrio* committees.[11] 'The women play a much greater role in the CDSs than the men,' asserts Gladys Martínez, co-ordinator of a *barrio* CDS in León. In 1987, the business of her CDS was dominated by the need to control the local unofficial market and help women cope with the economic crisis:  'As the war has advanced in the last six years there has been more economic destruction. Life is getting more and more expensive.' One serious problem is that if something is worth 300 *córdobas*, such as a loaf of bread, people will resell it for as much as 1,000 *córdobas*. Consequently, a food supply committee (directed by the *barrio* CDS) keeps an eye on prices, trying to ensure that products are distributed through secure channels, that is, through the '*expendios*' (government stores). Another objective of Gladys's CDS was encouraging families to secure their food supply by growing their own vegetables.

There are about 100 family gardens and one communal garden in this *barrio*. Growing one's own food is another way of helping to make ends meet. What we're trying to do at the moment is survive, so if you can cook up a meal using your own vegetables that's something, you feel the inflation a little less.[12]

Clearly, Nicaragua's urban women, in common with their rural counterparts, are fighting hard against economic crisis. At the time of writing (1989), however, many women were wondering just how much longer they could survive. Until US destabilization ceases and the country's fundamental economic problems are solved, conditions are likely to deteriorate rather than improve.

# Women in the urban workforce

## Market sellers

To a greater or lesser extent, most family units depend on the informal sector, either to supplement their income from waged labour or, more commonly, for their major financial support. By the 'informal sector', Nicaraguans generally mean private individuals or families, trading in goods and services, usually on a relatively small scale. This can be roughly divided into two categories: larger-scale commerce engaged in by middle-class people with some capital, who may own a shop or a small business; and petty commerce dominated by the popular classes who have next to no capital. The latter mainly takes place in streets or markets and the goods on sale are often home-produced: popular foods and drinks etc., vegetables, clothes, and crafts.

Here, we are concerned mainly with the popular classes' informal sector. A 1982 study of Nicaragua's markets revealed that 84% of such retail traders were women.[13] It may be asked why this is primarily a female activity. Part of the answer lies in the discrimination that exists in much of the 'formal' labour force where, because of their lack of education or formal training, women are often relegated to the most undervalued and badly paid jobs; in the informal sector, women are not subject to such discrimination. To sell in the markets, especially if the merchandise is home-produced, no particular qualifications and relatively little capital are needed.

In Somoza's time it was primarily poor, uneducated country women who made their way to the markets. Many came to supplement their menfolk's incomes during the so-called 'dead times' between harvests when there was almost no work to be had on the cash-crop estates. As conditions worsened in the countryside, others settled permanently in the markets. The growth in the informal sector is thus a by-product of the general wave of migration from the country. In many cases, market sellers began as maids in middle-class suburbs before moving to the relative economic freedom of the market. Out of 70 market women from Managua's Roberto Huembes and Oriental markets surveyed in 1986, the majority had worked as maids ten or 20 years previously.[14]

Since the early 1980s, there have been some major changes in these patterns. Firstly, the informal sector is expanding even faster than in Somoza's day. The investigative journal, *Pensamiento Propio*, estimates the growth rate at around 24% annually.[15] Secondly, skilled and professional women are now swelling the ranks of those market women who were previously maids and peasant farmers.

These developments may surprise those who regard petty commerce as anathema to popular socialist governments. Yet, in the context of war and economic crisis, it seems logical that women should seek solutions to their financial problems in the informal sector. As the war and the economic blockade have dragged on, money in state coffers has dwindled and wages in the state sector have dropped sharply. Private sector wages have also failed to keep pace with inflation. On average, urban wages are estimated to have fallen by 90% since 1979.[16] At the same time, the number of formal urban jobs has fallen. In May 1988, the government had to make thousands of state workers redundant in the cost-cutting process known as '*compactación*' (see chapter 3). For thousands of city dwellers it has therefore become impossible to make a living in the formal, waged sector. One of the quirks of the economic crisis is that someone selling fruit drinks on the streets may well earn more than a professional employee in a high-up government office. A woman now working as a market seller claimed in 1986 that, 'as an accountant, I didn't earn enough to support myself and my children'.[17]

Yet market sellers interviewed in the Huembes and Oriental survey stessed that money was not the attraction. There were other advantages, such as being one's own boss and working more flexibly with less intensive timetables than in the formal sector; being able to care for one's children 'on the job' is an added bonus. All but two of the 70 women from the sample had children (the average number being four) and some 70% were heads of households. All felt quite capable of managing without husbands; indeed the majority preferred it that way, 'because without a husband, I am free, independent and my own boss'.

As inflation spiralled in the mid-1980s, the popular classes dedicated to informal commerce were sometimes singled out as the main perpetrators of the mushrooming illegal, unofficial market, but this is a myth. Selling at a high price and speculating are quite different. High prices, are a result of inflation: for example, a sweetmaker who must buy her sugar at a high price is forced to reflect this in her sale prices, otherwise she will be unable to buy the next lot of sugar at the next round of price increases.

Speculation is not simply selling at high prices but rather hoarding products until they double or triple in value due to inflation. The small traders of the informal urban sector obviously cannot do this, as they lack the capital to buy up large quantities of goods. Most speculative trading had been at a higher level, amongst the middle classes and often inside the more formal commercial and distribution channels.

Women market sellers and street vendors are often as much producers as traders. Admittedly they are self-employed and do not work in a factory or a farm. Nonetheless, the sale of *tortillas*, sweets, *frescos*, and other basic consumer goods involves productive work. Managua's small traders are therefore contributing to the government's overall target of increasing production.

The self-employed producers of the popular classes cannot control inflation, but they have at least tried to improve the situation. Many women market sellers are involved in Sandinista Defence Committees (there are several in Managua's Huembes market), which have worked hard to control the speculative market.

Most market sellers are actually part and parcel of the state-controlled distribution system. After the Triumph, the new government decided to make use of existing retail outlets rather than create a whole new state network. Part of the policy was to channel basic supplies through market sellers who were organized into 'associations' or federations of legal vendors. The associations purchase their supplies wholesale from the government distribution department, MICOIN, and then share them out equitably amongst all members of the association. In this way speculation can be controlled and production more securely maintained. The associations also operate as quasi-trade unions, representing and negotiating with the government on behalf of their members over prices and distribution of supplies.

Obviously, this is not a foolproof system. In times of extreme scarcity, market sellers receive insufficient supplies from MICOIN and must turn to the private sector, where prices are high. Nevertheless, women interviewed in the Huembes market in December 1987 saw the new system as a great improvement on the previous state of affairs.

> Before, it was chaos [remarked a sweet-seller]. The people who had more money got the most sugar. Now we share, now we organize so that supplies get to the people . . . After the Triumph, all those who used to make sweets were called together to form an association. In this association, they give us the bags, all the materials and these come directly to us at the market at low prices. When some sackfuls of sugar come they have to be shared out between everybody so that we can all carry on working. We all have to solve these problems.[18]

## Conditions in the markets

The Huembes is a model market: its covered premises are equipped with running water, electricity, cemented and tiled surfaces and scrupulously clean toilets. But it is not unique. In the first two years of the revolution, 36 new local markets were built in Managua alone, as part of the government's plan to stimulate the local economy. Considering the improvement in their working conditions, it is perhaps not surprising that women working in these markets should support the FSLN:

> When people get to know the way things work here, especially the hygiene and cleanliness, they see that it's better. Produce lasts longer because it's not out in the sun or the rain . . . In the market there used to be a lot of crime — here, no. The government has arranged 24-hour security and people can see that it's much safer here . . . Next to the market we have a crèche where the children can spend the day while their parents work.[19]

In contrast, the Oriental market, only a few miles from the Huembes, exudes an atmosphere of decay: kitchen stalls are black with grease and dirt, gutters are clogged with rubbish and children scream in the heat of the midday sun as there is no enclosed area for stalls. Unlike the Huembes market, the Oriental has traditionally been both a haven for speculators and an organizing ground for counter-revolutionaries. For this reason, it has not been rebuilt

Nevertheless, in 1987 and 1988, great efforts were made to clean up speculation in the Oriental, not only by the Sandinista police but also by local Sandinista Defence Committees incorporating women market sellers opposed to the speculation of a few. As in the Huembes market, a large proportion of women in the Oriental also belong to associations. In 1988, the Oriental's association of meat-sellers, for example, organized protests outside Managua's town hall against the high price of meat supplies. A committee representing 28 associations in the Oriental actively supports the FSLN. 'None of us are ever going to side with the landlords and perpetrators of the counter-revolution or with the Reagan administration', exclaimed one woman at a market-sellers committee meeting in May 1988. 'We don't want to be confused with those who form the black market and those who are receiving money from CUS [counter-revolutionary trade union].'[20] Also in May 1988, a health sub-committee of this commission, all of whom were women market sellers, collaborated with local AMNLAE officials to try to improve sanitation in the market. The market sellers' children are plagued with diarrhoea caused by the flies, mud and decaying food that abound in the Oriental.[21]

## Domestic workers

In Nicaragua, women's unpaid work in the home is often combined with badly paid domestic work in other people's homes. By 1979, domestic workers accounted for a quarter of all Nicaraguan women working outside their own homes. Most of the women work either as live-in housekeepers or as day-time maids, but office cleaners and women who take in washing and ironing also fall into the category 'domestic workers'. Because domestic wages are so low, the employment of private domestics is a custom that extends far beyond the upper classes, which partly explains the large number of jobs in this sector. But, as in other parts of Latin America, the concentration of women in domestic work is also related to the steady migration of peasants to the urban areas. For women migrants without skills, education or money to spend on hotels or rents, domestic work in private houses is initially the only option. After all, it is work in which poor women are usually experienced and that at least provides them with some sort of board and lodging (for housekeepers). Yet this is literally all such employment has to offer. Isolated from other workers and from all except the employer's family, domestics have been exposed to the most highly exploitative conditions. In Somoza's time, they worked at the whim of the employer without fixed hours for very little pay and enjoyed virtually no legal protection. Most of those entering domestic employment were young girls, some only 12 or 13, as the following testimony reveals:

> I was 12 when I went to work for the Alegria family. I used to clean the floors, grind the maize and coffee, and cook supper. And I had to work even when I was sick. Once when I refused, they took me off to the National Guard for a lesson. I slept in their cheese dairy and drops of butter would fall on me. The place stank; it gave me bad headaches. With all the grinding I did I can still feel the pain my hands.[22]

After the Triumph, however, domestic workers began speaking out about their working conditions. Towards the end of 1979, domestics from all parts of the country met with the FSLN's National Directorate to discuss their work situation. Their first demand was for the elimination of paid domestic work. 'We are sure that domestic service will cease to exist in the future, because as production increases, jobs will increase too,' said one representative.[23] To some extent, their predictions came true, as we shall see later, but as there was no immediate alternative for many domestic workers, this demand remained a more distant goal. In the meantime, with the support of AMNLAE, a Union of Domestics was founded in 1980, which by July 1981 could boast a national membership of 2,000.

Officially, the Union has won a 10-hour day (with one day off a week), the right to double pay for holiday work and extra hours, a minimum wage and six months salary following dismissal. This latter law has been particularly important to domestics as many are dismissed when their employers discover they are pregnant. In recognition of the difficulties isolated domestics would face if they had to confront their employers directly, a special procedure for negotiating these rights was also set up. Women were to take their grievance to the union, which would then file a claim at the Ministry of Labour which, if the employer was seen to be violating the new regulations, would intervene on the worker's behalf.

Needless to say, implementation of these laws and rights has been no easy task. 'Some women say that little has been achieved in practice,' claimed one domestic in 1981.

> The 10-hour day hasn't been fulfilled and often in the Ministry of Labour the complainant does not get the support she seeks. Another thing is the wages. The recent decree stipulated a minimum of 400 *córdobas* — for the supposed 10-hour day — but it is clear that this salary, especially for a mother with children, or for someone who comes from the provinces and who regularly goes to see her family, is insufficient.[24]

Under the state wage controls (abolished in 1988), domestics were always on the lowest scale.

Employers' reactions to the new laws were generally hostile. Carmen Talavera, secretary of the Domestic Workers' Union in Estelí, recounts how in the early 1980s her union organized marches to particularly exploitative bosses' houses to demand that they comply with the regulations of the National Directorate. In response, employers then began spying on the Domestic Workers' Union, sometimes even attending meetings. If they saw any of their employees present at the meetings, they immediately fired them. Not surprisingly, this discouraged other domestics from becoming involved in the Union or, indeed, from doing anything to fight for their newly gained rights. By 1981, in Managua, out of a total membership of 1,200, only 30 women were actively participating in the Union.

The isolation characteristic of domestic work is the main impediment to organizing women into the Union. 'The struggle to get out of the house and come to the meetings seems too great for such small rewards,' commented one worker in 1981.[25] Carmen Talavera of Estelí holds a similar view: 'We don't like this situation where our workers are sleeping in their workplace because they never overcome anything. They don't have the spirit to get out . . . or do anything.'[26]

Significantly, most of the active members of the Estelí union work as cleaners in the state sector or in commercial offices — Carmen, for example, cleans the offices of a regional trade union where she clearly has a great deal of contact with other workers. She regrets that, 'very few of our members are working in private homes'. Part of the problem is that domestic workers in private houses rarely have anywhere to meet each other outside their workplace. This is why the Estelí union has been trying to set up a sewing school, which would not only enable women to learn a skill but also to get to know each other.

Working towards the abolition of paid domestic work, the Domestics' Union placed great emphasis in its early years on encouraging women to study or train for alternative employment. In may cases the literacy crusade of 1980 had simply passed them by. According to Esperanza González, a full-time official for the Union in 1981, 'Many of the domestics didn't learn to read because when the [literacy] census was taken the employers would say that they were their daughters or nieces, that they didn't have any workers . . .'[27] To combat this problem, the Union set about organizing special classes for domestic workers. In Managua, for example, sewing and reading classes were held in the Union's headquarters.

## Decline of the Domestics' Union

Despite the great efforts made to improve domestics' working conditions and future prospects, most of these initiatives date from the early 1980s. By the mid to late 1980s, it seems that the domestics' movement had stagnated and faded away. In 1988 Carmen Talavera claimed that the Estelí union was the only branch still functioning, that national union structure no longer existed and that even the Estelí union was barely managing to continue.

How do we account for this decline in activity? For Estelí it may have been partly force of circumstance: union meetings must be held on Sundays because this is the day that domestic workers have free. But Sunday is also the day when women from Estelí (a town in the war zone) go up to the mountains to visit their sons and husbands in the army. Hence the poor attendance at union meetings since 1983, when military service was introduced.

But there is a more fundamental reason underlying this decline. Despite the support, by AMNLAE and the government in 1979, for the aim of ultimately eradicating domestic employment, the work of domestics has, ironically, played a vital role in the revolutionary process. It has freed up time for other women to work outside the home and engage in political activities (as the revolution instructs them to do). Thus the interests of organized domestic workers have clashed with the interests of other women of other classes and with the goal of incorporating more women into productive and revolutionary activities. This contradiction was recognized by AMNLAE as early as 1981:

> The domestic in Nicaragua has been the subject of brutal over-exploitation. [But] in this stage of the Revolution, domestic work is necessary and indispensable as it . . . enables others to integrate into productive activities.[28]

In the opinion of Canadian researcher Beth Woroniuk, however, AMNLAE failed to resolve this conflict of interests. In the early 1980s, 'A fundamental restructuring of responsibilities in the home that would distribute the tasks more equally among all family members was thought to be out of the question, as was a major state initiative to socialize reproductive tasks.'[29] Hence the need for domestics to continue in their traditional roles, and from the domestics' point of view, traditional roles constituted bad working conditions, long hours and low pay. It was this contradiction that effectively killed the domestics' movement.

But the story does not end here. Since the early 1980s, it could be argued that events have overtaken AMNLAE's position. As predicted by domestic workers themselves in 1979, revolution and war have changed the face of the labour force. In the new Nicaragua, young teenaged women who previously would have had no option but to work as domestics are now studying and training for jobs in other sectors. Towards the mid-1980s when more and more men were away fighting the Contra, alternative employment open to women increased even further. Women who worked as domestics in the past have also drifted into other jobs. There has always been a traditional progression from domestic work to petty commerce, but economic crisis and inflation have accelerated this process.

Whatever employment women now choose to engage in, domestic work is definitely a last resort. Despite the introduction of legal minimum wages, they are not sufficient to live on in these times of economic crisis, and the working conditions remain poor. As a result, far fewer Nicaraguan women were working as domestics in the late 1980s than there had been in the late 1970s.

While creating day-to-dy difficulties for Nicaragua's professional women, the shortage of domestic workers has at the same time helped to identify the solution to the dilemma of domestic work, as highlighted in *Barricada* by Alicia Torres of the Women's Governmental Office:

'A slave', I replied to a friend who asked me about my Sunday activities. Because that is how it feels — crinkly hands, dirty washing, and other distasteful domestic things. It never used to be like this, some think it's the Revolution's fault and that is true . . . Of course, the Revolution comes and teaches the people how to read, divides up three million *manzanas* of land, sends more than 5,000 young people to study abroad and in general creates a new feeling of dignity and confidence. Peasant and working-class women have expectations which go beyond looking after other people's children and inheriting odd bits of clothing and shoes from the boss. So what shall we do, we women who are workers, housewives, members of some sort of organization, and students on top of all that? In the developed countries . . . it is also difficult to get domestic workers: they barely exist. However, there women have at their service washing machines, dishwashers, pre-cooked food and other things beyond our reach. Apart from the historical backwardness of our country, we also have war . . .

It is possible that the social responsibilities we Nicaraguan women have assumed will determine that we can no longer devote ourselves solely to husband and children. I guess the solution — in fact I don't see any other option — is to divide up and share out the household chores.[30]

Judging by the FSLN *Proclama* of 1987 on women's emancipation, and AMNLAE's Platform of Struggle for 1988, Alicia Torres' views may now be the general line of thinking amongst the country's policy-makers. Both of these documents stress the need for domestic work to be shared equally between men and women. If this were to become a reality, then clearly the dilemma described above would cease to exist.

## Prostitution

Long before the Triumph, the Historic Programme of the FSLN had specified that a future Sandinista government would 'eliminate prostitution and other social disgraces so as to raise women's dignity.' But why, with so much other business facing the new government, was the designation of prostitution as a criminal offence one of the government's first measures only months after the Triumph?

In Somoza's days there had been no laws against prostitution, rather it had flourished under the patronage of the regime itself; Somoza's National Guard were also deeply implicated. 'The brothel owners used to give the *Guardia* a cut,' explains an ex-prostitute from the port of Corinto. 'If the prostitutes managed to escape, the *Guardia* would seek them out and return them to the owners.'[31]

Somaza's corrupt economic policies were also perceived as an underlying cause of the dramatic growth in prostitution during the latter years of the dictatorship.

> With the big shift towards cotton production in the 1950s [says FSLN Comandante Tomás Borge], thousands of peasants were thrown off their land. Many moved to the cities and became workers. But not all could find a market for their labour. Families broke up. Some of the peasant women were abandoned by their husbands and had to make their own way. To feed and clothe their children, many women were forced to sell their bodies.[32]

Ideologically, the FSLN has associated prostitution with the exploitative relationships of capitalism. Borge describes it as:

> A war of prejudice, discrimination, a war in which capitalism tries to turn women into trash, buying and selling them like merchandise, like a luxury item or cheap vegetable, depending on the quality of the merchandise.[33]

In short then, for the Sandinistas, prostitution epitomized all the wrongs of the Somoza regime.

Of course, this oldest trade in history has yet to be eradicated from Nicaragua. With the worsening of the economic situation it is even thought to be on the increase. Around 800 prostitutes are said to be currently operating in Managua alone.[34]

A study of prostitution published by CIRA in 1987 claimed that at least 50% of Nicaragua's prostitutes had entered the trade because of their desperate economic situation. In common with market sellers, 50% had previously been domestics. Many became prostitutes so as to be able to provide their children with a better future: 'I want my children to study and to be something in life so that they don't end up like me.'[35]

Economic factors were also stressed by Xanthis Suárez, a social worker, who conducted a two-year study (1986–88) of prostitution amongst young women in Managua's Camino del Oriente, pretending to be a prostitute herself for three months.[36] Most of the prostitutes she met told her they had children to support or that they came from a big family and had to help 'Mama'. They blamed unemployment and low wages for having driven them to prostitution.

Veronica, aged 24, is typical of those analysed in Suárez's study. Since her husband left her, Veronica and her mother have had to care for her own two children, two children of an irresponsible brother, and two children of a sister kidnapped by the Contra. The family first failed to support them all, and Veronica was worried by how thin her mother was becoming.

In Nicaragua, prostitution is not a clear-cut profession. As pointed out previously, urban women's survival strategies frequently depend on a variety of incomes. Very few of the women in Suárez's study were full-time prostitutes and went on 'the game' only two or three times a week. Out of the three women with whom Suárez became most closely acquainted, one studied, another worked in a school, and another made cakes. For many, prostitution provides a supplement to other incomes.

Perhaps this raises the question of how to define 'prostitution'. It is not uncommon in Nicaragua — especially with the current economic crisis — for a single mother to sleep with a neighbour or a man she knows for a bit of sugar or some beans. Similarly, women often have sex with an unfaithful and sporadically appearing *compañero* in the hope that he may have brought something for the children.

## Rehabilitation

Recognizing that most prostitutes turn to the business primarily for economic reasons, AMNLAE and the social welfare ministry, INSSBI, have made some efforts to rehabilitate and retrain prostitutes in the hope of steering them towards alternative employment. The first rehabilitation hostel was set up in 1982 in Corinto — an apt setting as Corinto was the centre of Somocista corruption and it was here that high-ranking officials of the National Guard owned brothels. Within a year of opening, the hostel had already catered for about 80 of the 120 local prostitutes, providing daily educational and training classes in such occupations as sewing, typing, and broom-making. Although these are the traditional, low-status occupations to women they have boosted the women's self-confidence and realization of their potential.

> In Chinandega . . . in El Viejo, in León, in the sugar mills of San Antonio in Chichigalpa . . . where men are paid in cash a woman is more or less certain of work, so she goes prepared. And me, I used to drink a lot, I used to smoke marijuana and everything . . . Now I don't feel the same. I feel a different person . . . Once accepted here, they even gave me the opportunity to teach adult education classes. I am going to prepare myself to teach. From nine to ten I get music lessons; from two to four I get typing lessons; and from seven to nine I give adult education classes.[37]

In Managua, the 'women's psycho-social rehabilitation centre' is the only project aimed at helping the capital's prostitutes. Run jointly by INSSBI and the Centro Ecumenico Antonio Valdivieso (CAV), this centre is highly successful in persuading women to give up prostitution. By the end of 1986, out of 168 women participating in the centre's programme, 107 had decided to abandon prostitution. The centre operates not as a hostel but as a drop-in centre where women can go for group therapy sessions two or three times a week. The aim of these sessions is first to get women to recognize their condition as prostitutes and then to bring them to the realization that they are not 'bad' women but that prostitution is a problem caused by society at large. The centre also helps to place prostitutes in alternative jobs.

### Police practice
Co-operating with INSSBI's rehabilitation projects is the Sandinista Police. At the Corinto hostel, for example, police representatives serve on the management committee and the local police recommend prostitutes to the hostel when they arrest them. All the studies on prostitution point out the contrast between current police practice and that of Somoza's National Guard. Despite the fact that prostitution is illegal, most prostitutes are arrested not because of their trade but because of petty crimes associated with it, such as robbery, drunkenness, fights, or scandalous behaviour. The Sandinista Police are not involved in prostitution rackets and prostitutes can now denounce individual policemen who abuse them and, in line with national directives, such policemen are supposed to be punished.

Suárez noted that the prostitutes she studied in the Camino del Oriente now regard the police as their friends, but there have been isolated incidents of police brutality. In Managua in February 1981, for example, police smashed their way through prostitutes' huts around the Oriental market at the request of local community organizers.[38] Much work is still needed to change the attitudes of individual policemen. 'These women don't do it out of necessity, they do it because they like it,' is a typical remark made by one policeman in Managua.[39] In order to challenge such attitudes, the INSSBI-CAV centre has organized a series of seminars specifically for policemen.

**Prevention versus cure**

Despite the important initiatives undertaken by the various rehabilitation centres, some researchers in this field have begun to express doubts about the potentiality of such work to eradicate prostitution. 'The rehabilitation centres may become nothing more than repair workshops where women damaged by society are put back together and overhauled before returning to the system,' warns one researcher.[40] Likewise, Xanthis Suárez asserted that 'we have to carry out preventive work, not only curative work. It's not just an affair for the police but for the whole of society.' In her view, INSSBI has merely identified the problem and has not moved far towards its ultimate solution.

In 1987 the co-ordinators of the INSSBI-CAV programme also began to realize the limitations of their projects and to favour more preventive work.

> Prostitutes barely represent 2% of the female population of Managua between the ages of 15 and 23 [comments one co-ordinator]. But the economic crisis means that the number of girls at risk of prostituting themselves is much higher. For this reason, we are now dedicating ourselves to prevention and re-education.[41]

The INSSBI-CAV centre also began to realize that a major obstacle preventing women leaving prostitution altogether was the attitude of the rest of society. On the one hand they are regarded as social lepers and on the other hand they are thought to be necessary in order to reduce rapes. To change social attitudes was thus identified as a major priority and to this end the centre set about organizing a series of seminars in state schools; significantly these seminars are primarily for boys.

'There is no prostitution without men,' comments Xanthis Suárez. Similar assertions have been made by the co-ordinators of the INSSBI-CAV centre: 'Why does the father of the family advise and order his daughter not to leave the house and then at the same time go himself to look for a prostitute as soon as he is round the corner?' These double standards have become the theme of the school seminars.

'What we are now trying to do with the boys,' explains an organizer of the programme, 'is not just to look at the problem of prostitution, but to look at the problem concerning women in its entirety.'[42]

**Women and the Law Conference, 1988**

The 1988 Conference on Women and Law organized by CONAPRO (see chapter 8) was even more outspoken in denouncing those who saw prostitutes as the only problem. The absence of research on men's motives for becoming prostitutes' clients was noted. Whilst recognizing the economic causes of prostitution, the delegates identified the fundamental cause of prostitution as ideological, stemming from the continuing notion of women as sexual objects at the service of men. 'It is the man who pays to touch her, rape her, and take away her dignity.'[43] (Xanthis Suárez's study of prostitution in Managua was first presented at this conference.)

At the subsequent Latin American Conference on Women and Law a few weeks later, some women proposed that prostitution be decriminalized, but that promoters of prostitution be apprehended or punished. Parallel to legal action, they suggested setting up a system of prevention through grassroots organizations, political parties, and the church.

The debate around prostitution went quite a long way beyond this Conference floor. Amongst the many issues raised there the Sandinista press regarded the discussion on prostitution as the most important and several articles focusing primarily on Suárez's study subsequently appeared in *Barricada* and *El Nuevo Diario*.

*Sweet Ramparts*, a study of Nicaraguan women published in Britain in 1983 observed that, 'because the public issue is prostitutes, not prostitution, questions of sexuality, *machismo* and attitudes to sex that create a demand for prostitutes are simply not raised'.[44] This quotation illustrates just how far the whole debate has come in six years, for now the reverse conclusion could be drawn. By the late 1980s, prostitution was being discussed in Nicaragua within the context of social relationships between men and women and not simply as a problem for prostitutes.

## Urban women's co-operatives

### Employment creation scheme

The lack of adequate employment for Nicaragua's urban women was a problem the government was keen to rectify in 1979. Waged work outside the home was regarded as the key to women's emancipation. But before the Contra war broke out (and jobs left vacant by mobilized men were made available to women), there was a question mark over how this work was to be created. In the countryside it was possible, at least in theory, to incorporate relatively large numbers of women into production, as Nicaragua's economy is primarily agricultural; in the towns, it was a more difficult task. Apart from cottage production, market selling or domestic work — jobs that were either highly exploitative or very insecure — there was no large-scale employment for urban women. The small amount of industry in existence employed very few female workers.

To generate new employment for urban women, the government hit on the idea of light industrial co-operatives manufacturing basic consumer goods and crafts. This model tallied with Sandinista ideology that favoured collective production controlled by workers themselves. As well as creating new jobs, it was considered that co-operatives would have advantages for local urban populations by 'mak[ing] available to the people a series of basic goods at the lowest possible price . . . because sales will leave out the middlemen, the speculators . . .'[45] Compared to large-scale factory production, it was also recognized that small co-operatives would be relatively cheap to set up.

One of the first co-operatives was founded in Estelí during the literacy crusade. It produced the rucksacks in which the *brigadistas* carried their teaching materials and provided work for 90 unemployed women living nearby. Since then, a women's jam-making co-operative has also been formed in Estelí, which will eventually cater for 200 women selected with the help of INSSBI and AMNLAE. Special priority has been given to untrained and unemployed women, women with socio-economic problems, single mothers and war widows.

In general, however, the women's urban co-operatives do not operate on quite the ambitious scale originally envisaged, mainly because of the lack of resources. Having been established with a motley combination of state credit, foreign donations, and women's own limited funds, by the late 1980s a large proportion of the co-operatives were struggling to keep afloat and retained only a handful of members. The main problem is one of supply. As the economic shortages have become more acute, the co-operatives have found it increasingly difficult to purchase raw materials; hence recurrent requests by women's sewing co-operatives to international solidarity organizations for fabric and thread.

Since price controls were lifted in 1988, everything has become much more expensive. On top of this, state supplies frequently run out, forcing co-operatives like the informal sector's petty traders to buy on the unofficial market, where prices are even higher. In 1988, a women's poultry co-operative in Estelí had to fold, only a year after setting up, when the price of chicken feed suddenly rocketed. In some cases women have paid for supplies out of their own wages. Additionally, buying at a high price also means selling at a high price and this has caused business to flag. Most of the co-operatives are situated in poor working-class *barrios* where there is precious little to spend on manufactured goods.

## Stereotyping women

One criticism levelled at the women's co-operatives is that they simply reinforce the division of labour. The vast majority, for example, are sewing co-operatives and sewing is traditionally a woman's job. It is laudable that women have been encouraged to participate in paid production using skills they already possess but there may be nothing new in this. Untrained and underemployed women have always made clothes and other goods at home, not only for their own family but also for sale. One could say that the co-operatives are simply a more elaborate version of the petty commerce and cottage production of the informal sector.

Nevertheless, in co-operatives there are benefits for women not to be found in the informal sector. With the help of local community organizations and AMNLAE, women in co-operatives have learnt new skills in administration, book-keeping and management — skills that previously would have been beyond their reach. Women from the Estelí jam-making project, for example, initially received ten hours a week of management training. In many cases women setting up co-operatives have been obliged to build or renovate their own premises with minimal outside help; a task these women would not have contemplated in the past. But most importantly, the experience of working together outside the home has given them a new strength and sense of identity.

Before, we used to live shut up behind four walls [comments a jam-making co-operative member]. We were unconfident and shy, but now we have overcome those attitudes and know how to live and share as a collective. We have improved our feelings about each other and are fighting individualism.[46]

The fact that these co-operatives are comprised solely of women has clearly helped women build up their confidence, in sharp contrast to the mixed agricultural co-operatives where women are generally marginalized.

\* \* \*

## Mery de Beredo sewing co-operative in Barrio Sandino, Ocotal

*Initially founded in 1983, the co-operative was quite disorganized in the first three years. At that time, the women made toys and dolls which they sold at various craft fairs in Managua. But the work was very insecure. As they were all based at home, however, they didn't really work co-operatively. Gradually women started to leave and the co-op was reduced to four members.*

*But the remaining four were determined to carry on. Barrio Sandino is very poor and its inhabitants suffered a heavy Contra attack in 1984, thus adding to the hardship. The women could see that many families were unable to clothe themselves because of the expense, so they decided to start making cheap clothes for their own barrio. With assistance from the US Maryknoll Foundation, they renovated a workshop and bought two sewing machines. The co-operative has since expanded to 18 members. The wages are not enough to live on, but the women at least have secure work.*

*There are, however, problems of supply: the women have to work extra hard to sell enough clothes to buy more material. When they fail to make enough money, they have to close the co-operative for a few weeks. The women are very reluctant to increase their prices, but at times they have little choice. Space — or lack of — is another problem. The workshop is so small that the women must work in shifts, thus reducing productivity.*

*What is men's attitude towards the co-op? 'Some of the women are either single or don't have a man in the house, so for them the issue doesn't come up', says one worker. 'But for me with a husband, it has been a bit of a struggle. He's envious. He doesn't like me being economically independent.'*

*But despite their difficulties, the women want no more help from outside because they dislike being dependent on other people.*[47]

\*     \*     \*

## Women's building co-operative, Condega

*Most co-operatives are engaged in work traditionally undertaken by women, but there are a few exceptions of which a women's building co-operative is one.*

*Chica Ponce is the single mother of six children aged 4 to 13. She is also the driving force behind a women's construction co-operative recently established in Condega. 'At first I thought it would be hard. It's no easy decision to leave your house and become a builder,' she confesses. To encourage the others, she hid her doubts, telling them that nothing in life was hard.*

*The co-operative began life as a joint brigade with a group of North American women. Throughout 1987, eight Nicaraguan women and approximately 15 'gringas' worked on constructing a primary school, funded by US solidarity organizations. The idea was for the North American women to train the Nicaraguan women in basic building skills. They had to dig ditches half a metre deep, then mix the cement, lay the bricks, cast the earthquake-proof beams and instal electrical and plumbing systems.*

*When the North American women went home, the Nicaraguan women decided to carry on working as builders. Apart form the shortage of materials, the main problem has been one of confidence. Chica agreed to become the new 'Director of Works' but still felt apprehensive and unsure about giving orders. A minor disaster with a zinc roof had shaken her confidence and the gaping hole along the central ridge of one roof is a painful reminder. Mistakes cannot be afforded when building materials are in such short supply.*

*The co-operative has also become the target of 'machista' abuse. When the first school building was finished, local men came and jeered that the women did not know how to bricklay and that the roof would fall down on the students. 'They had to eat their words when the walls held up through the tremor a few months back.' Meanwhile a Nicaraguan foreman assisting the women is always absent because of illness — or so he says. Chica suspects that he simply feels uncomfortable working with women. 'The men don't like us doing work that the men normally do. They think the role of women is simply to have children and look after the house.'*

*Yet, despite the difficulties, the co-operative has given the women a new sense of their own worth; they are now building houses in a nearby settlement for people displaced by war.*[48]

\*　　\*　　\*

## Women as industrial workers

Traditionally, US policies have been designed to maintain Central America as a captive market for US manufactured goods. Indigenous industry has been minimal. Of the small amount of industry that existed in Somoza's time, a large proportion was bombed by his own forces shortly before he fled the country. Meanwhile, as the Somoza dictatorship crumbled, Nicaragua's leading entrepreneurs were amongst the first to shut up shop and leave. Some of the factories abandoned by Somocista owners have been reclaimed by the State, while others remain in private hands. With next to no capital, a limited domestic market and a dire shortage of raw materials, profit margins are small. Nevertheless, in times of war and economic crisis, *all* productive sectors are vitally important, including the industrial sectors.

Few women are involved in industry, but, as a result of integrating women into production and scarcity of male workers during wartime, they have become more prominently involved. The plywood processing plant, PLYNIC, for example, now routinely employs women to operate machines and supervise the production process — jobs that in the past were exclusively the domain of men. Until 1985, 7% of PLYNIC's workers were female; by the end of 1986, women represented 54% of the workforce.

The textile and clothing industry is the largest employer of female labour, with women now accounting for some 70% of the 4,000 workers. The concentration of women in this sector also prompted the Women's Governmental Office (OGM) (see pp. 151–2) in 1986 to conduct a study of women textile workers.[49] The OGM's remit was to examine the extent to which women workers were still suffering discrimination. At a more pragmatic level, the study also aimed to establish whether there was any connection between the high turnover of staff, low productivity, and absenteeism in the textile industry and the specific problems affecting the female workforce. If the problems could be identified and solved, it was hoped that the resulting disruption to production would be minimized. Textiles are a priority area for Nicaragua; the economic blockade has meant a desperate shortage of cloth and clothes. With more and more people joining the defence effort in the mid-1980s, the state-owned textile factories also had to meet the growing demand for military and khaki fatigues. Thus, in the textile factories, as on the cash crop farms, women's productivity had become a matter of national strategic concern.

**Sexual division of labour**

The OGM study focused on five state-owned textile/clothes factories, all based in Managua. Published in May 1987, the study revealed that discrimination in the industrial workplace was still rife; sexual division of labour was cited as the hallmark of this discrimination. Certain jobs such as the maintenance of machinery and the transport of materials were delegated to men, while women were engaged in 'auxiliary' jobs, such as the operation of looms and sewing machines and the cleaning of machinery. Replying to why this division of labour existed, the managers of the companies said: 'Women are more dextrous. The men's jobs require more force.' But Berta Arguello, a textile worker and AMNLAE representative, said: 'Because of our lack of experience and training, we end up doing jobs similar to our traditional roles, such as cleaning and sewing.'[50]

The OGM study also showed that there was a sexual division between those who supervised and those who carried out the work. In Texnicsa, 70% of the workers were women, 80% of the supervisors were men; in Fanatex 100% of the supervisors were men. Management's attitude towards women taking up supervisory posts together with their domestic responsibilities more or less excluded women from supervisory positions.

The study also questioned the relevance of the 'equal pay for equal work' law, as it was evident that in this case women were not doing the same work as men. The work undertaken by men was better paid than that carried out by women; 50% of male workers received the highest wages offered in the productive sector, while only 8% of the women were into this category. In one factory, Cotexma, it was estimated that women's wages were approximately 70% of those of the men. The OGM study thus concluded that company managements overvalued 'masculine' jobs and undervalued 'feminine' jobs. There was a failure to provide equal pay for work of equal *value*.

Clearly, if women are to cut through the sexual division of labour, training is essential. Moreover, as long as women — the bulk of the workforce — are not trained, the technical quality of textile production cannot be significantly improved, but the OGM study revealed that few training opportunities existed for women textile workers. During the two to three weeks most courses ran, trainees were not always paid; single mothers with no other income support were thus unable to participate. Some training courses took place outside work hours but, again, domestic responsibilities prevented most women from participating. In 1987, outstanding women textile workers chosen to undertake a special mechanical training course were unable to benefit from this opportunity due to childcare problems. Such comments as: 'Women don't like to get covered in grease,' that OGM researchers encountered from male managers suggest that their attitudes contribute to women's difficulties in gaining access to training.

## Staffing problems

When the OGM women discussed general productivity with managements the major obstacle to increasing production proved to be personnel problems: a high turnover of staff (around 34% a year), absenteeism (around 15% a day in Texnicsa) and a lack of discipline. A high turnover and absenteeism are to be expected in an industry with such poor physical conditions. 'Textile workers work in conditions as bad as miners,' commented one trade union leader. The cotton fluff in the air causes respiratory disorders and the loud noise produces occupational deafness. Yet it seems that the physical conditions on the shop floor are not the decisive factor in personnel problems.

Through their interviews with ex-workers, the OGM researchers discovered it was the low salaries that had led many to seek alternative employment. Women could not feed their families on their meagre wages. In addition, textile factories work 24 hours a day and employees, must, therefore, work shifts; for women, the night shifts make childcare very difficult. One worker, described as an expert machinist held in high esteem by the supervisors, had to leave her job when her child fell ill: 'I left because of my child . . . I asked them to put me only on the day shift but they didn't want to because they said it would affect production. I then asked them to put me on the day shift just for two months while my child got better but they still said no . . . I would have stayed if they had let me work days.' The strain of women's double day, in the factory and in the home, thus appears to be the root cause of the productivity problems in Managua's textile factories.

In response to this situation, a wind of change has filtered into the textile industry. After the OGM report was published, pregnant women were prohibited from working the night shift and, with the support of AMNLAE and the CST trade union, women in the factories have managed to set up a number of childcare centres, although these have not been provided totally free of charge. In most cases women have to do extra voluntary work in the factories to compensate for the financial costs to the companies. But the moral authority such voluntary work gave them 'was the spark for people to start taking us seriously,' comments Berta Arguello.

In 1986, ENAVES, a factory directed by a woman, created a brigade of women mechanic trainees, despite a lukewarm response to the proposal from the Ministry of Industry. 'The Ministry doesn't think that women mechanics will develop very quickly,' comments director Ruth Herrera. ENAVES has ensured that the courses are in waged time and accommodating to women's busy schedules. The OGM comments that the ENAVES experience could signify the start of a new policy in the textile industry.

## Conclusion

'We can't just change things through our attitudes or through propaganda campaigns,' concluded the OGM report. 'We need practical and real changes.' To this end they proposed that the factory managements re-evaluate the skills needed for the jobs done by women, in order to raise women's salaries. They argued that those working the night shift should be paid a bonus and that all factories should have a childcare centre. Women should also be given technical training in order to break with traditional structures 'which until now have been considered natural'. The study's final word of caution reads as follows:

> Women have conquered a space in the labour market . . . closed to them in the past. But still they have something much more complicated to achieve and that is access to the better-valued jobs with higher salaries. This would make the daily struggle to feed the family and particularly children less hard.

The results of the OGM study were shared in a meeting between union leaders from the textile industries and the women who had been interviewed for the study. Apparently the women were surprised to learn that their feelings were so widespread. 'Since then the women workers have felt more involved in their work,' claims Ivonne Siu, the Director of OGM (now called the Women's Institute). 'The management had become more aware of women's issues, and AMNLAE's work in this sector has been reinvigorated.'[51]

\*       \*       \*

### Sandinista Workers' Federation (CST)

*The CST is the major union representing industrial and urban workers. Some 37% of CST members and 40% of the union's leaders are women. Although compared to the Agricultural Workers' Union (ATC), the CST has been slower to look at the specific situation of women workers, several women's meetings were held in the late 1980s, primarily in the Managua region. The first, in April 1986, was attended by 208 delegates.*

*By 1989, CST women had become much more forthright in making known their demands, particularly in relation to the process of compactación (government redundancies). Speaking at the Fundamental Forces meeting on International Women's Day in March 1989, Sandra Ramos, the CST representative on AMNLAE's National Executive, declared that her union would fight for women's right to work, which was currently being threatened by the process of compactación. She also said that the CST was calling for a re-evaluation of women's jobs and skills and for a clause to be included in the Collective Agreements between union branches and workplace managements that would allow for the immediate dismissal of those who had sexually harassed women workers.*

\*       \*       \*

# Notes

1. Massey, 1987.
2. *Envío*, October–November 1988.
3. *Independent* (London), 23 January 1989.
4. Gladys Martínez, interviewed by Rachel Stringfellow, 7 September 1987, unpublished.
5. Maxine Molyneux, in Walker (ed.), 1985.
6. Paola Pérez and Ivonne Siu, 'Cambios y desafíos: la mujer en la economía nicaragüense', OGM, Managua, 1986, p. 2.
7. University of Central America (UCA) study analysed in *Envío*, December 1986.
8. *El Nuevo Diario*, 17 June 1988.
9. *El Nuevo Diario*, 3 May 1989.
10. *Envío*, December 1986, p. 44.
11. FSLN *Proclama*, 1987.
12. Gladys Martínez, interview, op. cit.
13. Aida Redondo, 'El sector informal: la mujer en el pequeno comercio', analysed in *Pensamiento Propio*, 31 March 1986.
14. Ibid.
15. Ibid.
16. *Financial Times* (London), 6 January 1989.
17. *Cuadernos de Investigación*, INIES, No.1.
18. Sweet-seller, interviewed by Helen Collinson and Elaine Ginsburg, Huembes market, Managua, December 1987, unpublished.
19. Market seller, Huembes market, Managua, February 1982, quoted in Deighton et al, 1983, p. 78.
20. *El Nuevo Diario*, 4 May 1988.
21. Ibid.
22. Adela Cruz, in Angel & Macintosh, 1987, pp. 81–3.
23. Nicolasa Morales, quoted in Deighton et al, 1983, p. 88.
24. Domestic worker, quoted in *Ventana*, August 1981.
25. Ibid.
26. Carmen Talavera, interviewed by Helen Collinson and Elaine Ginsburg, January 1988, unpublished.
27. Esperanza González, quoted in Deighton et al, 1983, p. 84.
28. *El Nuevo Diario*, 6 December 1981.
29. Beth Woroniuk, 'Women's Oppression and the Revolution — The Nicaraguan Debate', CUSO, 1987, p. 5.
30. *Barricada*, 28 July 1987.
31. *Documentos sobre la mujer*, CIRA, October–December 1987.
32. Tomás Borge, quoted in *International Socialist Review*, October 1985.
33. Ibid.
34. *Amanecer*, May–June 1988.
35. *Documentos sobre la mujer*, op. cit.
36. Xanthis Suárez García, 'Las muchachas del camino', paper to Nora Astorga National Seminar on Women and the Law, 4–6 August 1988.
37. Adela del Carmen Martínez Velázquez, quoted in Deighton et al, 1983, pp. 88–9.
38. Deighton et al, 1983, p. 88.
39. *Documentos sobre la mujer*, op. cit.
40. Ibid.
41. *Amanecer*, op. cit.
42. Ibid.
43. *El Nuevo Diario*, 9 August 1988.
44. Deighton et al, 1983, p. 88.
45. Ibid, p. 76.

46. *Barricada*, 28 June 1987.

47. Ocotal sewing co-operative, visited by Helen Collinson and Elaine Ginsburg, January 1988.

48. Condega women's building co-operative, visited by Helen Collinson, Stephanie Williamson and Elaine Ginsburg, January 1989. Also featured in *Barricada Internacional*, March 1988.

49. See 'Fuerza Laboral Feminina en la rama textil-vestuario: segregación, salarios y rotación', OGM, Managua, 1987.

50. *Barricada Internacional*, 7 April 1988.

51. Ibid.

# 6. Religion and Revolution

The engagement of progressive sections of the churches in Nicaragua with the revolution has presented the challenge of reconciling new definitions of women's roles and questions of sexuality and reproduction with traditional Christian teaching.

## The Roman Catholic Church

In examining these issues, the Catholic Church is of central importance; 80% of the population are Catholic, if only nominally in some cases. In Nicaragua the Catholic Church is divided between those in the church hierarchy whose aim is to preserve a traditional, authoritarian form of religion, and radical sectors outside the hierarchy known as the Church of the Poor, who believe that 'between the Revolution and Christianity there is no contradiction'.

Traditionally the official Church has accommodated itself to whatever regime has been in power, accepting US interventions in the early 20th century, and coexisting with and even legitimizing the Somoza dictatorship. But relations deteriorated with the growing repression and abuse of human rights during the 1970s. Convinced that Somoza must go, Archbishop Obando y Bravo (Head of the Nicaraguan Church) allied himself with middle-class sectors to plan an alternative government, but one that would prevent the FSLN from taking control.

In 1979 the conservative church hierarchy initially welcomed the defeat of Somoza, but soon joined the bourgeoisie in distancing itself from the Sandinistas. As the counter-revolution gained cohesion during the 1980s, Obando y Bravo became increasingly identified with the opposition. Lacking effective and respected leadership, the Internal Front (political counter-revolutionaries) frequently looked to him as almost a *de facto* spokesperson. In this context it is not surprising that bitter conflicts have repeatedly arisen between the government and the hierarchy. The latter has tried to convince national and international opinion that the church is being persecuted by a totalitarian Marxist state.

**Church of the Poor**

'The people are the Church, the Revolution is the people.'
'For peace and for our Church, we are Revolutionaries.'[1]

With slogans such as these, the Church of the Poor expresses compatibility of Christianity and the Revolution. It is neither a parallel to the Catholic Church, nor a breakaway section. It is a new model *within* the Catholic Church that has taken 'a preferential option for the poor', the position recommended by the Latin American Bishops' Conference in Medellín in 1968 for Christians in an unjust, class-ridden society.

The new religious practice emerged in Nicaragua in the 1960s and centred on Basic Christian Communities (CEBs). These were initally small study groups in marginal urban *barrios* and remote rural areas set up to discuss the Bible and its relevance to ordinary people's daily lives, particularly their social problems. In the late 1970s, the communities became drawn into the struggle against Somoza, taking part in protests, occupying churches, collaborating with the FSLN and in some cases even taking up arms.

For thousands of working-class and peasant women in Central America, the radical church of the poor has been their first contact with politics. It has played a crucial role in revealing the reality of their oppression, particularly in situations where few opportunities have existed for women to develop their ideas in any other forum. Invariably grassroots church groups like the CEBs have acted as a springboard from which women have ventured into more organized politics. Elvia Alvarado, a prominent Honduran peasant leader, is a classic product of this process. Like many others, her political activism began in a local church women's group:

> After I'd been living with Alberto for 15 years, I began to work with the mothers' club the Catholic Church was organizing. At the meetings we'd talk about our problems and try to help each other. We also did practical things like distribute food to malnourished children, make gardens, and go to talks about food and nutrition. And we'd pray together too . . . It became the high point of my week because it was a chance to get together with other women and talk about the problems we had in common — like how to feed our children and keep our husbands sober. We learned we had rights just like men did. We learned that we had to stop being so passive and start sticking up for our rights.[2]

The Basic Christian Communities played an important part in politicizing and giving a sense of dignity to their women members. Reinterpreting the Bible included highlighting a positive role for women and replacing the passive models of the traditional church. According to an article[3] in a pro-revolutionary Christian magazine, women have played an outstanding part in the Nicaraguan communities: they have held the communities together, just as they hold together their own families.

At the same time, women have not always found it easy to take an active role in the communities. 'Women shouldn't be put in a submissive role or treated like slaves,' asserts Corina, a member of an Estelí basic community.[4] But she admits that:

> These views caused some break-ups in the CEBs, as some men didn't like their women going out and being active. Part of the aims of our community work is to encourage women's participation and confidence, but in a subtle way, not to destroy marital harmony. We tell women directly they don't have to suffer a bad husband, for instance if he's always drunk, and that it's better to separate and be independent. The traditional church emphasizes women's role in the home and that we should be submissive to our husband's wishes.

Because of the shortage of priests in the 1970s, particularly in rural areas, lay catechists known as 'Delegates of the Word' were selected and trained in religious studies and community development in order to fulfil what was now seen as the Church's dual role. This training was open to men and women, the only criterion being that the selected person should be a highly respected member of the community. Women's involvement in this work has probably varied from area to area. According to Vida Esperanza Cerrato, a Catholic nun who has worked on the Atlantic Coast since 1972, these training courses were initally only for men. To counter this, she and another nun began to run courses for the Delegates' wives to enable them to operate on an equal level with their husbands. Later, they extended this work to all women in the communities.[5]

## Middle-class Christians in the Revolution

While the Basic Christian Communities were a forum for the radicalization of the working-class and *campesino* communities, middle- and upper-class Christians were influenced through special religious courses that taught liberation theology, and encouraged students to make a preferential option for the poor. For some middle-class women involved in the struggle against Somoza, their Christian beliefs were the starting point.[6] Nora Astorga who, before her death in 1987, was the Nicaraguan Ambassador to the United Nations, became a Catholic activist in the marginal *barrios* of Managua soon after leaving convent school.[7] Another radical middle-class Catholic to take a position in the new government was Maria del Socorro who gave up a private business to work, for a relatively low wage, as general secretary for the Ministry of Housing: 'For me sharing the hope of those who get a parcel of land free is one way of putting a preferential option for the poor into practice.'[8]

Before the Revolution, there were early links between women in this radical movement of intellectual Catholics and the Nicaraguan women's movement. Two active catechists, Teresa Cardenal (wife of the General Director of the National Administration of Ports) and Zela Diaz de Porres (President of the 2nd Regional Appeals Court) were founding members of AMPRONAC, the progressive women's organization that preceded AMNLAE.

## A new sexual morality?

Revolutionary Catholics' move away from set rules and rituals has also led to greater flexibility on 'moral' issues concerning sexuality and the family. The revolutionary Catholic publication, *Tayacan*, which devoted an issue to sex education, provides clear evidence of an attempt to come to terms with the concrete reality facing women.[9] In a popular, comic-book format, responsible parenthood, contraception, abortion, virginity, and divorce are addressed. The discussion takes place within the framework of Catholic doctrine but without recourse to an immutable, inflexible morality.

While life-long monogamous marriage is portrayed as the ideal, it is recognized that this is not always possible and that divorce is a 'remedy for an illness'. *Tayacan* also emphasizes that virginity should be neither fetishized in terms of preserving it at all costs nor be lost as a rejection of *machista* society; pre-marital sex calls for maturity and a level of consciousness that young people lack. *Tayacan* advocates responsible parenthood — having only the number of children you want, and using careful family planning. There then follows an outline of the main forms of artificial contraception, but the magazine also states that none of these methods is approved by the Catholic Church. In practice, revolutionary Catholics apparently take a quite pragmatic approach to contraception. Sex education courses for mothers run by one group of progressive nuns include information on natural methods of birth control. 'Our position is that women aren't just baby machines or supposed to stay shut in the home,' says Corina of Estelí. 'As regards contraception, we analysed the situation and asked which is the greater sin, to give birth to hungry children or to avoid this with contraception? We decided that contraceptives had to be better than nothing.'[10]

There is no such ambiguity in regard to abortion. *Tayacan* argues that abortion, even in the first 12 weeks, means taking a life; the following is, however, noted: 'We shouldn't promote abortion as a right, a conquest, as a responsible method of controlling birth. [But] we must avoid backstreet abortions in which in addition to the baby losing its life, the mother may also lose hers.'[11] For the writers in *Tayacan*, abortion is never right, but sometimes it is a lesser evil: 'We aspire to live in a world and in a country in which women never have to have an abortion. Not because it is illegal but because it isn't socially necessary.'

As part of the developing debate within the Church on sex and the role of women, *Tayacan* has also published a revised version of a Costa Rican book, *Learning to be a Woman*, which looks at gender roles and inequalities between the sexes.

In 1986, Christians from various denominations participated in a series of *cabildos* or open meetings specially convened for them to put forward their views on the draft constitution. Of particular relevance to women was the hotly debated question of the proposed legalization of abortion. According to *Amanecer*, 'There was openness and flexibility in approaching the diverse problems involved in better family planning and the decriminalization of abortion.'[12] The most popular position taken at the Christian *cabildos* was that abortion was part of a larger problem and that what was needed was better sex education and more freely available contraception.

\*     \*     \*

### Virtues of virginity

*The participation of committed Christians in the process of transformation can lead to debates on a perhaps unexpected level in a secular revolution. One example was an article on virginity by a Baptist lawyer, Adolfo Miranda Saenz.*[13] *The article arose from a radio programme that conducted a phone-in debate on the pros and cons of female virginity. Saenz complained that the programme was hostile to the idea of preserving virginity before marriage, although he claimed all the women who phoned in considered virginity a worthwhile virtue. Saenz believes that sexual activity should take place only within stable unions like marriage . . . He was however, careful to make the point: 'Of course I am against the idea that men should demand from women something we don't demand of ourselves. But the solution isn't to propose that nobody should be expected to follow a moral code; rather, it should be demanded of everybody.' His final point linked government policy with religion. Because at least 95% of Nicaraguans are Christian, he argued, the government must fulfil its promises to respect people's religious feelings, not simply by supporting religious festivals but also by respecting their religious values. 'We respect other people's values, other opinions on virginity, abortion and other themes. But the vast majority of Nicaraguans . . . continue to hold virginity as a virtue and abortion as a crime.'*

\*     \*     \*

## The Church in conflict

The aim of revolutionary Catholics is to transform the Church from within. But how dominant is this new model of the Church? To what extent is it in a position to create a less restrictive ideological framework for Catholic women? At the time of the Triumph in 1979 there were

300 CEBs and about 5,000 Delegates of the Word, suggesting that it was still at an early stage of development. Yet to some extent the advent of the revolution gave the movement a profile and responsibility far beyond its level of institutional development. Revolutionary Catholics have gained considerable credibility from the fact that three priests run government ministries: Ernesto Cardenal, Fernando Cardenal, and Francisco D'Escoto.

Nevertheless, the popular Church has still been vulnerable to attacks from the Church hierarchy. When the Pope visited Nicaragua in March 1983, he threw his considerable weight and influence behind the hierarchy, and publicly humiliated Fr Ernesto Cardenal (then Minister of Culture) by refusing to bless him. Up to 40 foreign priests and other religious people supportive of the revolution have since been forced to leave their posts by the Church hierarchy and all three priests in secular ministerial positions have been deprived of the right to carry out their priestly duties while they remain in government.

Under continual attack from the hierarchy, revolutionary Christians have often found themselves simply taking defensive measures — not a strong position from which to put forward modifications of conservative doctrines. Despite the initiatives mentioned earlier, in the mainstream Church it has been difficult to challenge key Catholic teaching on moral issues, particularly those central to the Church's social teaching, such as reproduction and the family. This would have fuelled the charge that radical Christians represented an infiltration of the Church by the Sandinistas; the hierarchy has already claimed that the Sandinistas are undermining the family.[14]

The conflict between the Sandinistas and the hierarchy has probably acted as a rein on the introduction of some changes. For example, it is thought that Church hostility is a factor that has militated against the decriminalization of abortion and a more positive attitude towards the issue of sexuality. In addition, the possibility of Church opposition provided an argument for those within the government not perhaps wholly committed to changes on these fronts.

From another viewpoint, however, the Church hierarchy has also been a loser in the conflict: their identification with the counterrevolution has lost them considerable moral authority. In some sectors, particularly among the youth, there has been alienation from the Church.[15] In addition, the conversion of Catholics to evangelical Protestant sects has greatly accelerated in recent years, particularly amongst more conservative Catholics. Thus the traditional Church is losing at both ends of the spectrum. Only amongst active opponents of the Sandinistas has the traditional Church raised its profile.

## The battle for the Virgin

For almost all the 659 million Catholics in the world, the religious landscape encloses at its very heart the powerful and most beloved figure of the Virgin.[16]

In Nicaragua the most important festival of the year is *La Purissima*, the Immaculate Conception of Mary, celebrated in the week beginning 8 December. This involves massive mobilizations in the streets in the evenings, people singing to the Virgin, letting off fireworks, and visiting each others's houses where there are altars to the Virgin. Gifts of food are given to visitors and toys to children. A newspaper report described the Sandinista response to the feast in 1988:

> The Sandinista government — Godless Marxists, according to President Reagan — gave full support to the feast of the immaculate Conception, with government ministries competing with each other for days to construct the most elaborate altars honouring the Virgin Mary. Thousands of Nicaraguans queued for hours by the altars, waiting to be given bags of sweets, calendars and little wooden toys by state officials in olive green uniforms. President Ortega, Vice-President Ramírez and Bayardo Arce handed out to children small wooden doves attached to a stick on wheels.[17]

Devotion to the Virgin Mary has particular implications for Catholic women. She is their model, someone to identify with. She provides an idealized picture of virgin and mother — passive, submissive, and asexual, the impression given is that sex is justifiable only in order to become a mother. Motherhood is the central theme defining Nicaraguan women's lives and identities (see chapter 2).

In the context of the polarized Church and the central importance of the Virgin Mary, it is not surprising that she has become part of the disputed ideological territory. The Church of the Poor has tried to establish Mary as a positive image for active women Catholics. Radical priests and nuns have used the slogan: 'With the Virgin on our side we will smash the bourgeoisie.'[18] An excerpt from a talk to a group of women by Sr Marta, a revolutionary nun in Matagalpa, shows her efforts to identify areas of Mary's experience relevant for modern Nicaraguan women: 'Today, Nicaraguan women hold Mary the Mother of God as their first model for promoting this Revolution. She, too, carried to the world a message of liberation . . . Mary isn't the sugar sweet stupid woman reactionary Christians so often make her out to be. At the age of 15 . . . she took an active part in the liberation of her people.'[19] Meanwhile, the Church hierarchy, who object to what they see as the 'politicization of Mary', still portray a traditional image of the Virgin.

The basis for women to identify with the Virgin Mary has been strengthened by the war. They see themselves as having a shared experience with Her, whose Son died to save the human race, while their sons died to bring peace to Nicaragua. Many women speak of this identification as a source of comfort when they hear of their sons' death. Dona Esperanza Cruz de Cabrera spoke of her anguish and despair when her son was killed but, 'then in that moment of pain, anguish and despair, you come to remember Christ's crucifixion. Mary felt this same pain.'[20] This theme is repeated in numerous interviews with Nicaraguan woman: 'When I saw my dead sons, I knew in my heart the pain Mary must have felt when she saw Jesus on the Cross.'[21]

The central space occupied by the Mothers of Heroes and Martyrs may be due to this, perhaps largely unconscious, recognition of the symbolic sharing of experience with the Virgin Mary.

## Mothers in conflict with the hierarchy

The search for comfort in religion when faced with the loss of their children has led women to demand from the traditional Church recognition of their sorrow and support. The official Church's mobility to respond adequately to the bereavement suffered by so many women has brought a new dimension to the polarization that exists within the Church. To comfort the bereaved has always been a traditional role of the clergy, yet the hierarchy has dealt very insensitively with what they see as the pro-Sandinista organization, Mothers of Heroes and Martyrs. An early, public rejection of an approach from mothers who had lost their sons came during the Pope's visit in 1983. At a Mass held in Managua's Revolution Square, the Pope did not respond to a request for a blessing from a number of mothers whose sons had been killed by the Contra.

In a pastoral letter in 1984, the bishops issued the following statement: 'The suffering of mothers who have lost their sons deserving of all respect, consolation and assistance is being manipulated to provoke hatred and lust for revenge.'[22] This statement illustrates the Church's dilemma when faced with the mothers' organizations. On the one hand rejecting them as pro-Sandinistas, on the other having to recognize the loss they have suffered.

The lack of response from Obando y Bravo (now a Cardinal) to the Mothers' request for his assistance in locating relatives kidnapped by the Contra has been a further area of conflict. In 1988, at a weekly vigil outside the Cardinal's Curia (see p. 162) the Mothers read from the Bible, sang extracts from the *Misa Campesina* (the popular version of the Catholic mass based on a rewritten liturgy to take account of the preferential option for the poor. The music for the mass was written by Carlos Mejía Godoy, a well known Nicaraguan singer) and planted wooden crosses bearing the names of their children.

These actions have yet to sway the Cardinal and the women feel abandoned by the Church, especially as Obando has made great efforts to get Somocista National Guard prisoners released. This has starkly exposed the Church hierarchy's partisanship, showing that political considerations take precedence over its pastoral role. The hierarchy has tried to conceal this partisanship behind the Christian-sounding concept of 'reconciliation'. But the Cardinal's failure actively to mediate between the Contras and the mothers of the kidnapped has revealed the emptiness of this concept.

## The role of the Protestant churches

The Protestant churches have grown rapidly in Nicaragua, particularly over the last 30 years: about 15% of the population are now Protestant, belonging to over 80 churches. A strong US influence has characterized the growth of Protestantism, with almost all the major denominations in Nicaragua receiving direct US assistance. This link has often resulted in a conservative theology together with virulent anti-communism. Nevertheless, the Protestant churches have reacted in a variety of ways to the Sandinistas: some support the revolution; others became part of the counter-revolutionary front (at least at an ideological level) soon after the Triumph. Many initiated an intense ideological, religious campaign against the revolution, encouraging passivity, political apathy and anti-communism, which had considerable success in the remote mountainous zones.

### The Moravian Church

The Moravian Church is both the largest of the Protestant churches and the principal church on the Atlantic Coast; 95% of the Miskito people are members. Because of the past neglect of the Atlantic Coast by governments on the Pacific Coast, there was very little institutional development, with the result that, according to Andy Shogreen, head of the Moravian Church, the Church effectively became the regional government even during the British Protectorate.[23] For this reason, the Sandinistas initially mistrusted the Moravians, especially when large numbers of Miskitos went to join Contra forces in Honduras. But a more co-operative relationship has developed over time. Although some ministers have gone to join the Miskito military camps, the Church has tried to mediate between the Sandinistas and the Miskito communities, taking an active role in the development of the peace and autonomy process in which women are very prominent. Regarding the attitude of men in the Moravian Church towards women, the words of one Moravian priest, Rafael Dixon, are revealing, despite representing the attitude of only one individual: 'I've never been drunk or danced a step. My only pleasures have been women and work, and because of this I have lots of children — but then I also have five women . . . I'm very bad, as they say, but all over the world men have more than two women. Even ministers like me.'[24]

## Baptists

Among the various Protestant denominations, the Baptists are the most committed to the revolution. They have also given some consideration to the position of women within their church. In an interview with *Amanecer*, Tomás Tellez, executive secretary of the Baptist convention, was asked about women in his Church.

> The strongest movement in the convention is the women's. Women are very active and contribute much of the financial and human resources. We have three women pastors at the head of their congregations. In our seminary 45% of the students are women. We would like to see more women become pastors and are encouraging women to enter the seminary.[25]

The priority the Baptists give to the position of women was evident when President Ortega visted their 50th anniversary celebrations in 1987. Among the questions he was asked was one about the elimination of *machismo*, not perhaps a predictable question from a Church convention to a country's president. Unfortunately the President's reply was not recorded.

### CEPAD and the women's ministry

There was no Protestant equivalent to the CEBs in terms of the role these played in supporting the Sandinista fighters, but since 1979 a positive relationship has developed between the government and some Protestant churches, particularly through CEPAD. This is a development organization set up after the earthquake in 1972, which runs programmes in agriculture, training, health, housing, education, child welfare, community development, and pastoral studies.[26] Over half the Protestant churches are affiliated. As CEPAD co-operates with the government, its projects have been targets for Contra attacks and some of its health and education *brigadistas* (including women) have been murdered.

With the growing pressure to deal with women's issues, CEPAD set up a women's department in 1982; its directorate comprises teachers, a psychologist, a sociologist and a theologian. The department deals with issues of faith and also supports a number of projects that arise mainly from women's pastoral groups. There are 27 women's projects, spanning agriculture, health, sewing classes and sewing co-operatives. In 1988, CEPAD's president attended its women's convention and pledged that the organization would give priority to work with women.[27]

One project supported by the CEPAD women's department is an agricultural co-operative near Masaya run by five evangelical women.

Faced with the difficulties of economic survival, these women decided to take up farming and grow basic grains; two of the five are over 60 years of age. While the women have the support of their families, their churches have been critical; the pastors have complained that the women do not attend the nightly church services. There is also a feeling that the women have moved away from their appropriate position, that they are wayward (*vaga*). They have been unable to fulfil the rigorous programmes of prayer expected of them, but they continue to be active on the religious front. The women have developed good relations with members of the neighbouring co-operative that lent them the land to start their farm. Five members of this neighbouring co-op have since been 'converted to Jesus' as a result of conversations with the evangelical women.[28]

## Conclusion

The central role of Christians in the changes of the last ten years is one of the most specifically Nicaraguan features of the revolutionary process. For many revolutionary women, their links with religion encompass both traditional elements and radical religious practice. In this way, they have maintained a bridge between both forms of religion, suggesting that radical Christians may be the real mediators between Church and revolution, rather than the conservative Church hierarchy, despite its claims to be working towards reconciliation.

The radical grassroots Church of the Poor has begun to participate in the ideological struggle against *machismo* and is developing new concepts of morality, which aim to give women more flexibility in such areas as reproduction. The strong opposition of the still powerful Catholic hierarchy has, however, operated as a brake on change in this direction.

## Notes

1. *Encuentro*, No. 31, August 1987.
2. Benjamin, 1987, p. 11.
3. *Amanecer*, June–August 1986.
4. Corina, interviewed by Stephanie Williamson, 1987, unpublished.
5. *Amanecer*, May–June 1988.
6. Randall, 1981, pp. 60–61.
7. *Envío*, June 1988.
8. Cabestrero, 1986, p. 41.
9. *Tayacan*, August 1988.
10. Corina, op. cit.
11. *Tayacan*, August 1988.
12. *Amanecer*, July–August 1986.

13. *El Nuevo Diario*, 30 May 1988.
14. 'Right to Survive: Human Rights in Nicaragua', Catholic Institute for International Relations report, 1988.
15. *Encuentro*, No. 31, August 1987.
16. Warner, 1985, p. 1.
17. *Central American Monitor*, August 1988.
18. Deighton et al, 1983, p. 147.
19. Randall, 1983, p. 162.
20. Solà & Trayner, 1988, p. 51.
21. Amanecida collective, 19??, p. 51.
22. *Barricada Internacional*, October 1987.
23. Angel & Macintosh, 1987, p. 45.
24. Ibid.
25. *Amanecer*, April–May 1988.
26. Haslam, 1987, pp. 39–44.
27. Helen Stanton, reports of visits to Nicaragua, 1988, unpublished.
28. *CEPAD Newsletter*, September–October 1988.

# 7. Women and Health

## Women's changing role and health care

In 1983, Nicaragua earned the acclaim of the World Health Organization for the greatest advances made in health care by a developing country. Within four short years, the Sandinista government had transformed the inegalitarian services of the Somoza regime into a free, comprehensive, and broad-based health system. Built on the principles of preventive health care, the new system targeted those sectors most in need of primary health care: the urban and rural poor. In so doing, it profoundly affected the lives of women as recipients of services, as carers and as health workers.

The family structure in Nicaragua and the sharp division of domestic labour between men and women has meant that women do the worrying, the planning and the caring when it comes to health care. The Sandinistas' health strategy has attempted to use women's energy and involvement in such care to improve the general health of the population. But women's own health needs have also been addressed in this process — particularly in relation to pregnancy and childbirth.

## Breaking new ground: the Nicaraguan health service

Before the Sandinistas came to power in 1979, health care was provided by some 23 different organizations. These services were distributed unevenly between rich and poor, towns and rural areas. Of these organizations, the biggest spender was the Social Security Institute (INSS), which in 1974 spent over 50% of the health sector budget, although serving only 8% of the total population. In the same year, the Ministry of Health, which had formal responsibility for the entire population and sole responsibility for the rural population, spent 75% of its budget in Managua (where only 25% of the population lived).

By prioritizing expensive hospital care, health provision under Somoza offered little to the majority of the population, most of whom suffered from the diseases of poverty and lacked even such basic facilities as sanitation and an adequate water supply. An estimated 90% of all health care resources benefited just 10% of the population, with only 28% having regular access to qualified health care. In the absence of state provision (especially in rural areas) health care had to come from within the communities themselves, provided by traditional (self-taught) midwives and healers.[1]

Under Somoza:

- Infant mortality, a key indication of general health, was 120 per 1,000 live births (11 per 1,000 in Britain).[2]
- Two out of every three children under five years old were undernourished.
- Six out of ten deaths were caused by preventable diseases.
- Less than 20% of under-fives and pregnant women received health care.

I had ten children in all, but was left with only two boys and two girls. The others died as babies, from diarrhoea, temperatures, fevers. It's as though I wasn't meant to have a family. The boys should have lived because boys come out strong . . . Girls are born to work, but I'm ill now, trying to recover from tuberculosis. I shake when I go down to the river to fetch water, I have to rest on the way.[3]

The Sandinista government established free health care as a right for all. In 1979, under the direction of the new Ministry of Health (MINSA), it also became possible for the first time to plan, co-ordinate and implement a national health programme.

The new strategy, drawn up in 1981, aimed to tackle the causes of ill-health and poverty by using relatively simple, inexpensive techniques and local resources — principally, the community organization and the knowledge of ordinary people themselves. In the absence of basic services, such as clean water and sanitation, effective preventive measures could be assured only by the active participation of the community. The social aspects of health care were therefore indivisible from and as important as biological factors.

Given the number of deaths due to transmitted diseases and the lack of services (especially in rural areas), the most effective approach was to mobilize large numbers of people to carry out vaccination campaigns and improve basic sanitation. MINSA recognized the potential of the popular education campaigns as vehicles for the health programmes and sought to build on the success of the 1980 literacy campaign. To this end, literacy workers were trained initially in malaria prevention and treatment. Following their success, volunteer health *brigadistas* were given training in how to prevent disease, carry out vaccinations and encourage community participation. Tens of thousands of *brigadistas* carried out mass vaccinations against polio, measles, and tetanus, and took part in massive clean-up campaigns. At the same time, attention was given to the prevention of diarrhoea — a major killer of babies and young children — in areas where access to drinking water was difficult and sanitation facilities poor. Diarrhoea can be simply and effectively treated — if caught in time — by administering a mixture of salt, sugar and water; some 266 Oral Rehydration Centres were set up in various parts of the country.[4]

## Women in the health campaigns

Around 75% of the *brigadistas* recruited to these early campaigns were women.[5] Their role as community organizers, so essential in the overthrow of Somoza, meant that many of them had the skills and understanding to effect changes in relation to community health. As carers they understood many of the factors that contribute to poor health, for it is women who take responsibility for what their families eat, for washing clothes, for cleaning and general hygiene; and it is women who bring their children for vaccination and who nurse members of their families when they fall sick.

The mobilization of so many women in the early health campaigns enabled many to find dignity and value in their knowledge and skill that hitherto had not been validated. For some, the training they received as *brigadistas* served as a springboard for further training. The experience of leadership and organizational skills they acquired enabled them to participate in and influence the wider political process. Mailene Hernández from León is just one of thousands of women who benefited in this way:

Before 1979, it was impossible for a poor girl like me to leave the country and seek a professional training. But this started to change after the Revolution. A doctor started coming to the village and began training some of us so we could participate in the vaccination campaigns. A Spanish nun who came to the area taught us how to do dressings, treat wounds, do check-ups on pregnant women and laboratory examinations. I spent three years doing voluntary work at the health centre every week, after which I started to receive a small salary and became an official health worker at the new health centre in the village. I did that for two years and then last year I was offered a place to study as an auxiliary nurse in León . . . Every day I had to get up at 4 a.m. so I would have time to do the housework and get to León by 7 a.m. I have now been working at the health centre here in Lecheguagos as an auxiliary and local co-ordinator since February.[6]

Despite the validation women received from their participation in the health campaigns, however, it could be argued that these campaigns did not fundamentally alter the social relations of health care, in so far as they reinforced the idea that the caring element of health care is primarily women's responsibility.

* * *

### Health workers and FETSALUD

*In addition to the health campaigns, the vast majority of professional health staff are also women, most working as nurses and auxiliaries rather than as doctors (although in 1983, 40% of those enrolling in medical schools to train as doctors were women). Not surprisingly, women make up the majority of the membership of the Sandinista health trade union, FETSALUD. This union has become increasingly vocal in its criticisms of government health cuts introduced in response to the economic crisis. In 1989 FETSALUD denounced MINSA for protecting certain administrators accused of corruption and for the deterioration of medicine stocks through negligence and inefficient management. There were complaints that a MINSA redundancy package affected rank and file workers (most of them women) whilst irresponsible high officials (many of them men) were let off or moved to another centre. Towards the end of the 1980s, FETSALUD also started to hold women-only meetings, such as those in preparation for the Fundamental Forces meeting in March 1989 (see p. 35).*

* * *

It is undeniable that the improvements in family — especially child — health, and the wider benefits brought about by the public health campaigns, have made domestic life pleasanter and easier for many women. At least they have been relieved of the anxiety and despair of seeing so many of their loved ones sicken and die from preventable diseases. By 1983, infant mortality had fallen to 80 per 1,000 live births; the incidence of malaria had fallen by 50% and polio had been effectively eradicated.[7] Following through the resolve to move away from centralized, hospital-oriented care, by 1984 a network of primary health care centres and simple health posts had been created around the country, giving some 80% of the population regular access to primary health care. The total number of primary health care facilities increased from 172 in 1977 to 487 in 1984.[8]

But what of women's own health needs? Just as women's traditional role as carers was used to recruit health *brigadistas*, so too were the early health campaigns aimed specifically at women because of their reproductive role. Mother/child health programmes have been a constant theme in the past ten years of health care policy.

Nevertheless in the area of mothers' health, there is still a long way to go. In 1987, the maternal mortality rate in Nicaragua was almost three per 1,000 (compared with 0.5 per 1,000 in most developed countries). This figure is very high, according to Dr Marta Norori, obstetrician and gynaecologist at Managua's Fernando Velez Pais Hospital and is linked to the lack of contraceptives and education on birth control, as well as to the (illegal) abortion rate.[9]

The average Nicaraguan woman has five or six children. Pregnancies in very young women can result in maternal death, because a young woman's body is too immature to withstand the demands made upon it by pregnancy and birth. Women under 15 are five to seven times more likely to die in childbirth than are women of 20–24.[10]

## Childbirth policy

In Nicaragua, more than 55% of all births take place in the home and of those, 80% are attended by traditional midwives. The latter tend to be rural women who have learnt their skills attending to their own births and those of other women in their communities. From 1980 to 1984, it was MINSA policy that every pregnant woman should have at least three checks in a health centre. If any problem was detected, the woman was referred to a hospital or health centre with beds for the birth itself. If the pregnancy was normal, the woman was simply encouraged to have the baby in hospital (although many preferred to stay at home and be attended by friends and family members). This emphasis on hospital care was based on the notion that to institutionalize birth was the best way to reduce peri-natal deaths. Although there was recognition and support for home births and the role of the traditional midwife, there seemed to be an assumption that with increased institutionalization of birth, the traditional midwife would simply disappear over time.

At the beginning of 1985, the norms which had regulated mother and child health programmes were revised. It was apparent that there was neither the money nor staff to institutionalize birth in the country. It was now stressed that women could choose between home or hospital delivery. The emphasis therefore shifted to better equipping the midwives to detect high-risk pregnancies in time and refer women to hospital if necessary. As part of this new policy, the Bertha Calderón women's hospital in Managua was to be the main referral centre for women with high-risk pregnancies.[11]

### Training popular midwives
Little by little, there has been an integration of traditional medicine (midwives, healers and the use of medical herbs) into 'modern' medicine. Since 1980 the mother/child health programmes have included training for traditional midwives with the purpose of incorporating them into the primary health teams. Training traditional midwives is a classic example of how the revolution has utilized the resources available in the people themselves.

For the traditional midwives, incorporation in the revolution has brought official recognition and a new relationship with trained health personnel. The process has been assisted by the involvement of AMNLAE and Basic Christian Communities, who collaborated in the early training programmes. The validation from the Sandinistas proved important, because many midwives had feared that the new government would prevent them from practising.

Drawing on the methodology of popular education, the one to two weeks training culminates in midwives receiving a certificate, an identification card and a basic delivery kit; they are then known as 'people's midwives'. They are not paid by MINSA, but women who call on them for childbirth traditionally give them some sort of material offering, such as food or animals. It is estimated that there are some 15,000 women who have worked as traditional midwives.

Health workers found they had very little quarrel with the way the midwives delivered babies but there were a few areas of disagreement as is illustrated in the description (below) of a training project for traditional midwives in Jalapa and Ocotal in the early 1980s.

The collaboration between traditional medicine and the new Unified Health System has facilitated a rich exchange of knowledge and expertise. Mondita, a nurse in Estelí explains:

> We have an important exchange of ideas with the midwives. One example is the positions for labour and childbirth suggested by the *parteras*. We've learned the value of these from them and started introducing them in the hospital. Also the *parteras* give a lot of loving care and emotional support to the women, whereas in the hospital, it's just part of the work of the doctors and they can seem indifferent. Traditionally, the hospital has given very little emotional care, but the national guidelines for health care that have just come out now specify that the women should be given emotional support.[12]

The project workers were very worried by the habit the midwives have of advising a diet of black coffee, toasted *tortilla* and cheese for 15–20 days after the birth. The diet can very easily produce anaemia. But . . . the midwives see milk (proposed by the project workers) as the cause of a fungus disease that produces vaginal discharge rather like sour milk; they think that fruit and vegetables produce colic and that meat might make the mothers vomit. The project workers also challenged the habit of singeing the umbilical cord with a red hot nail, believing this to be the main cause of infants dying of tetanus. The midwives don't agree because, they argue, the deaths take place some 15 days after the nail burning . . .[13]

### Natural Childbirth Centre, Estelí

Opened to the public in May 1986, the Centre was set up as a pilot project aimed at raising the quality of home birth and institutional delivery in the region and reducing the level of peri-natal death. It was built on the successes of the midwives' training programme and brought together the educational and training aspects of natural childbirth for pregnant women, popular midwives and health service workers. It has managed to establish this approach to childbirth as a firm alternative to the more impersonal, more medicalized approach that typified the health service.

The Centre psychologically and physically prepares pregnant women and their companions for childbirth with relaxation, breathing and stretching exercises and discussions; the women are referred from health posts or centres. The staff see 100–150 pregnant women per month, and the Centre is promoting the idea of fathers participating in childbirth.

The Centre is officially recognized by MINSA and maintains an important link with the hospital in Estelí. Staff time is shared between work in the Centre and attending deliveries at the hospital. There has been some resistance from doctors accustomed to treating women who are active and conscious during their labour. Nevertheless, the staff perceive the exercise as one of consciousness-raising that will prove to be worthwhile.

In 1988 the National Congress of Graduate Nurses supported the idea of extending and promoting the ideas of natural childbirth nationally. A new post-graduate course for nurses in maternal and child health has requested copies of a manual produced by the Estelí Natural Childbirth Centre.[14]

## Ocotal Mothers' House

In 1987, AMNLAE and INSSBI in the northern Nicaraguan town of Ocotal colloborated to set up a 'mothers' house' in premises that had accommodated a brothel under Somoza. Today it caters for rural women with high-risk pregnancies for whom it would otherwise be very difficult to find somewhere to stay near the hospital around the time of labour and who would probably give birth at home under dangerous circumstances. The women come a few days before the baby is born and, if necessary, will stay for up to one month after the birth. The objective of the Mothers' House is to reduce maternal and child death rates, educate women in hygiene and nutrition, and promote 'woman-to-woman solidarity'. In 1988, the House cared for 216 women from the surrounding areas, many of whom had heard about it on local radio.

The House is managed and directed by AMNLAE, with support from international aid agencies. There are insufficient funds to pay the staff a proper wage but the co-ordinator, Martha Antúñez, claims that she and her colleagues work there because they are conscious of the need to build solidarity with peasant women. In order to reduce costs, the women who use the service are expected to do some work in a sewing workshop.

**Puerto Cabezas Maternity House**
When the Moravian hospital in the North Atlantic Coast town of Bilwaskarma was closed by Contra attacks in 1981, Myrna Cunningham (then regional co-ordinator for the Health Ministry) and Mildred Levy, a *costeña* nurse, designed a Maternity House where women with high risk pregnancies could deliver their babies under the care of a midwife. The idea was resurrected in 1984 when two Swiss nurses decided to adopt the Maternity House as a solidarity project. By September 1988 the House was almost ready to open.[15]

> The idea is that the midwives will come to the house with their patients and also receive additional obstetric training [explains one of the Swiss nurses]. With more education, the midwives will be able to determine in time high-risk pregnancies . . . Too often women arrive at the Puerto Cabezas hospital and the foetus is already dead. In other cases a difficult birth can affect a child for the rest of its life.[16]

**Masaya women's centre**
In January 1988, a new private Women's Health and Advice Centre was founded in Masaya by a group of professional women attached to the professional workers' association, CONAPRO, who were concerned to provide services catering specifically for women. Staffed by a team of professionals — a psychologist, a lawyer and a nurse — it offers legal services, physical therapy and counselling. Contraception is available and tests can be carried out for infections and the early detection of cervical or uterine cancer. Clients have to pay for the centre's services but there is a sliding scale which enables a broad spectrum of women to use the centre. The centre's philosophy rests on separating women's sexuality from reproduction.[17]

A second centre with a similar remit opened in Managua in January 1989. It has secured funding from the British Marie Stopes foundation.

## Child health

The launch, in 1988, of the Campaign for the Defence of the Life of the Child was MINSA's response to what was still a relatively high infant mortality rate in comparison with other countries in similar circumstances. Neo-natal death through diarrhoea has been a particular concern in the past few years, especially during the wet season. To minimize the risks, advice on the treatment of diarrhoea has been disseminated via public announcements on TV, billboards, and simple leaflets. Several cautionary tales of mothers who failed to get their dehydrated children to hospital in time have also appeared in the daily press.

To prevent the recurrence of such tragic stories, MINSA has also promoted breast-feeding for the first six months of life (Nicaragua is still dealing with the legacy of a massive campaign by the baby-milk manufacturers in the 1970s), and nutritional and basic hygiene education.

Attempts to improve child health, and indeed health in general, have, however, been all but paralysed by the massive budget cuts forced on the Ministry of Health by war and economic crisis. Merely defending the gains already made has become a bitter struggle. Because of a breakdown in the vaccination programme, for example, polio is starting to creep back in rural areas. Meanwhile, even the most routine surgical operations can no longer be performed. In 1989 MINSA announced that only women over 35 with six or more children would qualify for sterilization. A woman in Estelí was told that the hospital could consider her for sterilization only if she provided her own supplies of thread and any other equipment needed. 'The situation in the hospitals and health centres is really appalling,' commented a resident British teacher in April 1989. 'Sometimes there isn't any cotton wool or alcohol even, let alone certain drugs, and prescription costs are so high that many patients can no longer afford to follow the doctor's advice.'[18]

A concurrent drop in living standards has had inevitable repercussions on the health of the population. In December 1988, for example, *Barricada* announced that some 68% of children under six had some degree of malnutrition, principally those in the rural regions of northern Nicaragua where at least half a million children were affected. In March 1989, Dr Armando Mendoza claimed that the problem of diarrhoea amongst children had moved beyond the usual pattern of seasonal fluctuation and had become endemic.[19] According to Dr Jorge Arostegui, 'the victims [of diarrhoea] are suffering malnutrition which makes it difficult for them to resist illness. Of those infants that die of diarrhoea in Managua's hospitals, 80% were underweight at birth.'[20] Such are the distressing indicators of the toll that dire shortages, reduced wages, and inflation have taken on people's health.

## Mental health: living with war and change

According to Dr Amparro Gutiérrez, a woman clinical psychologist, Nicaraguans are living in a 'permanent stress condition'. This condition is the product of the war, the economic situation, and the rapid social changes that have taken place in the country. Virtually every family has experienced the loss of one member through violent death. Families have also been separated — some members leaving the country to try their luck in the US. Others have been divided by ideological differences — perhaps the children supporting the goals of the Sandinistas and their parents opposing them. Invariably, adult male members of the family are away on military service. Many of the young people returning to civilian life from the war have experienced profound and severe shock as a result of the fighting.

The traumas of war go back far beyond the present crisis. The atrocities of the Somoza era and the dramatic events leading up to 1979 took their toll on the mental state of the general population. Thousands of people suffered depression in response to the deaths of loved ones, panic disorders due to repression at the hands of the National Guard, and a range of conditions directly related to the stress and upheaval caused by civil war.

Some of these disorders were reduced by the overthrow of Somoza. It is common to hear health professionals speak of the revolution as the main healer of the Nicaraguan people and the 'fountain of health'. But, if the liberation of the country enabled psychological reparation to begin, it also threw up new tensions, as people started to take up new roles and form new identities. Much of this tension has manifested itself within personal relationships between men and women, as gender roles and women's expectations have shifted.[21]

Between 1985 and 1988, regional studies by a team of psychologists to identify the relationship between war and stress revealed that 32% of the population were living with high levels of anxiety — higher than the average in other parts of the world. There was a strong relationship between the economic situation and the level of anxiety, especially amongst women.[22] The economic crisis has meant that tasks normally considered routine, such as buying food, travelling, clothing the family, and maintaining waged work have become almost insurmountable problems.

The frustrations, anger, grief and desperation produced by the present circumstances in Nicaragua and the responsibility for coping with them weigh heavily on women who are the focal point in the family for nurturing, caring and providing. Tired, angry and frustrated people usually have to find something or someone on which to vent their frustration. For men, wives are often the targets of such frustration and the violence it engenders. For mothers, children are invariably on the receiving end. In 1988 there were a number of press reports about women who beat their children (although this may just have been part of the general debate about child abuse at that time and does not necessarily reflect an increase in such abuse). A British volunteer worker describes the case of Silvia Toruna:

> Maltreatment of children was something that Silvia and I talked over a lot. Her mother beat her when she was young and she didn't want to do the same with her kids. However, being in the house with four hyperactive children stretches her patience to the limit sometimes . . . Silvia would wallop the kids when she was tired or angry. She recognized that it was almost a reflex and it was a problem she had to deal with . . .[23]

**Mental health care — starting from scratch**

The Somoza regime's contribution to the field of mental health was a single psychiatric hospital in Managua, greatly influenced by the US in its approach to caring for the mentally ill: patients were controlled by drugs and electric shock treatment. Out of 12 psychiatrists in the country at the time of the revolution, four left for the US. Although a few psychologists remained, there were only between 30 and 40 in the entire country in 1979.[24]

MINSA aims to integrate mental health care with other health services through the network of hospitals, health centres and health posts. A few specialist services — known as CAPs (Centres for Psychosocial Attention) also exist, although all these are in Managua. There is no overall strategy for providing services and each region works out its own plan. In the absence of resources to build an effective mental health care system, maximum use is made of community health workers.

Community health workers are encouraged through training courses and manuals to recognize signs of depression from people's behaviour. These signs are identified as: acute anxiety, disturbed sleep patterns, physical problems such as aches and pains, sadness and apathy. Mental stress can be detected amongst women by irregular periods, eating disorders, child beating, and neglect of personal hygiene, such as forgetting to wash or comb hair. Treatment is suggested through people coming together to share their common experience and to undertake routine tasks from their daily lives. Community health workers are also encouraged to devote time to listening to people's problems.[25]

Amparro Gutiérrez has identified a number of key areas in the new thinking on mental health in Nicaragua that health workers are attempting to develop. One area is the prevention of mental illness that involves equipping families and individuals with the ability to recognize the 'signals' of distress in themselves and others so as to understand their own needs and the needs of those around them.[26]

One source of influence has been the Internationalist Team of Mental Health workers, based in Mexico, whose input has been mainly in the field of group therapy. Marie Langer, co-ordinator of the Internationalist Team until her death in 1987, was particularly concerned with the stress suffered by women. In one group she was working with in León in 1984, all the women present were taking potent tranquillizers, prescribed to them by doctors trained in pre-revolutionary Nicaragua. The women complained bitterly both about the drugs and about the undependable, abusive behaviour of the men in their lives. Another point of stress was the relationship of many women with their children. Because so many families are headed by single women, the women form their closest emotional ties with their children, consequently women often feel threatened by their children's normal striving for independence.[27]

Marie Langer's group provided an opportunity for women to talk these things through. The women also had a source of support beyond the group in the form of such local mass organizations as the Sandinista Defence Committees which were involved in the programme. In Langer's view, this was how an integrated service should operate.[28]

A large proportion of women's mental health problems stem from abusive husbands or *compañeros*. To counter these problems, the Women's Legal Office (OLM) in Managua offers free sessions with a psychologist to women suffering severe stress within the family. The OLM also provides joint counselling for both partners in a relationship. The philosophy of the OLM is that legal support should go hand in hand with emotional and psychological support (see p. 12).

## Traditional support mechanisms

Mental health provision is a recent phenomenon in Nicaragua and, because of the shortage of resources, has yet to be made comprehensive. To a large extent, Nicaraguans have thus had to rely on their own defence mechanisms. Ironically, the family, whilst presenting women with enormous problems, is nonetheless where much support is to be found, especially as it extends into the life of the community. Another major strand in Nicaraguans' mental survival strategies is religious faith. The interlocking of the Popular Church with the revolution has meant that for many people actively involved in the revolutionary process, religion remains a source of emotional support.

Religious customs related to death, for example, enable Nicaraguans to discharge their grief. Traditionally the dead body is displayed in the family house for about 24 hours so that the local community can pay their last respects — lighting candles, which are placed on a makeshift altar in front of the body. It is a common sight in Nicaragua to see groups of weeping women filing out of a neighbour's house after such a ceremony.

Conversely, this custom can make things doubly difficult for families who have never managed to retrieve the body of their loved one (as in the case of 'disappearances' or kidnaps). In this situation they are left in a sort of limbo with no outlet for their grief and fewer possibilities for sharing their grief with their communities.

The government is now trying to promote the idea that mourning the death of loved ones is essential to the mental and physical well-being of the nation. This was not always recognized. In the early years of the revolution and the beginning of the Contra war, the dead were heroes and martyrs — the death of a loved one was often a flag for family and friends to continue the struggle. Grief was transformed into political action; but it was frozen and hence unresolved rather than transformed. Amparro acknowledges the truth of this:

We were very hard on our feelings . . . Now we say people have permission to cry. We say now in official speeches, 'We cry in the morning, we bury our dead in the afternoon and the next day we have to work and to celebrate.' Somehow people have come to learn that they have to do this and combine the discharge of feelings with active social bonds with their *barrios* and relatives. Now we can call them 'our dead' instead of 'my dead' — even if it is not a political death . . . When someone dies, people gather — invited or spontaneously — and stay all night in the street and in the house, supporting the family. The next day, they accompany the family to the burial and for nine days there is official, religious praying which is social, active. Then the *barrio* comes again, and provides things which the family needs. The support of friends and strong social ties have helped Nicas a great deal to 'unfreeze' their grief.[29]

## Conclusion

Attempts to improve the health of the Nicaraguan population have hinged on women as the implementers of new programmes and policies. In the process, thousands of women have had the chance to receive training and gain confidence in community organization and leadership. Nevertheless, the idea that women are society's 'carers' may have been reinforced along the way.

The improvements in women's own health can largely be attributed to the general improvements in health services since 1979. The transfer of expertise and resources from inaccessible hospitals in the towns to local health posts in rural areas is one example of this. In view of the number of children most Nicaraguan women have, the emphasis placed by the new government on mother/child health has been of particular benefit to them.

As far as mental health is concerned, much of the burden of coping with economic crisis and caring for the mental illnesses of family members has fallen on women, causing acute stress. 'It is not possible for women to manage alone,' comments the psychologist, Dr Gutiérrez. 'Women have more propensity to endure and suffer — leading to illness.' In her view, the reduction of this stress rests on co-operation between men and women to solve the sexual division of labour: 'In the home, in work and in the street, men have to be educated, incorporated. They have to be part of the solution.'[30]

## Notes

1. 'Health and Health Care in Nicaragua', Nicaragua Solidarity Campaign (NSC) 1987, health study tour report.
2. Figures from Sivard, 1985.

3. Rita López, in Angel & Macintosh, 1987.

4. 'Health and Health Care in Nicaragua', op. cit.

5. Deighton et al, 1983, p. 117.

6. Mailene Rugama Hernández, interviewed by Rachel Stringfellow, 1987, unpublished.

7. 'Nicaragua Special Report — Health', NSC, 1986.

8. 'Health and Health Care in Nicaragua', op. cit.

9. Report of a workshop on 'Health Issues', organized by British Residents of Nicaragua Women, Managua, April 1987.

10. *Barricada*, 9 March 1989.

11. Susana Veraguas, Catholic Institute of International Relations (CIIR) report, March 1988, unpublished.

12. Nursing staff at Natural Childbirth Centre, Estelí, interviewed by Ginny Baumann, January 1989, unpublished.

13. Deighton et al, 1983, p. 122.

14. Susana Veraguas, op. cit.; also report by Sue Murray, CIIR volunteer at Natural Childbirth Centre, Estelí, July 1988, unpublished.

15. *Barricada*, 25 February 1989.

16. *Barricada Internacional*, 22 September 1988.

17. *Barricada*, 8 January 1989; *Barricada Internacional*, 24 November 1988.

18. Stephanie Williamson, letter to the Sheffield–Estelí Society, April 1989, unpublished.

19. *El Nuevo Diario*, 17 March 1989.

20. *The Militant* (USA), 14 July 1989.

21. Langer, 1989, p. 12.

22. *Barricada Internacional*, 24 November 1988.

23. Silvia Toruna, interviewed by Rachel Sieder, 1988, unpublished.

24. See Debbie Pickvance, *Changes*, January 1987.

25. *La Depresión*, MINSA manual for mental health workers, Managua, June 1988.

26. Dr Amparro Gutiérrez, interviewed by Maria Boniface, 23 July 1988.

27. *Barricada Internacional*, 24 November 1988.

28. Langer, 1989, p. 18.

29. Dr Amparro Gutiérrez, op. cit.

30. Ibid.

# 8. Women and Law

Some feminists in the West feel, understandably, that working to change the law is futile because the state is basically antagonistic to women's interests. For Nicaraguan women, however, the law is a crucial area of struggle in which the institutionalization of men's power over women is increasingly challenged. The long-term effects of the Contra war and the deepening economic crisis make material advances virtually impossible; women are thus demanding advances on the ideological front.

Nicaragua is a remarkable example of a democracy in which the mass of the people really do participate in the national decision-making process. New laws are widely discussed at grassroots level and suggestions for change are taken into account before they are passed. It is in this context that women in Nicaragua have made equally remarkable use of the law and the Constitution as an instrument for their emancipation and in particular to challenge *machismo* in its many forms.

In a country such as Nicaragua, with very limited resources with which to fully implement legal changes, the role of the law as ideology becomes paramount — it opens up debates and raises consciousness. Because new laws are discussed and people participate in making them, legal changes tend to *affect* social attitudes as much as they reflect them. There is at the same time an awareness of the importance of educational work and of the dangers of imposing change from above, without it first having been adequately discussed, understood and supported at grassroots level. This can be best illustrated by considering legal changes, and debates toward such changes, specifically relevant to women in Nicaragua.

## Laws inherited from Somoza's time

In the time of the Somozas, women's position of 'abject slavery' was reflected in the civil and criminal law. Until 1955 women were not even granted the right to vote, for what little it was worth in pre-revolutionary Nicaragua's fraudulent electoral process.[1]

Women's rights on marriage and divorce, though not of practical importance for a large proportion of Nicaraguan women in 'common law' unions, were nonetheless symbolic of women's status in *machista* society. Marriage was a contract that obliged the woman to follow the man to wherever he decided to make his home and to submit to his decisions as head of the family on their children's education and upbringing and the use of family assets. Adultery by the woman was grounds for divorce whereas for the man it was grounds for the woman to divorce him only if it could be proved to have taken place in a public or scandalous manner. Remarriage by a person found guilty of adultery was forbidden but only the woman concerned could be convicted of such an offence (for which the sentence was two years imprisonment).

Possibly more important in practice was the law relating to children born outside marriage. A woman was denied legal rights over a child if she was not married to its father and he opposed her, whereas the father could be granted legal rights over his child whatever the circumstances.

There was no civil protection (such as injunctions) for battered women except divorce (if the woman was married) which was obtainable only on grounds of excessive cruelty or other serious offences. These charges were difficult to prove and needed the services of a lawyer, who had to be paid. As criminal accusations between spouses were prohibited, a married woman could not use the criminal law against a battering husband. Even if she had had recourse to the criminal law, the police (who must almost always be involved in criminal cases) would be the last people to whom she would turn for protection against domestic violence: the National Guard, Somoza's military force of repression, would probably have been even more feared than a violent husband. The non-military police force introduced by the Sandinistas (together with the voluntary police) is an entirely new concept in the Nicaraguan context.

Neither prostitution nor pimping were criminal offences; on the contrary, prostitution was positively encouraged under the Somoza regime (see pp. 69–73).

## Transitional developments 1979–85

In the early years of the revolution, new legislation was debated in the Council of State, a transitional body composed of representatives from the FSLN and the Sandinista mass organizations, private enterprise and opposition political parties, left-wing organizations and unions and independent organizations such as the Church. In this transitional period (which ended in 1984 with the elections to the National Assembly, which replaced the Council of State) many laws were passed specifically affecting women, particularly their position as mothers.

On the very day after the Triumph over Somoza, the use of images of women for commercial purposes (for example, in advertising) was prohibited and prostitution was made a criminal offence. Both of these measures have more recently been the subject of controversy, for very different reasons (see sections on *Semana Comica* and prostitution in chapters 5 and 12) but the speed with which they were introduced undoubtedly reflected widespread anger about the commercialization of women's bodies, which had been a hallmark of life in Nicaragua before the revolution.

These and other transitional measures are listed below:

**1979:** **Provisional Media Law** — prohibited the use of images of women's bodies for commercial purposes (ie., in advertising). **Prostitution** made a criminal offence.

**Fundamental Statute of Rights and Guarantees** — declared equality for all and outlawed sex discrimination (now embodied in Articles 47 and 48 of the Constitution). Specifically established the right to investigate the paternity of illegitimate children.

**1980:** **Adoption Law** (AMNLAE's first proposal to the Council of State) — made it legal for single women to adopt fully; prohibited the export of Nicaraguan children for adoption by people abroad.

**Law promoting breastfeeding** — and banning advertising of powdered milk substitutes.

**1981:** **Law regulating relations between mothers, fathers and children** — abolished the old automatic status of the man as head of the family (known as *Padria Potestad*, literally Father Power); — created equal rights over children for mother and father; — established that in a custody dispute over a child under seven where both parents are equally suitable, the child will stay with its mother, and that the views of children over seven will be taken into account in deciding which parent should have custody.

**Co-operatives Law** — aimed to promote women's active participation in agricultural co-ops and granted women the right to hold title to land.

**1982:** **Law of Nurturing** ('*Alimentos*') — meaning in this context provision of a home, food, clothing, education, attention etc. (Note: This law was passed by the Council of State but never ratified by the transitional Junta.) — eliminated the different classes of children (that is, abolished status of illegitimacy) stating that all children have equal rights and all parents have equal obligations; — imposed a legal obligation on men to discharge their family responsibilities including childcare and housework;

— charged children, parents and grandparents with the duty to look after each other.

**Old law** — enabling the state to force salaried fathers to pay maintenance for their children was *reformed* to make it easier to enforce and expand its use. The fathers concerned can have their salaries deducted at source if they refuse to pay maintenance.

**Employment laws reformed** — equal pay introduced; women allowed to appear on farm pay rolls; nursing mothers allowed one hour off a day to breastfeed.

**State pensions introduced** for the elderly, disabled, war widows and those injured at work.

## Women's Legal Office

In 1983 the first AMNLAE Women's Legal Office opened in Managua. This was at a time when the country was having to shift on to a permanent war footing; it reflects the commitment to increasing women's rights, in even the most adverse conditions.

Dependent on foreign aid for all funding other than staff salaries, from 1985 onwards the Office expanded its role to include education, research and work on proposals for the Constitution. In 1985, a second office was opened in Estelí, followed by offices in León, Granada and Masaya. Most of their casework is on domestic violence, child maintenance and custody. Counselling for individuals and for couples is also offered, with the aim of achieving reconciliation. In 1987, over 2,000 agreements for couples were drafted, laying down ground rules for a new marital relationship. Educational work ranges from organizing workshops for groups such as women health workers, mixed groups of police officers, and Sandinista Youth groups, to participating in a television programme on domestic violence, and publishing leaflets on women's rights.

In areas where there is no Women's Legal Office, a woman can go directly to the local police if she is being beaten or to the local Office of Family Protection (OPF) in INSBBI (the Ministry of Social Welfare) if she wants to try to obtain child maintenance from a biological father. The OPF has offices in 22 towns but it cannot do the outreach work that the OLM tries to do.

## Debate on the Constitution

The Nicaraguan Constitution was drafted during 1985 and 1986 and inaugurated in January 1987. In its brief history as a republic, Nicaragua has had a fair number of constitutions, mostly written in close collaboration with US officials and handed down from above. This time it was different; the new Constitution was not simply a formal document, it was a focus for a nationwide debate on how the revolution should proceed. Nicaraguans were able to participate in designing their Constitution and protecting their rights by attending open meetings (*cabildos*) organized by the Constitutional Commission, with separate forums in each region of the country for peasant farmers, for soldiers, for young people and for women. Aware that this was to be a statement of national principles containing all the basic rights and duties of every Nicaraguan, many ordinary women displayed an interest in influencing its contents. Maria Lourdes Bolanos (then director of the Women's Legal Office) commented: 'This is the first time women have been consulted in the writing of a constitution.' For that matter it's the first time people have been consulted.[2]

The mood of some of the women participating in the open meetings is best highlighted by an incident at a meeting in the northern Nicaraguan town of Ocotal. Towards the end of the meeting a male member of the presiding committee announced that although this was a women's forum, if any men present wanted to express their opinions they were welcome to do so. The women present quickly shouted him down with a gigantic, 'Hoooooo!'[3]

The following eyewitness account of one of the open meetings organized by the Constitutional Commission for women, in Managua, conveys the exhilaration felt by women voicing their demands to a government which was prepared to listen and respond to pressure from below. The Managua meeting was broadcast on national radio.

> The hall was crammed with well over 1,000 women, seated in rows and standing in all the aisles, many with their children. . . . Six members of the Constitutional Commission arrived to listen to them including two prominent government leaders, Dora Maria Tellez and Carlos Nuñez, who invited anyone who had a point to make to step forward. There was a sudden rush as 75 women stood at once and poured to the front of the hall while the rest of us burst into applause. . . . One by one they came up to the microphone and said their piece. . . . The majority made very specifically feminist demands — insisting again and again that the Constitution must enshrine a woman's right to control her own fertility, including the right to abortion: 'I am a mother of ten children and a worker and a student. We have the right to be mothers but men want us to get pregnant just so they can feel macho . . . *we* must decide whether to bear a child.'
>
> Men were attacked for rape and domestic violence, for leaving housework to women, for abandoning women with children, for being responsible for prostitution and for failing to understand that the Nicaraguan Revolution includes women . . . The open meeting began before six and was still going strong when I crept out at 10 at

night after some 50 speeches. Every woman was given space to speak. As one said: 'I feel a deep emotion at participating in this open meeting, adding my voice to the Constitution. This really is *our* revolution.'[4]

The outcome of the open meetings was a Constitution that contains more than ten Articles referring specifically to women's rights. The previous Constitution of 1974 (in Somoza's time) had contained none. The new Constitution (written in non-sexist language) establishes the right to 'absolute equality between men and women'. The legal advisor to the National Assembly, Milu Vargas, has pointed out[5] that this is equivalent to the Equal Rights Amendment in the USA, which North American women have been struggling in vain to insert in their own country's Constitution since the 1960s.

## Women and Law Conference

In August 1988 the women's section of CONAPRO (the organization of Nicaraguan professionals) held a three-day national seminar on Women and the Law. They clearly felt that after so much had been achieved on paper in the Constitution, it was necessary to keep up the pressure to ensure that the principle of equality was translated into practice by a radical overhaul of the old laws in every field. Their conclusions and recommendations were reported in detail in the daily papers *Barricada* and *El Nuevo Diario*.

One recommendation was that if a man battered a woman he should be denied active participation in a political project. Other recommendations made more specific demands: for example, that domestic violence be treated as a crime, punishable as severely as an act of violence committed outside the family. In the field of labour legislation, it was proposed that the old 'protective' laws, which regulated hours and conditions of work for women, should be abolished, as they were seen as running counter to the institutionalization of equality between men and women embodied in the Constitution.

The seminar also proposed a new law that would enable an unmarried couple, or one of the partners, or any of the children born of a common law marriage, to request a judicial declaration establishing their relationship before a local district judge.

Further proposals included stiffer sentences for rape and sexual assault and flexible sentencing to take account of the circumstances and age of the victim. A strong statement was made in support of the decriminalization of abortion (see pp. 118–21). Delegates pointed out the hypocrisy of arguing that it is the woman's social responsibility to continue with an unwanted pregnancy, yet when the child is born the responsibility for its upbringing is hers alone and not seen as a social responsibility. The delegates also strongly opposed state regulation of prostitution (see also Chapter 1).

Hard on the heels of the CONAPRO seminar, the first Latin American conference on women and the law took place in Managua in October 1988. It lasted five days and more than 200 legislators from Latin America, Europe, the US and Canada attended to compare experiences and formulate proposals on all the issues mentioned above.

## New demands

Fired by the inspiration provided by both conferences, AMNLAE and CONAPRO followed up the theme of law in January 1989 by making detailed submissions to the National Assembly on reform of the civil, criminal and labour laws. Amongst their proposals were the extension of the definition of rape to all forms of vaginal, anal or oral penetration by the penis or any other object, and increased sentences for rape to 20–25 or 30 years in cases with aggravating features, such as where the man is in a position of trust or authority over the woman or where he is or has ever been married to her. AMNLAE also demanded the decriminalization of abortion (pp. 118–21), and asked that maintenance payments be linked to the man's salary level and index-linked to inflation, and in the event of separation for stable unmarried couples to have the same rights over children and shared property as married couples in divorce.

## Population and reproductive rights
(See also Chapter 7)

### Birth control and imperialism
Reproductive rights and better access to contraception are now major demands of the Nicaraguan women's movement. But until the mid-1980s birth control was a private issue, discussed very little either by AMNLAE or any other Sandinista organization. There are a number of reasons for this silence. First was the Church's opposition to birth control and abortion and the belief that to have children was reflecting God's will. Second, the war that preceded the Triumph had strengthened the general commitment to creating families. 'After years of bloodshed, splitting up of families and deaths of relatives, people wanted to create new life, and re-establish the security and bonds of the family.'[6] Also, economically many family units relied on their children's labour for survival and because of high infant mortality rates, it seemed that only a large family could ensure economic security. Meanwhile, the FSLN argued that the country was underpopulated and that Contra war casualties exacerbated this situation. A population of

only three million, it was argued, was particularly vulnerable to foreign interference. Large-scale migration, mainly to the US, probably added to these fears: between 1979 and 1987, 140,000 people left Nicaragua.

The sense of vulnerability must be seen within the context of US birth control programmes introduced during the Somoza era. These aimed to 'kill the guerrilla in the womb' by means of enforced contraception and sterilization; in 1968, a major US aid programme was conditional on Nicaragua accepting family planning. By 1970 the birth control programme was wholly funded by the Somoza government, even though previously the cultural mandate that women should have lots of children had actually been encouraged by Somocista landowners themselves so as to guarantee a supply of seasonal labourers on their plantations. Somoza's birth control programme focused on areas where the guerrillas were known to be strongest. Doris Tijerino, Head of the Sandinista Police, claims that US volunteers put agents into anti-polio vaccines to sterilize women without their knowledge or consent.[7]

Family planning was thus associated in the public mind with imperialism. Against this backdrop, AMPRONAC, the women's organization of the pre-revolutionary years, called for the elimination of the use of birth control. Once in power, the Sandinistas likewise put greater effort into improving conditions for mothers and children, rather than promoting birth control.

But the FSLN's fears need to be offset against the population statistics that indicate that Nicaragua has one of the highest fertility rates in Latin America. Half the population is under the age of 15, and in 1988 the average number of children born to Nicaraguan women between the ages of 14 and 45 was 5.5. The reduction in the infant mortality rate means that the population is likely to exceed five million by the year 2000.[8] The highest birth rates are in rural areas where they are three times higher than in the towns.[9]

In relation to women as the bearers of children, the Sandinistas face a dilemma. As much as they may welcome the growth of the population, there is also a very practical need to involve as many people as possible in production, and women are a source of productive labour. This labour is more difficult to tap as long as women are tied up with childbearing. A large proportion of babies are born to young women who may be just coming into the economy as productive workers. A high birth rate thus perpetuates a sharp division of labour between the sexes and limits women's involvement in the economy. Frequent pregnancies amongst adolescent women — especially in the rural population — also strain the health service as obstetric complications are common in this age group.

## Contraception

Contraception is free in Nicaragua and — theoretically — available to everyone. But the theory and reality rarely coincide. Supplies come from abroad and tend to be sporadic. In 1983, 22.1% of women between the ages of 15 and 49 were using contraception provided by government health facilities, of whom 75% were using the pill, and 15% the IUD and 'other methods'.[10] These figures, however, do not give the full picture as many women prefer to buy their contraceptives from market stalls to avoid the embarrassment of going to a state health clinic.

Depo-Provera (an injected contraceptive, administered every three to six months), used in the past, was quite popular with women who found it difficult to conceal other forms of contraception from *machista* husbands. But this method is no longer promoted because of its dangerous side-effects.

In the late 1980s, condoms were beginning to be used in Nicaragua, although *machista* attitudes stood in the way of their popularity. The increasing use is due mainly to concern about the spread of AIDS; by mid-1989, two Nicaraguans had died of AIDS.

Sterilization by cutting the fallopian tubes was available to women over 25 and in 1988 it became possible for women to be sterilized without their husbands' permission. Because of cuts in government health spending, however, state provision of this service was limited in 1989 to women over 35 except in cases of emergency. Even then women were eligible only if they already had six children.

### Women take the initiative

In the mid to late 1980s, grassroots discussions amongst women started to force the issue of contraception on to the agenda. In October 1988, for example, a conference of women farm workers, organized by the ATC and co-sponsored by AMNLAE, called for low-cost contraception to be made available throughout the country. Lea Guido, then National Secretary of AMNLAE, addressing the conference, said that contraception should be as accessible as a quart of milk.[11]

Clearly the opportunities in employment and in the mass organizations opened up by the revolution combined with the general reassessment of women's role in society have led many women to question traditional attitudes towards contraception. Maria Cecilia, a Colombian nurse working in a rural clinic in 1984, noticed that more and more women were asking for whatever contraception methods were available. Flor Ramírez, head of the tobacco section of the Agricultural Workers' Union (ATC) comments:

Just imagine, had I been taking the pill I would never have had 7 children. Now I'm more in control of my life, but that's me. Many others aren't and abortion isn't the answer. Some women tell you it's

God's will. Is God going to provide dinner for all her children? I'm not criticizing anyone's belief, let them believe in the devil, but we want to have the choice whether to be pregnant or not. I mean, if the conditions aren't right because of the war and the economic blockade, why burden yourself with another mouth to feed?[12]

Inevitably, contraception has aroused fierce passions within relationships, largely because of men's attitudes. 'All methods have met with resistance from some of the men,' commented one woman. 'When they feel the IUD strings, they send her back to the clinic to take it out. They won't let her plan her family . . . they think if she's protected, she'll go out with someone else. So the women come and take the pill secretly.'[13]

## Abortion

Nicaragua's 1974 Criminal Code (which is still in force) makes abortion illegal, except 'therapeutic' abortion on strict medical grounds. A woman cannot ask for this herself; the request must come from her husband or nearest relative who must later also give formal permission. The decision is made by a three-member medical panel, usually all men.

Although the law has not been changed since 1979, it has been FSLN policy not to prosecute women who have illegal abortions, or those who perform them. There have been reported cases of the police arresting and detaining both parties involved, but they have been released without charges a few hours later.

Instead of introducing new laws on abortion, official emphasis has been placed on improving the supply and distribution of contraceptives, developing sex education and challenging traditional attitudes, such as the sexual double standard and men's irresponsibility.

The FSLN leadership has argued that because Nicaragua suffers a labour shortage exacerbated by war casualties, legal abortion is unthinkable. There is also fear of a political backlash organized on religious grounds, as the Catholic Church hierarchy and the political parties to the right of the FSLN are vociferous opponents of legalization. And of course many Catholic supporters of the FSLN and some party members themselves have strong religious convictions which make them reluctant to support legalization of abortion. Indeed some actively oppose it.

### Illegal abortions
Many Nicaraguan women still die from botched illegal abortions and many others need hysterectomies in order to survive the illegal operation. This state of affairs emerged for the first time in November 1985 when a study by doctors and social workers was published in *Barri-*

*cada*,[14] which showed that from 1983 to 1985, 45% of the admissions to Bertha Calderón Women's Hospital in Managua were as a result of illegal abortions. Of these, 10% died and 26% were left sterile.

There followed in the pages of *Barricada* an intense public debate on whether or not abortion should be legalized. The argument that legal abortion and safe contraception were necessary for women's health was forcefully put. It was pointed out that the government's attitude to abortion, of 'semi-legality', made it impossible either to control abuses or to introduce such safe (and cheap) methods as vacuum sunction. Doris Tijerino, Head of the Sandinista Police, argued that if legal abortions were freely available, the police would be able to prosecute the backstreet abortionists who were currently maiming women. 'I'm in favour of legalizing abortion,' she announced, 'not only as a woman, but also as Chief of Police.'[15] She made it clear that the Sandinista police did not prosecute women because it was understood that many of them had no alternative. She opposed changing the law by decree, however, stressing the need for discussion and education first.

The debate in *Barricada* appears to have been closed prematurely because the issue was seen as too explosive, but shortly afterwards, in the open forums for women to discuss the draft constitution the two topics they raised most often were sex education and abortion. The Constitution is silent on abortion, but the Conservative Party proposal that the 'right to life' Article banning capital punishment should be extended to declare that life begins at conception was defeated.

The discussion on abortion did not end there. In 1987 the Sandinista leadership was caught in an increasingly uncomfortable compromise between the growing 'legalization' lobby and the forces of the Church hierarchy and the right in their claim for the 'moral high ground'. In September 1987 at a 'Face the People' meeting to mark AMNLAE's 10th anniversary, President Ortega, 'used the authority and discourse of the revolution and the war to attack and demobilize campaigners for women's reproductive choice.'[16] US policy, he argued, had been to 'freeze the population growth . . . to avoid the risk of an increase in the population that could threaten a revolutionary change.' Nicaragua was subject 'to a policy of genocide' through the US-sponsored Contra war. 'One way of depleting our youth is to promote the sterilization of women in Nicaragua . . . or to promote the policy of abortion.' He said that some women, 'aspiring to be liberated', decide not to bear children. Such a woman 'negates her own continuity, the continuity of the human species.'[17] Nicaraguan women did not allow this expression of Ortega's personal views to go unchallenged. At the end of his speech many angry women gathered around him to argue and later a meeting was called with women from different organizations to put to him their views on the subject.

Meanwhile, women were also taking the law into their own hands. In January 1988 the newly-opened Ixchen Women's Centre in Masaya started to offer legal, psychological and gynaecological services to women. The women involved had surveyed 70 women in Masaya, Granada and Rivas; 50% of them had attributed their need for abortion to economic problems or irresponsible paternity and most of them were aged 30–35. The Centre is a private institution, which charges for its services, but on a sliding scale and within the reach of poor women. A similar Centre has since opened in Managua.

In late 1988 the public debate again opened up, partly in response to more research studies and partly because of a resounding demand for legalization from the CONAPRO Women and the Law conference (see pp. 114–15). In his closing speech to the Latin American conference on Women and the Law that took place in Managua in August 1988, President Ortega appeared to have retreated from his vehement anti-abortionist position of the previous year. On this occasion he side-stepped the issue by proclaiming that it was the revolution's wish that abortion should be reserved for extreme cases and that through proper sex education women should be able to avoid the need for it.

Soon after the Women and Law conferences, Dr Maria Pizarro, a gynaecologist at Bertha Calderón Women's Hospital, produced a study in which she highlighted the waste of scarce medical resources resulting from the treatment of women who had had botched abortions. Between July 1985 and September 1988, 531 women were treated at the hospital due to illegal abortions; 30 of them died and of those who survived 98% needed surgery to save their lives or repair the damage. A typical woman in this group would be aged 20–35, in a stable relationship, and prior to this (her first) abortion, would have had between four and six pregnancies.[18]

There are now strong signs that such research is likely to lead to legalization, or at least decriminalization of abortion. In September 1988, Carlos Núñez, President of the National Assembly, indicated in an interview in *El Nuevo Diario* that the issue was likely to come before the next session of the legislature, 'Not because it is the invention of some feminist organization or association, but because it is a demand of the specialists in gynaecology, who point out that it is one of the main causes of death in Nicaragua.'

The National Secretary of AMNLAE, Lea Guido, was more specific when she spoke to the ATC Women's Assembly in October 1988. She said that abortion should be decriminalized so that, 'when a woman is pregnant, and for whatever reason wants to have a voluntary abortion, she can have it done in a hospital and not like an animal.' This represented a breakthrough at an official level and was followed in January 1989 by the inclusion of the demand for decriminalization of abortion in the AMNLAE submission to the National Assembly on Law Reform. In the past, AMNLAE had been wary of supporting demands to change the law, even when large numbers of women were voicing such demands at events like the open meetings in 1986.

If safe legal abortion facilities are introduced in Nicaragua, not only women's lives, but also scarce medical resources will be saved.

## Conclusion

Contraceptive supplies and provision for women seeking sterilization remain inadequate while abortion is illegal. This is as much to do with deep-seated attitudes towards women's role as mothers and with the supposed need to maintain the population in a war situation as it is to do with the lack of medical resources. In the late 1980s the Nicaraguan women's movement began to challenge these attitudes and to demand more rights in relation to reproduction.

## Notes

1. Heliette Ehlers, speaking in London, May 1987.
2. 'Central American Historical Institute Update', 29 October 1985.
3. Beth Woroniuk, 'Women's Oppression and the Revolution — the Nicaraguan Debate', CUSO, December 1987.
4. Lucinda Broadbent, in Managua on 10 June 1986, quoted in *Nicaragua Today*, Autumn 1986.
5. Milu Vargas, interview, 'ANN: Women in Central America', bulletin No. 2, March 1987.
6. Deighton et al, 1983, p. 124.
7. Ibid., p. 153.
8. *Barricada*, 18 September 1988.
9. *Barricada*, 21 September 1988.
10. Lauren Poole, 'Nicaragua: Nation of Births' in *WIRE*, November 1984.
11. *The Militant* (USA), 16 December 1988.
12. Angel & Macintosh, 1987, pp. 127–8.
13. Lauren Poole, op. cit.
14. *Barricada*, 19 November 1985.
15. *Barricada*, 9 December 1985.
16. Maxine Molyneux, 'The Politics of Abortion in Nicaragua', *Feminist Review* No. 29, May 1988.
17. *The Militant* (USA), October 1987, quoted by Maxine Molyneux, op. cit.
18. *The Militant* (USA), 30 December 1988.

# 9. Women and Education

Education has been seen as a key to emancipation in the new Nicaragua. Indeed one of the first priorities of the new administration in 1979 was to teach the people to read. Within a year illiteracy was reduced from 50% to 12% — earning Nicaragua the 1980 Krupskaya Award from UNESCO. But education in Nicaragua extends beyond reading and writing. It is regarded as a life-long process, an essential element of the revolution, and a participatory process that should help the people solve both their own and their country's problems.

The Sandinistas inherited a hopelessly poor education system. In 1979 there was no education for children under six; there was only 64% enrolment in primary education, and for the majority of children over the age of 13 schooling was rare. Education was particularly bad in rural areas where 90% of schools had only one teacher and not more than one in 20 children completed the top primary grade. Textbooks bore no relation to life in Nicaragua. Universities served only 3% of the population, and the wealthy sent their children abroad to be educated (Bianca Jagger is perhaps the best-known example of this). Following the Triumph in 1979, a poster distributed in Nicaragua showed a shoe-shine box traditionally used by child workers, under which were the words: 'This is the symbol of childhood before the revolution. We will put an end to this tyranny'.

For girls, schooling was particularly inadequate, as Gladys Martínez, Co-ordinator of the Barrio Committee in Clavarito, León, recalls:

> I was helping my mother in the bakery by the age of seven. My mother was on her own by then because my father left her with us three girls. As the oldest I had to help her although this meant that I often didn't go to school. So I got as far as 4th grade primary. My mother's attitude was that she was too poor to get me a proper education so all she could do was to teach me her profession, which is breadmaking.[1]

# Traditional constraints on women studying

Girls and women wishing to study have faced varying degrees of opposition at all stages of education. Parents of young girls have often felt that the family would be better off to have their daughters working and bringing in money, even if they are still in primary school.

For older girls, this pressure continues, either to get married or to go out to work. Unmarried female students at university experience pressure from parents who do not believe that girls should be involved in education at such a high level. 'Husbands put indirect pressure on their wives, saying that they shouldn't neglect their household duties', comments Nancy Arostegui, Director of the Humanities Faculty at the University of Central America in Managua.[2]

Married women who want to continue studying also have to cope with their husbands' jealousy. It is not unusual for women to go out alone at night, but women who do are viewed with suspicion. Some students are discouraged from going to the class by their husbands who believe that they go to meet other men. But as a popular education teacher notes, some men are changing their attitudes: 'At the beginning my husband wanted to object [to her becoming a teacher], but after a while he accepted it and in the end he became my student.'[3] Similarly, Otilia Cruz, a *campesina* woman asserts: 'Tacho [husband] wants me to study. . . . Our friends are surprised, saying "How can you go off and abandon your children?" But I tell them that if my children are all right with me then they'll be all right with Tacho'.[4]

Childcare is the biggest single problem women face when trying to educate themselves. At the secondary school level it is still fairly common for girls to leave after the third grade (aged 15) because they are pregnant. In August 1988, *El Nuevo Diario*[5] reported that university teachers did not take their women students seriously once they had babies. Around 40% of families are headed by single women and naturally this presents problems for them if they want to study, particularly those without mothers or relatives to help with childcare. There are no crèche facilities in Nicaragua's schools and only minimal childcare provision at colleges.

The Revolution has, however, made strenuous efforts to overcome some of these constraints. Because women, and primarily rural women, formed the majority of illiterate people in 1979, they have been the main beneficiaries of the massive education drive since the revolution. Literacy for women in Nicaragua is not only about learning to read and write: it is about finding a voice after centuries of invisibility, building a sense of dignity and self-confidence and participating in the political process on an equal level with men.

## Literacy Crusade and Popular Education Collectives

Most illiterate Nicaraguans learnt to read and write during the Literacy Crusade launched by the FSLN in 1980. Based on the principles of Brazilian educationalist, Paulo Freire, the Literacy Crusade had a twofold aim: one, to teach the population to read; and two, to show country people the revolution in action, using education as a tool for development.

Each lesson was designed to stimulate a dialogue based on pictures and key words representing crucial issues in the learners' lives. Lesson four of book one, entitled simply 'Woman', looks at the central part played by women in the revolutionary process and their arduous domestic routine.

A further aim was to enable people from the towns — the teachers, known as *brigadistas* — to experience the harsh rural conditions in which the majority of Nicaraguans lived. The introduction to the primer for literacy teachers reads:

> We should be the motivators of the [learning] process, who teach and learn at the same time. The learners are people who can think, express their ideas and teach what they know from experience. In many cases they are extremely creative. All of us will learn from this epic adventure.

Sixty per cent of the teachers were women and in some areas there were brigades wholly of women.[6] Mercedita Talavera of Estelí recalls:

> We worked from sunrise to sunset, classes for kids in the morning and for adults in the afternoon and evening, and even at weekends we'd do things like decorate the room we used for classes . . . and we'd plan little activities. And we worked alongside the *campesinos* in the fields.[7]

At the end of the first leg of the crusade, after only five months, more than 300,000 people could at least read a daily newspaper. The Crusade had an immense impact on women's morale. In 1984 a newly literate woman wrote to *Barricada*:

> Already since the Crusade we working-class women have shaken the idea that there is nothing for women to study for; some of us want to become dressmakers, midwives . . . but we have also found a new occupation . . . before long we became . . . teachers.[8]

After the Literacy Crusade, Popular Education Collectives (CEPs) were established so that students who had just learnt to read and write could maintain these skills. The Collectives were also designed to teach those who, despite the crusade, remained totally illiterate. As with the first literacy campaign, popular education for adults is not simply about learning to read and write; it starts from the premise that everyone should have the chance to learn about Nicaragua's history, and understand its problems today — from the war to the lack of milk and food shortages. Once informed on these issues, it is hoped that the students themselves will join in the discussions to solve these problems.

The 'popular teachers' leading the classes are themselves still learning, having been chosen from among fellow students to lead the study sessions; 95% of the popular teachers are women. Because of their importance to the revolution, popular education teachers have, arguably, received more validation than primary and secondary teachers, the majority of whom are also women.

Adult education classes are free. They take place in isolated villages, in towns, factories and farms (often during worktime), in schools during the evening and in people's homes. The teaching methods are those used in the literacy crusade, based on pictures with a simple text and designed to stimulate discussion. One lesson has a picture of a skilled woman working a machine, accompanied by the sentence: 'We must support everyone, particularly all women who could receive training in technical and union matters.'

## Illiteracy creeps back

Despite the extraordinary results of the literacy campaigns, however, the war has taken its toll, and illiteracy has crept back to 23% (1987) from the post-crusade figure of 13%. In 1988 David Archer and Alan Murdoch, of the British Oxford Community Education Direct Research Unit (CEDRU), conducted a study of the current state of the CEP.[9] They concluded that drop-out rates were high and enrolment was falling. Eight hundred and fifty centres had been closed and 100 CEP teachers killed by the Contra. Illiteracy has risen particularly fast among women. A Ministry official was quoted as saying:

> Although we have no precise figures, we have been alarmed by the number of women who have returned to virtual illiteracy since the brigades because the follow-up collapsed — maybe the teacher didn't show up or there were shortages of materials. Other women were just too tired — they worked in the fields during the day, then did the housework, grew crops on their own small plot of land. When are they going to study? This is not just a women's problem — men also find it hard to do the follow-up, but women's situation exacerbates it, the number of illiterates is increasing.[10]

To combat this, new literacy crusades were launched during 1988 in León and Estelí. In Estelí all 4th and 5th year secondary students must teach literacy or basic education to adults. An encouraging aspect of the current campaign in Estelí is that many of these 'teachers' go to their students' homes as women find it difficult to attend regularly at a centre.

Not only the Ministry of Education is taking measures against illiteracy. A report from the 1987 Women's Assembly of the Agricultural Workers' Union (ATC) says:

> Our CEPs are passing through a difficult time, and we have not been participating fully. This is because we have not been able to solve the problems of childcare while we attend the classes and the burden of the double shift [work and domestic life] which women face.

The ATC magazine, *El Machete*, has incorporated these problems into a popular education lesson format, so that students discuss illiteracy within the process of learning to read. Thus in one lesson there is a picture of women attending a class accompanied by the text: 'We must restart CEPs where there aren't any, and we must find solutions to the problems of the timing of the class, and of childcare.'

## Primary education

The Sandinista government provides universal, free education for all children from the ages of 6 to 12. Between 1979 and 1985 (before the school building programme was frozen because of the war) 3,934 new classrooms were built and, as a result of special training courses, the number of trained primary school teachers had tripled by 1983.[11]

Despite these efforts, by 1982 only 82% of those eligible had enrolled in primary education. This low attendance reflects the legacy of underdevelopment from which Nicaragua was suffering. In many cases, girls have still been kept back from school, as 14-year-old Joanna explains:

> Sometimes I miss school because I have to help my mother, maybe to stay and do the washing. When that happens my sister lends me her notebooks so I can copy down what they've done that day. Today, for example, my sister had to stay at home and do the housework.[12]

In isolated rural areas, where transport problems have made school attendance very difficult, the Ministry of Education has had particular problems in fulfilling its aim of universal education for all children. Additionally, many rural people attach more importance to learning practical skills than to learning to read and write. Thus some parents have had to be positively encouraged to send their children to school. In the early years of the revolution, orientation classes were offered to parents to show them the importance of education, especially for girls. That enrolment of boys and girls in primary education is now equal is evidence of the success of these orientation classes in discouraging sexist attitudes to girls' education.

## Child labour

Many more children go to primary school than in Somoza's day, but a large proportion must still do remunerated work. Indeed during these times of economic crisis, working-class and peasant families invariably depend on the earning power of their children. The jobs undertaken by urban children range from selling *tortillas* or chewing-gum in the street to helping their parents on market stalls and making cakes or bread for sale. In the country, children often pick coffee and work on the land at peak times alongside their parents. Ironically, parents (often single mothers) engage the labour of their children precisely in order to provide more for these same children. Silvia Toruna, a mother of four, told a British voluntary worker in 1987 that it was an increasing struggle for her to provide materials and clothing to enable her children to continue going to school.[13] Some mornings they left with only a glass of *pinol* (maize and sugar drink) for breakfast and consequently could not concentrate on studying. This situation has driven more and more women in Silvia's *barrio* to send their children to sell drinks and chewing-gum in the Oriental Market.

Work of this nature has gradually taken up more and more time and schools have seen serious decreases in their rolls. Nevertheless most children still manage to combine such work with school attendance. This is made possible by the fact that Nicaraguan schools (both primary and secondary), like schools elsewhere in Latin America, operate a morning and afternoon shift system. Consequently many Nicaraguan children perform a juggling act between school and paid work, as verified by a boy from Managua:

> I'm up at five usually and off to the market with my little sister Mercedes or my older sister Nubia. We buy fruit there to sell at break times at the school next door. . . . We're back by 7 for school. Saturdays and Sundays are different. Then we're usually out all day selling dumplings.[14]

## Secondary school education

By far the largest educational funds have been spent on improving primary education ($2300m — 1979 figures), but the budget for secondary education doubled following the Triumph in 1979. In Nicaragua, secondary school education caters for children aged 13 to 18, and all children are now encouraged to complete the first three years at least.

By contrast, in 1978 only about 18% of those eligible enrolled in secondary school.

The attitude towards secondary education is flexible, in that it incorporates large numbers of adults who have missed out on education, either because of the war (pre-1979), compulsory military service (1984-present), or because of work, pregnancy or childcare commitments. In some cases young women of 18 plus, sometimes new mothers (often wearing school uniform!), attend morning classes, or more often in the evening.

\*   \*   \*

*Azucena is 19, she split up with her husband who left her mainly because she refused to give up studying. As a result she moved back to her mother's, with whom she leaves her 18-month-old son for much of the time. Her work day is from 7 a.m. till 4 p.m., with an hour at home before she goes to night school in first-year secondary. She gets home at 9.45 p.m. Not surprisingly, she finds it hard to get all the homework done as the house does not have electricity. Azucena is her class's representative in the Federation of Secondary Students and has recently got a job as a cook in the army.*

\*   \*   \*

At the secondary school level, the attendance of young women is higher than that of young men. According to a Ministry of Education spokesperson, there is now a relatively high enrolment rate among girls: between 60% and 70% of those eligible attend secondary school.[15] This is mainly because men from the age of 18 are called up for military service and some volunteer earlier; once they have turned 18, they cannot enrol for classes unless they can prove that they have registered for military service, a factor that undoubtedly deters draft dodgers from attending secondary school.

According to a British teacher in Estelí's biggest secondary school, the girls are the highest achievers in the female-dominated daytime classes; they are also very confident and take a leading role in the class. The small number of boys in daytime senior classes (maybe between five and 10 out of 40) allows girls to participate more fully, and most class 'presidents' are girls. In contrast, at the same level at night school, classes are more mixed and the men take over, with many of the young women remaining completely passive. Women students also predominate in the evening classes, but most of the class representatives are men.[16]

Whilst the Ministry of Education has incorporated anti-imperialist and anti-racist ideology into its textbooks, there is no such obvious anti-sexism or positive imagery about women. In theory, boys and girls are expected to participate equally in school activities, but in practice the traditional gender divisions persist. For events like the annual International Food Day, the girls do the cooking or buy the food. Meanwhile, sport is still mainly organized for the boys. Beauty queen contests are an integral feature of school life, promoted by the teachers, the student federation and the Sandinista Youth. The School 'Band of War' always includes a squad of majorettes in the briefest of miniskirts.

Parental concern for their daughters is undoubtedly a factor in hampering girls' involvement in activities such as school vigilance patrols, end-of-term parties and fund-raising concerts. Nevertheless the very fact that so many girls are attending secondary school has inevitably increased their self-awareness and development.

## Higher education

Between 1979 and 1984 there was a 105% increase in Nicaragua's higher education student population (from 21,000 to 43,000). Since July 1979, 300 technicians and technical assistants have finished their courses and are now working in rural areas. This figure represents 42% of the technical personnel to have graduated in the last 50 years.

As part of the strategy to recruit more women into university courses, 50% of places are automatically reserved for women.

**Proportion of Women in Applied Subjects**

| Subject | 1979 | 1983 |
|---|---|---|
| Civil Engineering | 0% | 35% |
| Agriculture | 0% | 11% |
| Technical | 0% | 57%* |
| Professional studies | Not known | 47% |

* 50% of courses reserved for women

Women now make up by far the majority of university students, largely because of male military conscription. Enrolment in higher education actually fell from 36,000 in 1983 to 29,000 in 1985, but the proportion of women students rose dramatically from 45% in 1985 to 85% in 1987. According to Jackie Barry, who taught English at the Autonomous University of Nicaragua in 1986, men were not allowed to register for her courses because the class would have been interrupted by students being called up. It remains to be seen if the proportions of male and female students change dramatically once the war is over.[17]

But although women predominate among the students, it is still difficult for them to attain positions as elected representatives within the universities at high levels, and there is only one woman who is a faculty president. According to Jorge Cerrato, President of UNEN (University Students Union), this is due to continuing opposition from men.

Women who attend universities and technical colleges still have huge logistical problems to face. One complaint of the better-off students is that with the rising expectations of poorer women, as a result of the revolution, domestics are hard to come by, making it very difficult to squeeze in study around household chores. 'It is not simply a choice for the women to work or study, but also the case that they must get up at 4 a.m. to do the housework', commented an article in *El Nuevo Diario* in August 1988. Other reasons cited in the article included looking after sick parents, childcare and childbirth. Although university women students are provided with a post-natal subsidy and a 40% absence allowance following childbirth, there is a high drop-out rate amongst women with small children. The University has a crèche, but there is strong competition for places. The strain of having a new-born baby coupled with male university teachers' negative attitude towards mothers are often too much to bear.

For many single young women, their lack of confidence outside the family structure, and parental concern about sending daughters away from home, automatically dissuades them from considering further education. Stephanie Williamson, a British teacher in Estelí, recalls that the only chance several of her fifth-year girls had of continuing to study was to get a place in further education in their home town as it was inconceivable for them to live away from home.

\*     \*     \*

## Women's Studies course

*Students and teachers at the University of Central America (UCA) are now studying the social problems affecting women as an academic subject. A Women's Studies course, run by the Sociology department, looks at the role of women in society, and the causes of their oppression in Nicaragua and elsewhere. The course is aimed particularly at those AMNLAE staff members and activists who are identified as needing a stronger ideological foundation from which to develop their work. Women in senior positions in the government have also participated in the course; for example, Olga Avilez, currently Ambassador to Vietnam. UCA students have also undertaken primary research into specific aspects of women's lives. In 1986, for example, a number of students took part in a study of people's survival strategies in Managua. Most of the material collected focused on women as those with prime responsibility for day-to-day survival.*

\*     \*     \*

## Nicaraguans studying abroad

Despite massive improvements, Nicaragua's higher education facilities remain limited and the country has had to rely on friendly governments, such as in Cuba, Mexico, Spain and the USSR, to offer scholarships in subjects not sufficiently catered for in Nicaragua itself. These scholarships are very important to Nicaragua, where there is an acute shortage of skilled professional and technical workers. By 1984, 1,800 Nicaraguans were studying abroad. But these opportunities have been taken up less by women than by men, as women are more likely to have prime responsibility for children, which prevents them from leaving the country.

For all Nicaraguans, the culture shock and homesickness of being abroad is overwhelming. The men at least will have experienced military service (a condition for obtaining their grant) but for some young women the change is too difficult to cope with and many women drop out. 'Boyfriend reasons' is often the explanation given by the families concerned. On the other hand, for single women, the experience of living away from the social pressures of marriage and childbearing has enabled them to develop and forge new identities, as reflected in the following testimony from Rosario Mora, a student in London:

Since the Revolution, ordinary Nicaraguan women have been able to get grants and study abroad. It was difficult to imagine that I would be one of those women. But now I can go back to Nicaragua and say, as a woman, 'I can do it!'

I remember the first letter I got from my father when I was in London. He went on and on about how proud he was that one of his daughters had crossed the 'puddle' to Europe. He made me cry. You see, I wasn't having a good time at all. I didn't speak English; I didn't understand the culture; the cold was awful; it was not compatible with my dreams. I realized that as a foreigner my rights were very limited and I was worried about money. In Nicaragua, if I don't have a job or money I can go to my family. But here if I don't have money I might not eat. If I try and find a job, I might get prosecuted.

I must admit my family was a bit worried when I said I was going to Europe mainly because at my age [late twenties] they thought I should be married. My aunt told me not to waste my time going off to study, because at the end of the day I'd settle down with children and nothing would have changed.

But recently she wrote me a letter saying: 'These days you're the only person in the family who's enjoying herself.' When I left Nicaragua, I had a boyfriend. I missed him a lot in the first few months but I never regretted my decision. I knew it was the end of the relationship.

The most important gain of my stay in Britain has been my personal development. Before, in Nicaragua, men made me feel like I wasn't attractive and since I couldn't attract men, I felt I had nothing to offer. But now I realise that I am a person, that I have a personality and a qualification and that is more important than my physical appearance. It's good to be a woman in Britain. Women have a lot more consciousness of their collective power; when I get back to Nicaragua, I want to get involved in a women's organization to develop awareness there. We women who are studying and pursuing our own goals — we are breaking the ice for future generations of Nicaraguan women.[18]

## Women teachers in Nicaragua

At all levels, women form the vast majority of teachers — 70% at primary level, 75% at secondary level, 55% at the university level and an astonishing 95% in popular education for adults.

At the primary and secondary levels the majority of teachers are 'empirical' teachers, who have had no training whatsoever. To overcome this, they are encouraged to go on training courses — either at weekends or for longer during the week. Jenny Watson, a British teacher, comments:

Government plans to train all teachers from rural areas and to persuade them to go to the 'Normale', the training school many miles away for a week's training, present teachers who are mothers with childcare problems. But teachers can't be promoted without this training.[19]

Despite training 200% more teachers, there are still shortages. For this reason students can move on to teacher training college after only three years of secondary education. To increase the number of teachers for rural schools, new teachers must now teach in rural areas for a period immediately after training. In August 1988, *Barricada* carried a long article about Ligia Garcia, a young teacher who went to teach in Los Nogales, a remote rural area. It tells of her initial problems, of how she overcame these and won the hearts of all her students. Such pieces are designed to highlight the importance for the Revolution of teaching in the country. The article claims that Ligia's resolve to stay for her two-year teaching stint was hardened by the murder of some of her friends at the hands of the Contra.

In general, however, morale among teachers is very low, and there have been many resignations in recent years. This situation is not helped by the low salary. All state jobs are relatively poorly paid but an average-level teacher was only in the middle of the national wage scale until 1988 (when it was abolished). It has been calculated that, in Estelí, a secretary in a private firm with two or three years of secondary schooling can earn more than a teacher with a university degree.

School teaching has always been seen as a women's profession in Nicaragua, which may explain the low wages and attendant low status. Until recent wage negotiations, a low-scale primary teacher earned half the wage of a university teacher, in spite of far more class contact hours. A recent article in *El Nuevo Diario*[20] made the point that in Nicaragua, teaching had less importance than the productive sector.

Nevertheless, on other levels, teachers in Nicaragua are held in almost the same reverence as that reserved for mothers. While their material rewards are scant, their role is imbued with great importance as instrumental in imparting morality and knowledge to the nation's youth. As in other parts of Latin America, there is a Teachers' Day every year, when pupils show their appreciation of them by putting on shows and parties. The fact that women dominate teaching has recently prompted AMNLAE to provide them with a specific quota of seats for the new Assembly of Women.

Women comprise 55% of university teachers, which is an unusually high figure compared with most universities in other countries. Probably the main reason for this is compulsory male conscription. It will be interesting to see if the proportion of university women teachers decreases when the war is over and the number of men bidding for relatively well-paid university posts goes up.

## War and economic crisis

The main problem still facing education in Nicaragua is war and the economic crisis associated with it. To undermine Sandinista support in the countryside, the Contras have set out to destroy new schools and kill teachers. By the end of 1984, 360 rural schools had been forced to close, over 170 teachers had been murdered and 180 kidnapped.[21]

Despite this, many teachers in rural areas have remained working. 'These women are the vanguard of the revolution,' commented a British education delegation. They sleep with their clothes on for fear of Contra attacks.[22] Yet not all teachers are so heroic and many have been deterred from working in the war zones. It is here that literacy levels are lowest.

The economic crisis associated with war has also affected standards of education. In attempting to provide secondary education for all, Nicaraguans have had to cope with chronic shortages of space, textbooks, and other resources, and almost everything is rationed. Because most of the study resources must now be paid for by the students or their parents, it is increasingly difficult for poor families to continue studying.[23] Students and teachers in the towns often have to study by candlelight in the evening because of frequent power cuts (although a large proportion of Nicaraguan families, particularly in rural areas, have never had electricity).

The mobilization of so many men in the army has meant that even more women than usual have had to take care of children single-handed; this creates immense problems for those who want to attend classes. State nurseries cater for a minority of children, and women must increasingly rely on their friends or relatives to care for their children when they go out to study. Severe cuts in public transport are another major problem due to the war. Students often have to walk long distances to their classes and women are more vulnerable to abuse and attacks than they would be on public transport.

But ironically, because many boys of upper secondary age have been doing military service and therefore missed out on schooling, girls have probably received a better education than boys in recent years. When boys return from the army they often seek work rather than complete their education.

## Conclusion

One in every three children in Nicaragua now receives education, which by law is free at all levels, and guaranteed by Articles 121 and 122 of the new Constitution.

These days, there is quite a strong feeling that women should take the educational opportunities their mothers never had. At secondary and university level enrolment is higher among women — although this may change substantially as men are demobilized. Also at this stage the age-old problems for women begin to assume prominence — pregnancy, childbirth, and childcare — coupled with opposition from husbands stemming from jealousy towards other male students, the need for them to share childcare, and fears of losing control over their women.

The 1987 FSLN *Proclama* on women in the revolution acknowledged women's right to full education. Yet as long as women have to take prime responsibility for domestic chores and childcare, they will continue to be at a disadvantage when trying to study. It may be that only general change in social attitudes will ensure for women equal access to education.

In the words of Ligia, the young woman teacher working in the countryside: 'I have learnt that women must be independent, take their own decisions without being scared to do so, and always be pushing themselves forward.'[24]

## Notes

1. Gladys Martínez, interviewed by Rachel Stringfellow, August 1987, unpublished.

2. *Barricada*, 1988 (precise date not known).

3. Reen Pilkington, in *Wallpaper*, National Federation for Voluntary Literacy Schemes, No. 11, 1984.

4. Otilia Cruz, in Angel & Macintosh 1987, p. 91.

5. *El Nuevo Diario*, 8 August 1988.

6. Literacy primer, quoted in Deighton et al, 1983, p. 103.

7. Mercedita Talavera, interviewed by Stephanie Williamson, 1987, unpublished.

8. Newly literate woman, quoted by Reen Pilkington, op. cit.

9. *Nicaragua Today*, No. 26, Spring 1987.

10. Ministry of Education official, interviewed by Duncan Green, 1988, unpublished.

11. Figures given by Milena Núñez, General Secretary of ANDEN (teachers' union), quoted by David Steed, 'Education in Nicaragua', in *Nobody's Backyard*, Teachers and Latin America and the Caribbean, Sheffield, No. 8, 1987.

12. Joanna, interviewed by Duncan Green, 1988, unpublished.

13. Silvia Toruna, interviewed by Rachel Sieder, 1988, unpublished.

14. Schoolboy, quoted in *Comeback*, Returned Volunteer Action, No. 4, 1987.

15. Figures given by Mary Stead in Dr Haleh Atsho (ed.), book as yet untitled, Longman, forthcoming.

16. Azucena, interviewed by Stephanie Williamson, 1989, unpublished.

17. Figures given by Marlena de Montes, Director of Training for AMNLAE, at workshop organized by British Residents of Nicaragua Women, Managua, April 1987.

18. Rosario Mora, interviewed by Helen Collinson, April 1989, unpublished.

19. Jenny Watson, interviewed by Daphne Davies, 1988, unpublished.

20. *El Nuevo Diario*, 5 May 1988.

21. *Barricada Internacional*, May 1985.

22. World University Service, *Less Arms, More Education*, 1988, p. 20.

23. Rooper, 1988, p. 186.

24. *Barricada*, 30 August 1988.

# 10. Luisa Amanda Espinosa Presente!
## Nicaraguan Women's Movement

Popular democracy has remained the hallmark of the Nicaraguan revolution despite war and economic crisis that many other governments would have seen as good reasons to restrict popular participation in the decision-making process. It is this willingness to listen to the demands of ordinary people that has enabled the Nicaraguan women's movement to flower, particularly during the mid and late 1980s. Women hold 40% of the seats in the National Assembly (Nicaragua's parliament), but there are only two women ministers, and only a handful of top government positions are filled by women; none of the nine *comandantes* of the FSLN Directorate are women. Getting more women into government positions has not been a major issue in Nicaragua. 'Imagine if we had nine Margaret Thatchers in the Sandinista Directorate,' commented a Nicaraguan visitor to Britain, by way of illustrating that women in power do not always further women's interests.[1]

It is at a more popular and grassroots level that women have asserted their demands and influenced government policy. Different sectors of the population are regularly consulted by the country's leaders before major decisions are made. Hence the nationwide grassroots *cabildos* meetings with women in 1985 to discuss the new Constitution, and the Fundamental Forces meetings in 1989, with women representatives from all the productive sectors, to discuss how the government's new economic measures were affecting women. Face the People meetings — often lasting several hours — in which ordinary women can voice their complaints and opinions to the President himself are also routine. Against this backdrop of popular consultation the FSLN has constantly revised its policies on women's emancipation and their participation in the revolution. A landmark in this process was the *Proclama*, a major FSLN policy document on women's oppression and participation in the revolution which was first announced on International Women's Day 1987.

The *Proclama* dealt with issues specifically affecting women, such as irresponsible paternity, the physical and moral abuse of women, and the domestic burden. By asserting that 'the struggle to wipe out discrimination against women cannot be separated from the struggle to defend the revolution' and that 'the solution to the specific problems of women . . . concern not only women, but all of society', the *Proclama* gave women the moral authority to voice their demands.

## What is the Nicaraguan women's movement?

Yet while the Sandinista revolution has given women the space and the confidence to start grappling with their oppression, it has not yet provided them with total liberation. To move forward, women have had to organize themselves into a collective movement: AMNLAE, the Luisa Amanda Espinosa[2] Association of Nicaraguan Women, the Sandinista organization that has co-ordinated most of the work relating specifically to women in the revolution over the past ten years. Most of this chapter therefore focuses on AMNLAE.

Strictly speaking, this movement sees itself as an umbrella organization incorporating women from all the different sectors, including the trade unions. The trade union women's sections, dealt with in chapter 3, are therefore part of AMNLAE and are represented on AMNLAE bodies. But the women's sections still maintain their separate identities outside AMNLAE, particularly in the case of the Agricultural Workers' Union (ATC) Women's Secretariat and the CONAPRO Women's Secretariat. By the late 1980s, there were also smaller groups of women, taking their own action on women's issues quite independently of AMNLAE, of which the Matagalpa women's theatre group and the independent women's centre in Masaya mentioned later in this chapter are just two examples.

## A 'feminist' movement?

'Feminism' remains a dirty word for large sectors of the Nicaraguan revolution. Seen as an anti-male doctrine, it is commonly defined as the opposite of *machismo* — in other words, extreme and unacceptable. A cartoon in *Barricada* in 1981 sums up the popular interpretation of feminism. It shows two fighters behind their sand-bagged defences shooting at each other. One bears the flag 'radical feminism' and the other, '*machismo*'. In the No Person's Land between the opposing armies sits a confused-looking baby. 'If we consider *machismo* to be deformed virility, feminism is its counterpart in the feminine sex', wrote a journalist in September 1988.[3] For him, feminism was merely a by-word for what he regarded as women's subtle and devious ways of conquering men.

Reactions like these may have something to do with the popular perceptions of Western feminism that predominated in Latin America in the 1970s. At that time the image of the rampaging 'bra-burning' anti-men feminist (as she was portrayed by our own sexist media) was often associated with the imposing, aggressive and alien culture of US imperialism. Many people were suspicious of this 'foreign' phenomenon — a suspicion men soon learnt to exploit to prevent discussion on the real issues underlying women's oppression. 'Capitalism has divided men and women so that we couldn't join together and change things', comments one-time AMNLAE propaganda worker, Heliette Ehlers. 'So sometimes, when people hear the word feminism, they are afraid because they see it as another way of trying to divide us.'[4]

Not surprisingly, Nicaraguan women have therefore chosen to avoid the term 'feminism', instead prefering the terms 'women's organization' or 'feminine movement'. Nevertheless, the sort of work now undertaken by AMNLAE would undoubtedly be regarded as 'feminist' in Europe. AMNLAE's Platform of Struggle for 1988, for example, commits the movement to combating violence against women, paternal irresponsibility, sexual harassment, and pornography. Comparing Western with Nicaraguan terms may thus be fairly fruitless.

### Women and men — together in everything

AMNLAE has argued that women are doubly exploited and marginalized, but its leaders are quick to point out that theirs is not a struggle against men. 'We are talking about a mutual liberation, of men and women, not a competition between men and women,' said Lea Guido in 1981.[5] Apart from encouraging 'paternal parenthood', AMNLAE's objectives rarely mention men directly and are couched in relatively neutral terms. For example, rather than demanding that men take on more housework and childcare, AMNLAE simply calls for domestic tasks to be 'shared between the members of the household.'[6]

The thinking behind this position is that men are not responsible for women's oppression. Rather it is part of the 'ideology of exploitation which was imposed upon us by imperialism and the dominant class in Nicaragua';[7] men are no more than 'the instrument used by their oppressors'.[8] The solution to women's oppression is thus seen as lying in men and women working together, as a task to be confronted by society as a whole. For AMNLAE's tenth anniversary celebration in September 1987 the slogan was 'Together in Everything' and posters produced for the event sported interlocking male and female symbols.

Considering the importance of unity in the struggle against Somoza, the dominance of the 'Together in Everything' philosophy is not surprising. Without a mass revolution involving both men and women, women would have had virtually no hope of emancipating themselves. Politically women have regarded men as allies, albeit sexist allies whose attitudes need changing. 'Together in Everything' can also be construed as a radical objective that Nicaraguan women have still to achieve: nearly half of all families are headed by single women who bear sole responsibility for the home and children and who do 'everything' alone without any support from men. The slogan is thus intended to encourage men to help their women with housework and childcare.

But if women's oppression is a problem for men and women together, why is there a women's organization at all and why have women been positively urged to become involved in AMNLAE, an organization that is exclusively female?

AMNLAE exists primarily to boost women's participation in the revolutionary process. In fact, it has never been a totally separate organization; to all intents and purposes it is the women's section of the FSLN. 'AMNLAE functions within the parameters defined by the party and shares the same national goals,' argues commentator Hermione Harris.[9] Until recently, the FSLN's revolutionary goals were deemed to be even more important than the fight against women's specific problems; only in the mid to late 1980s did the balance start to shift. Not that women's oppression has ever been totally ignored by the FSLN; point seven of the FSLN's Historic programme of 1979 pledged itself to the 'establishment of economic, political and cultural equality between men and women' and called for an end to the regime of servitude suffered by women 'that is reflected in the drama of the abandoned working mother.'

## Before the Triumph

Nevertheless, when AMNLAE's predecessor, AMPRONAC (Association of Women Confronting the National Problem), was founded by FSLN members in 1977, its primary role was not to work for women's emancipation but to draw more women into the struggle against Somoza and to denounce the human rights abuses of the regime. At that time, youth, students, workers and peasants had started to organize, but women were often left on the fringes of the opposition. Those who were involved tended to be young and without responsibilities. Lea Guido explains:

> We had many, many women who weren't going to participate in the struggle unless we could provide ways for them to organize as women. It was in April 1977 that . . . comrade Jaime Wheelock (now Minister of Agrarian Reform) suggested we organize a work commission to look at women's problems and work towards the creation of a broad-based women's association.[10]

Initially, AMPRONAC catered primarily for bourgeois women whose participation was greatly valued by the FSLN.

> Their class condition, and the image the dictatorship had of women in general and bourgeois women in particular, made it possible for them to go and see certain government officials. They were able to

get interviews with men like . . . the head of Public Relations of the National Guard, without fear of being arrested. They could also use international forums to denounce what was happening in Nicaragua.[11]

But to attract a broader spectrum of women, AMPRONAC soon realized that it would have to address not only the general demands of the liberation movement against Somoza but also the specific concerns of women. Thus, AMPRONAC's programme of 1979 mentioned: equality of civil rights and equal pay for equal work; an end to the commercialization of women; a need to combat prostitution; and the elimination of the use of birth control policies as a way of eradicating poverty. It must, however, be said that these demands were made after the general human rights demands already shared by other sectors of the opposition to Somoza.

Leaving aside its position on women's oppression, AMPRONAC was phenomenally successful. From 60 women at its first assembly in the autumn of 1977, it grew to over 8,000 in the final days of the insurrection. It organized demonstrations, occupied churches, circulated petitions, carried messages from political prisoners to their families, and lobbied the government to disclose the whereabouts of the 'disappeared'.

Even though there was no in-depth analysis of the specific situation of women in this period, the number of women involved in all levels of the opposition by 1979 was very striking. In this year, some 30% of guerrilla fighters were said to be women. Merely by participating in the insurrection women broke taboos. Magda Enríquez of AMNLAE claimed that: 'We never entered into a lot of theoretical discussions about women's liberation. . . . In fact we never said that we were equal — we simply demonstrated it in the battlefields, on the barricades, in the mountains . . .'[12]

## After 1979: identity crisis

After the revolution, however, these individual women's achievements had to be converted into the norm for the majority of women. This was not easy. Before July 1979, AMPRONAC had little time to think about its role in a revolutionary society; its primary aim then was to overthrow the Somoza dictatorship. Moreover there was still disagreement in the FSLN about the need for women's organization in *Nicaragua Libre*. Significantly the new women's organization, AMNLAE, was not formed until August 1979; it justified its existence in the following terms:

It is necessary that as women, we meet under the guidance of an organization in order to discover and understand our specific situation and organize ourselves to change our reality . . . move forward in the elimination of ideological chains that tie us to a form of behaviour that is dependent, submissive and that underestimates our capacities.[13]

AMNLAE duly set about creating several crèches for working mothers and launched a 'minimum programme' for women, demanding legal equality, responsible paternity, and equal pay for equal work. AMNLAE also helped to found a union for domestic workers after the Triumph.

Despite pledges to look at women's specific situation, however, AMNLAE's primary role was still to incorporate women into general revolutionary tasks. Most of its work in the first two years centred around the integration of women into the literacy crusade, health brigades (mainly of women), and small production co-operatives (see pp. 49–54, 73–77). The rationale that informed this participation in the revolution was that women would be emancipated. To some extent, AMNLAE was proved right. 'Just as participation in the struggle against Somoza earned self-confidence and the respect of others,' writes Hermione Harris, 'so activity in mass organizations . . . has had the same effect.'[14] To be part of a group helps to overcome domestic isolation. A few years later women did indeed start to campaign on issues specific to their sex but only after they had gained the confidence to confront such issues through their collective involvement in the wider struggle.

AMNLAE was relatively successful in its objective of integrating women into the revolutionary process. The majority of health and literacy *brigadistas* were women, as were most members of the Sandinista Local Defence Committees (CDS) which took on various social and revolutionary tasks at a *barrio* and street level. Nevertheless, the ambiguity surrounding the role of AMNLAE remained.

It faced problems that the other mass organizations did not face. For the most part the other organizations organized people according to their geographical position: the CST organized workers in factories, the ATC organized agricultural workers, the CDS worked in neighbourhoods and markets. Yet for AMNLAE it was not so easy. Their constituency was all women . . . They were to organize women as AMNLAE *and* encourage women to integrate themselves into other organizations. At the same time they were also charged with the responsibility of formulating and advancing women's interests.[15]

Turned in so many directions, AMNLAE frequently lost its way. In September 1981, its executive issued a frank self-criticism of its work. They cited the lack of clear objectives, administrative capacity, and experienced women, the best of whom were working in other areas. Despite subsequent attempts to streamline operations, the problem continued.

One reason why AMNLAE lacked clear direction in the early years of the Revolution was that it failed to connect women's specific situation with their participation in the Revolution and to recognize the possibility of particular problems, such as childcare or husbands' attitudes that prevented women becoming more involved in the revolution. Instead, these two aspects of AMNLAE's work seemed antagonistic, with its activists never really knowing if it was a movement *of* women or positively *for* women. Connected to this was the confusion about the image of the new Nicaraguan women AMNLAE should promote. AMNLAE's national magazine, *Somos* (shelved in 1987), for example, invariably contained articles about exemplary liberated women who had broken with age-old convention by joining the police, fighting in the reserves or setting up an agricultural co-operative, while the last few pages of each issue were always devoted to traditional feminine features, such as recipes, dress patterns, and tips for personal beauty. However practical the latter may have been in the short-term, the overall impression was that women who participated in production or took up non-traditional occupations should still stay feminine and retain their domestic roles in the home.

Part of the problem was that AMNLAE was never given the time or the space to develop an analysis of women's oppression. Its close ties with the FSLN meant that FSLN directives received priority over everything else, as illustrated by new developments in 1983 when, towards the end of that year, the military threat against Nicaragua was growing. After the invasion of Grenada, there was a strong feeling that Nicaragua would be next. AMNLAE was thus called upon to direct its energies single-mindedly to the defence efforts. With the introduction of the military draft, motherhood took on an aggressively political meaning. Contra propaganda now argued that the revolution was maliciously taking sons away from their mothers. To counteract this propaganda, AMNLAE was assigned the task of providing support for mothers of mobilized sons, primarily through the organization of Mothers of Heroes and Martyrs. This gave AMNLAE the sort of concrete focus it had not had since before the Triumph.

Yet AMNLAE paid a price for this abrupt change of direction. Work with mothers soon overshadowed all other work previously undertaken by AMNLAE, and action around the specific oppression of women stagnated. This was not the time to push women's specific problems, argued the FSLN. On 7 April 1985 Bayardo Arce told an AMNLAE assembly: '. . . the work around women [is] not strategic for women. Strategic for women is the survival of the Popular Sandinista Revolution.'[16] Since no one had identified the link between women's emancipation and the defence of the Revolution, this attitude was to be expected. As a result of the emphasis on the war effort and the mothers of mobilized men, AMNLAE lost touch with its original base.

By 1985, AMNLAE's popularity and membership had declined. In recognition of this situation, the Executive organized 600 local meetings of women throughout Nicaragua to discover what they wanted from AMNLAE. Around 40,000 women from all social sectors took part in this consultation process. Many common denominators emerged from the discussions: the demand for more information and access to birth control; the issues of sexual harassment at work, of rape and domestic violence; and men's failure to share the domestic burden of childcare and housework. Previously, AMNLAE had never fully explored these specifically women's issues.

The contrast between the feelings of women at the base and the National Leadership of both AMNLAE and the FSLN came to a head at AMNLAE's Second National Assembly in 1985. Participants severely criticized as superficial the official document presented to delegates. Bayardo Arce, the FSLN's guest speaker was shouted down by angry women workers and *campesinas* when he questioned the need for a women's organization within a revolutionary society.

## Women's organization under fire

The Second National Assembly sparked off renewed discussion within the FSLN about the role of AMNLAE. The position against the women's organization was led by Rosario Murillo, a prominent poet and *compañera* of President Daniel Ortega:

> I believe that in a Revolution, a specific women's organization can't exist as it would be a way of perpetuating inequality. We don't talk about creating specific organizations for men and of men, in spite of their unequal situation vis-à-vis the exploited or oppressed in a class society.[17]

Nevertheless, the grassroots meetings of 1985 clearly showed that specific problems in women's 'personal lives' hampered both their involvement in production and their participation in the political process. For women who had to bring up children single-handed, or were beaten and abused by their men, participating in anything was difficult. AMNLAE's policy of simply integrating women into the revolutionary process was therefore insufficient on its own.

> As women get involved and increase their conscious participation as active members of society [wrote Gioconda Belli], they have to confront a complex social and family situation. Women find themselves alone in resolving their problems; society has only concerned itself with integration, failing to deal with the ideological work that must be done with both men and women. It will require a long process before conditions are sufficiently improved so that women

can participate in the basic work of the Revolution on a massive scale.[18]

A week after AMNLAE's Second Assembly, members of the Sandinista Assembly (the top advisory body of the party) met with 100 women leaders from all sectors to discuss the future of AMNLAE. After a day of heated discussion, the need for a women's organization was reaffirmed.

In response to these criticisms, AMNLAE drew up a new agenda that included a serious investigation of issues which addressed power relations between men and women. AMNLAE's submission to the Commission drafting the new Constitution in 1986 included proposals for the prohibition of sexual harassment, domestic violence, rape, and for 'allowing women the right to decide freely as to when and whether to have children'. It also called for a new definition of the family, which did not discriminate against single mothers. The Open Forums organized in 1986 throughout the country in all sectors to discuss the Constitution served to strengthen AMNLAE's change of direction. In the Women's Forums, topics such as violence against women, sex education, and the right to freely chosen motherhood were mentioned frequently.

Nevertheless, there was still a time lag between AMNLAE's public airing of women's oppression and real change within the bureaucracy of the women's organization. In October 1986 Milu Vargas of AMNLAE's National Executive wrote: 'We must accept the blame for the fact that after a year we still have not been able to develop a plan of action for our work, even though we have had the contributions of thousands of women in this rich process of democracy.'[19] AMNLAE's thunder had largely been stolen by the Women's Secretariat of the Agricultural Workers' Union (ATC) whose grassroots work in 1985 and 1986 had encouraged thousands of women agricultural workers in the most marginalized sectors of the population to talk about their specific problems in a way that AMNLAE had never managed to do.

It was at this point that the FSLN itself publicly entered the debate on the problems confronting women. At the end of 1986 the Sandinista Assembly convened yet another special meeting to discuss the situation of women and AMNLAE's goals. On International Women's Day, 1987, the Party issued its long formal statement on women and the Sandinista Revolution, commonly referred to as the *Proclama*.

## FSLN *Proclama* on women: a turning point

The *Proclama* was the outcome of vigorous lobbying by certain women members of the FSLN and was regarded as official recognition of women's specific problems. The *Proclama* had a profound influence on AMNLAE's priorities and working methods. It acknowledged that women suffer additional exploitation specific to their sex and that their struggles within the revolutionary process were legitimate; it also roundly condemned *machismo*. Most importantly, it argued that women's issues could not be 'put off' till after the war. On the contrary, dealing with inequalities between the sexes would strengthen the revolution. Coming from the FSLN, this announcement had a significant impact. A few months after the *Proclama* was issued, Milu Vargas of the AMNLAE Executive declared (perhaps rather rashly) that, 'since the *Proclama*, *machismo* has gone underground in Nicaragua'.[20] Possibly no other party has issued such a major, mainstream policy document on women's specific oppression while in government.

As an FSLN statement, the *Proclama* meant that women's emancipation was no longer an AMNLAE ghetto but the responsibility of the entire FSLN. In fact the *Proclama* implied that everyone would have to think more about women's emancipation on the grounds that '*machismo* and other forms of discrimination against women inhibit the development of the whole society'.

What stimulated this change in policy? Commentators have argued that the social and economic repercussions of the war had had a major impact on the country's policy-makers. With so many men mobilized, it was imperative for the survival of the revolution that women's productivity be raised, particularly in the cash-crop sector. For this reason, there was an urgent need to remove the obstacles implicit in childbearing and childcare that prevented women from raising their productivity. In fact, the *Proclama*'s approach to women's emancipation, which involved extensive work on women's specific problems, had already been successfully operated in the Agricultural Workers' Union (ATC), precisely in the context of increasing rural production. The rise in coffee production in the 1985–86 harvest as a result of this strategy convinced many FSLN leaders that the solution of women's problems was not idealistic, but pragmatic.

In addition, grassroots discussions amongst women in 1985 and 1986 had made clear to the country's policy-makers that 'women's issues' were not the fabrication of middle-class feminists in Managua but of concern for ordinary peasant and working-class women throughout the country. The *Proclama* should also be seen as a triumph for women in the FSLN who for several years had been lobbying the male-dominated leadership of the Party. The *Proclama* should not, therefore, be regarded as evidence that the FSLN had suddenly 'seen the light'.

### Shake-up in AMNLAE

As part of the process of bringing women's issues into the mainstream, the *Proclama* proposed various structural changes to AMNLAE. In the past, AMNLAE had tended to operate as a separate body, often duplicating the work of the other mass organizations (trade unions,

CDSs, Mothers of Heroes and Martyrs and so on). It had always striven to be a broad-based movement, but its bureaucratic structure had not lent itself to such a model. It was now recognized that AMNLAE would have to be representative in a practical sense and not simply on the level of rhetoric. Thus, the three-member executive committee was replaced with a nine-member executive consisting of representatives from all the sectors and mass organizations, including the women's sections of the trade unions. AMNLAE was to be an umbrella movement, which would co-ordinate the work of the different sectors.

This approach was to be mirrored in AMNLAE structures at the base: instead of AMNLAE representatives going into trade unions from outside to mobilize women, women who themselves were already active in their unions or mass organizations would carry out this task. Women's issues would thus be raised from within the different sectors and within the context of women's day-to-day experience. In this way it was hoped that AMNLAE would penetrate all sectors of society.

With this in mind, AMNLAE planned a programme of mass education and training in the new strategy for its officials and active members. AMNLAE national officials, already trained, would train the AMNLAE representatives or '*promotoras*' in the regions. The *promotoras* had the crucial job of identifying and activating the 'natural leaders' at the base (in trade union branches and CDS committees, for example) whose task, in turn, would be to educate the women around them. In this way it was hoped that women's problems would emerge.

Training the *promotoras* is clearly a priority, but Melba Barrios, training officer at National AMNLAE, admitted in January 1988 that, 'lots of them still say, "I am AMNLAE" and don't want to work in the different sectors. They still see AMNLAE as a separate organization with its own identity.'[21]

Building on the *Proclama*, AMNLAE's Platform of Struggle for 1987 called for solutions to the problems of women's domestic burden, and paternal irresponsibility, and the elimination of all aspects of violence against women, and finally sex education.

Comparing the Platform of Struggle with a similar policy document produced in 1981, it becomes evident that AMNLAE has moved to a more assertive position, largely due to pressure from the base. In 1981, defence of the revolution headed AMNLAE's list of priorities; in 1988, emancipation of women came first. Apart from the actual policies proposed, there is also a marked change in the language; the injunction to 'fight' for each objective has replaced the call to 'promote'. 'The impression given is one of a much more assertive movement which is confident of support within society, rather than one that is continually looking over its shoulder.'[22]

Simultaneously, AMNLAE began to take more militant action in 1988 on some issues listed in the Platform. A well-publicized petition was presented to the Supreme Court, condemning violence against women and children; AMNLAE organized rallies outside the Supreme Court in order to raise the profile of this petition. In August and September 1988, Lea Guido, General Secretary of AMNLAE, took an angry stand in favour of closing the Sandinista comic magazine, *Semana Comica*, after it published pornographic pictures with captions taking an aggressive swipe at the women's movement (see pp. 168–71).

In the late 1980s, AMNLAE began to cater for the needs of its constituents on a more practical level. In Estelí, for example, the regional AMNLAE office has set up a women's training centre which offers courses such as poultry rearing, pig-keeping, sex education, journalism, cookery, project administration, small-scale production, women's legal rights, as well as special political training courses for AMNLAE activists. Training is now a major theme of AMNLAE's work.

In Managua, AMNLAE offices that previously had dealt only with administration are being converted into Women's Centres, aimed primarily at unemployed and underemployed housewives. In 1988, one of these was reported to be running courses on beauty and dressmaking, child and women's health, and on 'couple relationships' for adolescent girls.

## Towards democratization

As part of its metamorphosis into a broad umbrella body, AMNLAE changed its name to the *Movement* of Nicaraguan women 'Luisa Amanda Espinosa' (from its previous name of National Association) at a conference marking its 11th anniversary in September 1988. This conference also voted to give the movement a more democratic structure by introducing an electoral process. It was agreed that open meetings would be held in every region to elect representatives of the various sectors (trade unions, CDSs and so on) to a National Assembly of 1,200 women. The Assembly was to be the major decision-making body of the Movement and was to meet once a year. Regional Assemblies were to meet every six months, with elections every three years. Describing the new movement, Ivonne Siu, a member of the AMNLAE Executive, declared: 'Women are increasingly conscious of the fact that our movement cannot be the women's section of any party, sector, or institution.'[23]

A few months later, however, this democratization process was arrested by the announcement in early 1989 that the elections for the Women's National Assembly were to be postponed until November, ostensibly because of a lack of time and resources. As Nicaragua's General Elections were to take place in February 1990, there was speculation at the time of writing that AMNLAE's elections might never take place.

Our impression of AMNLAE in 1988 and 1989 was that there were two main currents within the movement. One, the representatives of the different sectors (rural workers, industrial workers, health workers, for example) who wanted AMNLAE to be directed by women at the base via the proposed new democratic structure, and who were wary of an over-powerful AMNLAE full-time staff. The other, the regional and national AMNLAE full-time workers who favoured a more hierarchical organization, in which they and ultimately the FSLN maintained the power to make decisions.

## Breakaway initiatives

### CONAPRO

While the women's sections of the trade unions have often been critical of the bureaucratic nature of AMNLAE, they have nevertheless remained committed to the formation of a strong, unified women's movement under the AMNLAE's co-ordination. But not all Nicaraguan women have been so patient. Frustrated by the slow pace of change within AMNLAE, some women chose to break away from the official women's movement almost entirely. The Women's Secretariat of CON-APRO, the Sandinista Federation of Professional Workers (such as lawyers, psychologists, and administrators), established in February 1988, is a case in point. On one level, CONAPRO continues to acknowledge the importance of AMNLAE as a co-ordinating body; the Head of the CONAPRO Women's Secretariat, Dr Milu Vargas, is an active member of AMNLAE's national executive, and CONAPRO also supports the FSLN. On another level, CONAPRO women have forged a separate identity, independently of AMNLAE and of the FSLN. AMNLAE was barely mentioned during two Women and Law conferences organized by CONAPRO women in 1988. Despite the prominence given to these events in the national press, no AMNLAE workers even attended the first of these conferences in Masaya. Ideologically, the CONAPRO Women's Secretariat has been prepared to take one step further than official AMNLAE. The Women and Law Conferences, for example, put forward proposals for the decriminalization of abortion several months before AMNLAE adopted this policy.

The CONAPRO Women's Secretariat for Region VI, based in Matagalpa, is breaking taboos in the Nicaraguan women's movement. Their magazine, *Apante*, contains hard-hitting articles on such topics as contraception and male violence, portrayed with a frankness that AMNLAE has never dared attempt, for fear of appearing 'out of tune' with the general population. CONAPRO, it seems, does not share these anxieties. The 1988 Mother's Day issue of *Apante* questions the basic motives for becoming mothers and analyses the obstacles preventing women from making free decisions about motherhood. It contains practical advice on contraception and a list of concrete proposals related to reproductive rights, including one which asks not for the decriminalization of abortion but for its legalization. In addition to *Apante*, the

CONAPRO women of Matagalpa have produced a series of simple and accessible feminist radio programmes for transmission on the local station. In 1989 they were in the process of setting up a women's centre in Matagalpa, which apparently is to be totally separate from AMNLAE. They also helped to found a feminist theatre company, Ciutlampha (see below). While the national CONAPRO Women's Secretariat is predominantly middle-class, the CONAPRO group in Matagalpa has attracted a broad cross-section of (mainly urban) women.

### Ixchen women's centre

CONAPRO was also the launch-pad for another breakaway initiative, the privately-run 'Ixchen' women's centre in Masaya, opened in 1988. Ixchen's team of professionals offer women a variety of services ranging from legal and medical advice to training, sex therapy, contraceptive and gynaecological treatment. Although it is a privately run commercial centre where women pay for its services (albeit on a sliding scale), Ixchen's aims remain fundamentally political. The Director, Maria Lourdes Bolanos, herself a lawyer, worked at AMNLAE's Women's Legal Office in the mid-1980s, when the Office was bombarding the government with proposals for major changes to the law as it affected women. When AMNLAE moved in to tone down the politics in the OLM, Maria Lourdes resolved to bring about change in her own way. Her belief in a 'woman's right to choose' was not to be deterred by the intransigence of AMNLAE or the government — hence the Ixchen centre. A similar centre has just been opened in Managua with money from the British Marie Stopes Foundation.

## Women's Theatre

### Managua

On a more local level, some women have spontaneously formed their own groups to deal with issues such as male violence, irrespective of AMNLAE. In Managua, for example, women in the *barrios* around the Carretera Norte formed a self-help group, in 1988, which now visits women who have been attacked by their husbands as well as the husbands themselves. Around 40 women attend their weekly meetings and they have now formed a theatre group called Dynamite.

### Cihuatlampa

The women of Cihuatlampa, in Matagalpa, originally met when they worked together in Nixtayolero — a mixed theatre company. When the men in the company were mobilized, the women carried on alone, incorporating more local women. The men returned to find the attitudes of the women had changed. Much internal wrangling followed, resulting in some women leaving to form their own all-women group in 1987.

In 1988 there were three members of the company — Ana, a Spanish woman who originally came to Nicaragua as a nurse, Gloria, who served in the army until 1984, and her sister Rosa who trained as an architect. All have children, and all have perpetual problems with childcare. It is hard to find local women prepared and able to make the degree of commitment necessary. Added problems include the building that houses the company, which remains primitive.

Ambitions for the building embody the aims of Cihuatlampa — to be not just a theatre company, but to promote women's position and awareness in society. Plans include turning the building into a centre for women's culture, with performance space, living quarters, café and resource centre providing books, journals, videos and contacts, and to hold conferences for women on a wide variety of issues. A Swiss workers' union has bought the building and provides salaries. Originally, the women were regarded with suspicion for living and working without men in what is an unusual occupation by Nicaraguan standards, but they have now established themselves within the community through running a creative arts group for local girls and working alongside local people.

The girls' group caters for girls from about 5 to 15 years old, and runs daily from 6 p.m. to 8 p.m. In September 1988, the group was working on a performance commissioned by MINSA, the government health ministry, looking at local peoples' experiences of the health services from the children's perspective. Despite the usual problems of regular attendance (often girls will be called out during a session to go and help at home), the sessions are well-subscribed.

The company performs at *fiestas*, conferences and community gatherings throughout the area. The pieces are devised and improvised by the women themselves, with masks and costumes, minimal props and no set. For pieces based on a particular area or culture, one or two company members will first live in the relevant community for two or three months to gather background information. One of the company's most popular and controversial pieces is *Y ahora que hacer?* (What shall we do now?), a play about domestic violence towards women. Audience participation is frequently encouraged and, towards the end of this play, the character of the policeman starts towards the audience to 'expose the man who has been beating his wife'. It is rumoured that at one recent performance 90% of the men in the audience rushed out. Criticisms of *feministas* abound, but, in the words of one critic, Cihuatlampa continue to revolutionize women'.

## Nicaraguan Women's Institute (INIM)

This organization bears little resemblance to its rather conservative British namesake. Originally called the Government Women's Office (OGM), the Institute was created in 1982 to help formulate, develop, and strengthen state policies on the incorporation of women into the revolution. In recent years, it has acted mainly as a research co-ordinating body, servicing the growing demand for information on women that has arisen with the growth in the Nicaraguan women's movement over the past few years.

> Above all, our research should give results that make it possible to draw up concrete proposals for making government programmes more effective (comments Ivonne Siu, director of INIM). 'Our proposal to the Social Security and Welfare Institute that it give priority to building child-care centres for urban and rural women was backed up by a study we had made. Until then the government had been setting up these centres in a rather haphazard way. At the same time, as a result of our research, we have formulated concrete suggestions for the Ministries of Labour and Industry regarding women's wages.[24]

In 1986, INIM undertook a major study on women textile workers, which was instrumental in identifying the nature of discrimination against women in the workplace (see pp. 77–81). In 1988 the Institute began a study on the impact of agrarian reform policies on rural women.

INIM emphasizes the importance of participatory research, in which women are not only the object of investigation but also the investigators. When studying the situation of women textile workers, for example, INIM tried to involve the women themselves. A similar approach has also been adopted by the Agricultural Workers' Union (ATC) and by AMNLAE.

INIM has paid particular attention to women workers in state institutions — institutions that theoretically should be an example to the rest of society. 'If we find that a state organization is not making basic changes that favour women, we can resort to the presidency, to which our Institute is directly linked,' Ivonne explains.[25] One of INIM's major projects has been to encourage the training of female state employees in non-traditional areas of work. With this aim in mind, INIM has persuaded the National Electric Company to train women in such jobs as installation.

The Institute has worked with the Ministry of Education on women's images in school language, textbooks, and general teaching. They have also helped instigate a national family planning programme with the Ministry of Health. Seminars have been organized on issues such as women's mental health, the situation of rural women, and women's sexuality. INIM is now in the process of setting up a women's reference library.

Ivonne Siu is particularly keen on promoting new approaches to the advancement of women. 'When we learn that creative forms have been implemented somewhere that advance women's goals, our goal is to learn from them and apply them in other areas.'[26]

## Conclusion

The revolution has created a space for a women's movement to develop in Nicaragua. This movement has undergone several metamorphoses, largely spurred on by pressure from women at the base. During the first years of the revolution, only AMNLAE appeared to represent the interests of Nicaraguan women. Yet, when AMNLAE declined in popularity in the mid-1980s, the void was filled by the trade unions whose newly-formed women's sections started to make known the specific demands of women workers in their various sectors. As the presence of women in production grew, so too did their importance in the political and social arena, giving rise to the FSLN *Proclama* of 1987. Since then AMNLAE has made a considerable effort to incorporate women from the productive sectors into what is now intended to be a broad-based co-ordinating umbrella movement with a democratically elected National Women's Assembly. Resistance to such a movement is, however, still to be found amongst members of AMNLAE's full-time bureaucracy. Many women are now organizing separately from AMNLAE, preferring to take their own action unbound by AMN-LAE's bureaucratic machinery.

Nevertheless, from the early days of the revolution when it was no more than an apologetic women's section of the FSLN, AMNLAE has grown into a self-confident movement representing large sections of Nicaragua's female population, and is asserting women's specific demands. AMNLAE's ability to carry out its democratization process and incorporate different forms of expression will decide whether it sinks or swims. Another factor in the balance is the continuing economic crisis that could well impede women's organization in the future. 'The key question for women themselves,' writes Hermione Harris, 'is whether their exhaustion at combining their additional responsibilities with trying to maintain themselves and their families under present conditions will erode their enthusiasm.'[27]

# Notes

1. Luisa Amanda Espinosa was the first woman to die in combat against Somoza's National Guard.

2. Heliette Ehlers, speaking in London, May 1987.

3. *Ventana*, 10 September 1988.

4. Heliette Ehlers, quoted in *Spare Rib*, July 1989.

5. Lea Guido (General Secretary AMNLAE 1987–89), quoted in *Barricada*, 13 May 1981.

6. AMNLAE, 'Platform of Struggle', 1988.

7. *Barricada*, 3 September 1981.

8. Soto Orlando Núñez, 'Machismo y Revolución', in *Revolución y Desarrollo*, MIDINRA, No. 3, 1985, p. 46.

9. Hermione Harris, 'Nicaragua' in *Third World Quarterly* Vol. 5, No. 4, 1983, p. 908.

10. Lea Guido, quoted in Randall, 1981, pp. 3, 16.

11. Randall, 1981, p. 3.

12. Magda Enríquez, speech, February 1984, reprinted in *Nicaragua: The Sandinista People's Revolution*, 1985.

13. *Barricada*, 15 April 1980.

14. Hermione Harris, in Isaksson (ed.), 1988, p. 199.

15. Beth Woroniuk, 'Women's Oppression and the Revolution — The Nicaraguan Debate', CUSO, December 1987.

16. Bayardo Arce, quoted in Beth Woroniuk, op. cit.

17. *Barricada*, 28 September 1985.

18. *Barricada Internacional*, 9 October 1986.

19. Ibid.

20. Heliette Ehlers, interview in *Cayenne* (Canada), Summer 1987.

21. Melba Barrios, interviewed by Helen Collinson and Elaine Ginsburg, January 1988.

22. Rosalyn Cooper, 'AMNLAE — The struggle for women's emancipation in Nicaragua', unpublished dissertation, Essex University, 1988, p. 85.

23. *Barricada*, 8 March 1989.

24. *Barricada Internacional*, 7 April 1988.

25. Ibid.

26. Ibid.

27. Hermione Harris, op. cit., p. 208.

# 11. Fighting for Peace

With the intensification of Contra attacks from 1982, defence of the revolution became a priority. Military mobilization became a way of life: not only men but women too (some armed, some pregnant), in military uniforms, became a striking feature of revolutionary Nicaragua. As defence absorbed up to half the national budget, the pace of revolutionary change in other areas slackened, at least at a material level.

Women's role in military defence of the Revolution is acknowledged in AMNLAE's emblem, which shows a gun against a woman's profile.[1] Women's apparent embrace of a military role may evoke conflicting feelings among women elsewhere, where the issues of war and peace have arisen in a very different — invariably pacifist — framework. The ethos of women's peace camps centred on the view of war as intrinsically alien to women's pro-life culture; only male power comes out of the barrel of a gun. But Nicaraguan women have been faced with a situation where peace can be achieved only by military action. In Nicaragua too, however, it has been difficult to achieve a consensus of women's military role; indeed, the issue has stimulated considerable debate.

## Insurrection against Somoza

Nicaraguan women are proud of their part in overthrowing the dictatorship; at the time of the victory, 30% of the combatants were women. There was some resistance to fully integrating women into guerrilla actions, but many took on leadership positions, heading units and battalions. In some columns the entire command was composed of women, which represented a real break with the traditions of Nicaraguan society. In addition to military activities, women were the backbone of the support networks for the guerrillas: they set up safe houses in urban and rural areas; fed, clothed and sheltered fighters and political workers; organized first aid and medical supplies; made bombs; hid arms and ammunition. They also operated as messengers and sent food to the fighters in the mountains. Members of AMPRONAC took part in the final insurrection and were heavily involved in organizing the local defence committees, which still exist today.

As a result of their experience in the struggle, a number of women of high standing in the FSLN took on positions of major responsibility after the victory. Doris Tijerino became head of the Sandinista Police, Dora Maria Tellez became Minister of Health, and Leticia Herrera directed the Sandinista Defence Committees during the first years of the revolution before going on to become vice-deputy of the National Assembly.

## After the victory

Women's active participation in the military has varied with the development of the revolution and its defence needs.

Soon after the Triumph, some women guerrilla fighters took the initiative and formed their own battalions or 'companies' as a positive statement about women's presence as fighters. To quote Maria Elisa Navas, second in command of the Juana Elena Mendoza Infantry (women's) Company in 1979: 'This company is something we thought up to show our ability and desire to belong to the army. Women want to organize militarily to defend our country. We want to show that women continue to have a role to play.'[2]

Yet, on the whole, women were unable to maintain the position they had held in the guerrilla army before the Triumph. In July 1979, most women fighters were demobilized, partly because many of the educated women who had been combatants during the emergency of the insurrection were now needed in administrative and political positions within the new state, and partly because it was thought that women were more likely to gain political awareness through civilian activities, such as the locally based Sandinista Defence Committees, than through the army. For men, on the other hand, the army was seen as playing an important role in political education. Many young, disaffected working-class men had spontaneously joined the insurrection but had not had any military or political training. The army was thus seen as the tool to educate these men and turn them into fully fledged Sandinista cadres. With women, the army's social control role was less relevant, as women were unlikely to become an unruly social force or pose a threat to stability.

Unease about maintaining women as fighters began to surface during the process of forming a new national professional Sandinista People's Army. In August 1979, Comandante Luis Carrion, a member of the general command, when speaking of the make-up of the new army said: 'There is also a notable number of women for whom *special* units [our emphasis] will be created.'[3] Soon afterwards separate training for men and women was introduced; this was a break with the traditions of the guerrilla war. 'In the mountains there weren't men and women, just fighters' is the nostalgic interpretation of the pre-insurrectionary period. To quote Ana Julia Guido who joined the Sandinistas while still at school: 'There was never any lack of respect on the part of our male comrades. On the contrary there was incredible solidarity.'[4] But even before the Revolution it seems that there may well have been some hidden differences.[5] Monica Baltodano, an ex-guerrilla fighter, remembers exploiting the fact that she was a woman in order to do less exercise. This was clearly easier than confronting the prejudices about the capacity of women as combatants.

Unofficially, it seems that a lack of confidence in women's ability to fight as competently as men may have been the root of the moves to discourage women from fully integrating into the army. At the time, however, the separation between men and women soldiers was justified by the fact that many of the new recruits lacked the experience of fighting with women in the mountains, and were thus likely to treat them as women rather than as fellow soldiers. Additionally, the Sandinistas were subject to certain conventional pressures now that they were in power. They had to appear responsible in the eyes of the community, and particularly the parents of young women soldiers who did not want their daughters sharing quarters with men.

## The popular militia

Women were more prominent in the popular militia than in the regular army. In addition to building up a professional army, the need to mobilize the mass of the people in defence of the revolution was high on the agenda in 1979, particularly after a few early counter-revolutionary attacks later that year. Hence the establishment of the popular militias at the end of 1979 to defend against internal aggression and to guard factories, co-operatives, and neighbourhoods. Membership was open to anyone between the ages of 16 and 60 who agreed with the aims of the revolution. Militia duties were part-time and fitted around ordinary day-to-day responsibilities. Participation in the militia was promoted by AMNLAE, and women comprised up to 60% in some urban areas. Because of the more restricted lives of women in the countryside, fewer were able to join the rural militias, but they were not totally absent. A co-operative member near Estelí reported: 'Some women take part . . . And we see that in training they do everything the same as a man, just as well.'[6] Militia training centres were opened in 1981 offering training early in the morning or straight after work. According to one participant, women were physically slower than men, probably because of the lack of sporting facilities for girls at school. But the market traders from the Mercado Oriental, who were used to carrying heavy weights and excelled at military training were an exception.

Although many women attended the militia training, their numbers gradually decreased because of such difficulties as providing childcare;

AMNLAE tried to organize group care for children, but this was only a temporary measure.[7] Many women also faced indifference or even outright hostility from male partners who objected to being left with the domestic responsibilities.

Meanwhile, in military circles, stereotypical views of women as irrational and unmotivated persisted. In 1983, for example, a comic-format booklet intended to attract people to the militias showed a man trying to recruit a woman by seducing her. An editorial in *Barricada* pointed out that this trivialized women's decision to enlist.[8]

### A place in the Reserves

The reserve battalions are part of the regular army and consist of volunteers who can be mobilized for a period of months, often at the war front. Training is more rigorous than for the militias and involves going up to the mountains for weeks at a time. Inevitably, the greater time commitment and mobility involved meant that, initially, the Reserves consisted almost entirely of men. Joining the Reserves poses great problems for women, as leaving home usually means arranging childcare. Nevertheless, there were women who began to ask why the government had not set up women's reserve battalions.

In 1981, AMNLAE mobilized 500 women in Estelí to demand a greater role for women in defence. In a meeting with Edén Pastora, then head of the Popular Militia, Marta Munguia, general secretary of AMNLAE in Estelí, said: 'We as women cannot limit our participation in defence to duties that will place us again in a secondary role, as we would be leaving empty the space left us by the women who died for the country.'[9] She added that while women formed a significant part of the Popular Militias, only one women's battalion had been mobilized. Pastora acknowledged their protest, confirming that women would shortly start to train in the region for the Reserves. By 1983 there were seven women's reserve battalions; a number that has since increased nationally.

## Patriotic Military Service (SMP)

In August 1983, two years of compulsory military service were introduced for young men between 18 and 25 years old. The law establishing the Patriotic Military Service was a response to the mounting threat from the US-backed Contras, who had now become a more cohesive force and aimed to create a 'liberated zone' on the frontier, with a provisional government. Up to this point, the defence of the revolution had fallen heavily on the volunteers in the militia, and particularly in the Reserves.

Although women were not to be called up for military service, they could register as volunteers in the Reserves. AMNLAE was not happy about this development and argued that it was in breach of the Statutes of Rights and Guarantees passed in 1979, which outlawed discrimination against women. The army disagreed, pointing out that the conscription of women and their full integration into the regular army would mean providing separate facilities in battalions dominated by men; women had special needs, for example, during menstruation, it was argued, and they were not as strong as men. '[Women's participation in SMP] would be like a man breastfeeding his baby or a woman lifting weights,' declared Humberto Ortega, Minister of Defence.[10]

But this was not simply a conflict between the women's movement and the army. While some women were keen to participate with men in the SMP, there was no guarantee that the majority of women around the country shared this view. Some prominent women, like Doris Tijerino, the Chief of Police, publicly opposed women's integration into military service because of their home duties and their 'biological limitations.' Other ex-guerrilla women fighters kept silent. A further complication was that the introduction of SMP raised strong protest from the Right, leading to one of the major clashes between the Catholic Church hierarchy and the government; the recruitment of women would have exacerbated this crisis. The Church would probably have seen such a move as a further blow to traditional values, and to the family in particular.

Eventually a compromise was reached whereby women could participate in active military service on a voluntary basis. Many women, however, were still of the opinion that to be given a secondary role in military service was a decisive break with the traditions of the revolutionary struggle.

**Women volunteers**
The first women volunteers to serve in the SMP were not called up until 1986, when the army was seeking solutions to a shortfall in the number of soldiers. Some 300 women were recruited at this point. Welcoming this move, Sofia Montenegro, in an article in *Barricada*, pointed out that not participating actively in defence

> Denied women an immense two-year opportunity to acquire military training and political, ideological and leadership development as professional cadres with equal capabilities and experience to guarantee the maintenance of a female vanguard in all fronts of the struggle.[11]

Major campaigns to recruit women into military service began in 1988, despite some continuing misgivings from the army. The recruitment drive was directed towards women living outside the war zones, as they were less involved in vital civil defence than were women living in areas under attack from the Contra. During 1988 about 1,000 women volunteered for military service or joined the Reserves. Perhaps it had then been accepted that without necessarily moving towards the full integration of women, they could usefully fulfil some roles, and thus release men for other duties. Women are mobilized for one year in specifically women's battalions, where they fill posts at all levels including military leaders and mechanics. Matagalpa, Chinandega, Jinotega, León, Managua, and Masaya were among the first towns to set up such battalions.

Volunteers' ages range from 13 to 63, but the majority appear in their late teens or early 20s. Many are secondary and university students and many are workers, state employees, housewives, and small private business employees. While men's recruitment is based on age rather than political conciousness, the women volunteers are activists, many having already participated in the literacy crusade, health campaigns, CDSs or coffee brigades. Typical comments from these volunteers are: 'Women volunteers are following the steps of the women who died fighting Somoza.' 'It is possible to vote at 16, it follows that it is possible to defend our country.'[12]

Women volunteers themselves have spoken of the importance of the experience for their political development, and mention practical benefits too. Asked why she was joining up, Zenelia Martínez, head of the Managua women's contingent, said, in an interview with *Barricada*, on 11 June 1988: 'When we finish our SMP, we will demand to be treated as equal to a demobilized man, with priority for studying, scholarships, work, medical attention, housing and all the same rights as the *cachorros*. ('*Cachorros*', or Sandino's lioncubs, is an affectionate name for drafted soldiers.)

Many volunteers are mothers of young children, some only babies. For example, Carla Lisset Castellon, 15, has an eight-month old child; she decided to join up when she heard a call to women on the radio. Eva Maria Chavez, 17, with a daughter of nine months, joined while still at secondary school. She plans to make a permanent career in the army after fulfilling her SMP. 'I've a daughter who's just a few months old but I know that by joining the contingent [in Rivas] I'm defending her life.'[13] Reyna Cruz from Jinotega, who lost three sons in the war, joined up to maintain her sons' example. Young children left behind are cared for by grandmothers, aunts, husbands and ex-husbands. That so many mothers of young children can volunteer highlights the strong support networks that exist in Nicaraguan families.[14]

Of course there is no way of knowing how many women have not joined up because of opposition from less supportive families. According to a newspaper article 'The Dilemma of the Mobilized Women', the first line of fire to be endured by women wanting to join the SMP is their family's prejudice. For this reason a regional campaign in León to recruit 300 women between the ages of 17 and 25 included meetings with parents. According to one volunteer, 'It's a hard struggle; first you have to confront society and your family, your friends. People say you are a runaway — that this is just for men.'[15] Johana Fonseca's family were worried that the women and men would be in the same units and together 'in everything'. 'People take a dim view of this,' she says, 'because they are always saying things about women in the military.' This reflects feelings of ambiguity about women in the army. On the one hand there is a great deal of respect for military women; on the other, it seems that there is some unease about the 'morality' of women in uniform, associated with their independence from protected family life. Special battalions alleviate these worries, and also avoid comparisons between men's and women's military merits.

## Women and the Sandinista Army

Women soldiers are not usually sent to the war front. In an interview with *Barricada* in 1988,[16] however, Major Rosa Pasos, public relations officer for the Ministry of Defence (and one of only five women to have attained this rank in the EPS), admitted that there were women now ready for combat and pointed out that there was a permanent women's unit specializing in anti-aircraft defence.

Women do, however, go to the battlefield as cooks and other auxiliary workers, often risking their lives in the process. Women's units have been assigned to important work in military communications, and mobilized to defend the coffee harvest, which have been targets for Contra attacks since 1982. Women now form 20% of the regular army and 40% of Ministry of the Interior staff (MINT personnel are uniformed and carry out many military-style security duties).[17] Thus, while men continue to be responsible for direct combat, women are increasingly filling positions in the rearguard.

It should also be remembered (as explained in chapter 2) that women's work in production, which has risen as men have been taken into the military, is seen as part of the war effort. Maintaining production levels, growing food to feed the population and the army, and raising the output of export crops such as coffee, cotton and tobacco, are all tasks that complement military action against the Contras. Women who stay at home can play a crucial role in keeping up the army's morale, for example through such organizations as Mothers of Heroes and Martyrs.

In fact, one of Nicaraguan women's strongest links to the military is as mothers of soldiers, and work with the mothers of combatants has been a major priority for AMNLAE. This has involved helping women to build up support networks, easing communication with their sons, and organizing them into a coherent force to overcome isolation while encouraging political mobilization. The Mothers of Heroes and Martyrs keep alive the memory of those killed, by organizing museums, photograph galleries and monuments. They also help bereaved families, visit the wounded in hospital or raise money to send them parcels. With economic survival as such a central issue, some mothers' groups have set up sewing co-operatives, popular eating places or street stalls. Political work has included demonstrations against a total amnesty for Somocista and Contra prisoners, and support for the mothers of the kidnapped. Not all the women in these groups are mothers; some are sisters, wives or other relatives, but the name endures because 'motherhood' carries such emotional resonance in Nicaragua.

For Nicaraguan women, the conscription of a son means the loss of a major support, both economically and emotionally. The right-wing has targeted the mothers as among those who may see themselves as losing rather than gaining from the revolution. Meanwhile, when conscription was introduced, the Church hierarchy made direct appeals to the mothers of young men to reject the drafting of their sons. Realizing the particular vulnerability of these women to right-wing influence, the FSLN were especially concerned to include them in the revolutionary projects.

The emphasis on women as mothers of combatants may seem to contradict the aim of changing women's role in society. Although many women became involved in the struggle against Somoza because of the arrest, torture, and murder of their children, women then participated as activists in their own right. The political activities of these women now are completely bound up with their identity as mothers and thus one step removed from the front line. It must, however, be stressed that a mother's role in Nicaragua is not a passive one, as women so often carry total responsibility for their children. Moreover, to confer a high profile on the Mothers of Heroes and Martyrs is symptomatic of the difficulty of changing women's position while simultaneously fighting a war. In the long term, war may lead to great change, but in the short term, it calls for the reaffirmation of traditional values and a seeking for stability in the middle of crisis.

## Mothers of the kidnapped

The politicization of mothers that developed through the movement of Mothers of Heroes and Martyrs established 'motherhood' as a meaningful focus for women's organization. Thus it was as mothers that the relatives of the kidnapped came to the fore during 1988. By the end of 1987, it was estimated that over 7,000 Nicaraguans had been kidnapped since the start of the Contra war. The impetus for the widespread organization of Mothers of the Kidnapped groups arose from the arrival of the Contra leaders in Nicaragua for peace talks with the government in early 1988. The strategy of the new groups has been to try to mobilize the support of national and international human rights organizations. They are also trying to document all the kidnappings, and hope to visit the Honduran Contra camps to establish who is being held there. In early 1988, they called on Cardinal Obando y Bravo, who was appointed head of the National Reconciliation Committee set up under the Esquipulas Peace Plan, to mediate for them with the Contra. Frustrated by his lack of response, from July 1988 the Mothers have held weekly vigils outside the Cardinal's Curia, demanding a meeting with him.

## Living in the war zones

This chapter, so far, has been concerned with women's *active* role in the war. But there are also many women who may not be directly involved with the army or with any Sandinista organization, but who nevertheless have found themselves on the war front, simply because the battlefields are the homes of many *campesino* families. The Contra's strategy has been to concentrate almost exclusively on civilian targets. Particularly vulnerable to attack have been agricultural co-operatives, state farms, schools, health posts, and even crèches — six children were killed in a dawn raid on a crèche in San Juan del Sur in 1987. State employees and those seen as government supporters, such as nurses, teachers, agrarian reform workers, technicians, and grassroots' church workers, have been singled out for kidnapping, murder, and torture. It has been common practice for women taken by the Contra to be raped before being either kidnapped or murdered. The Contra have also mined roads and ambushed vehicles, making travel extremely hazardous. Some of the victims have been women on their way to visit sons in army camps. In 1985, eight women died and 18 were seriously wounded when they were ambushed by the Contra. Between 1980 and 1987 women victims of aggression have been: killed, 355; injured, 1,603; kidnapped, 863.[18]

### Displaced people

The aim of Contra attacks on civilians is to instil terror in the population to deter them from becoming involved with the revolutionary process; this campaign has caused many families to abandon their homes.

Altogether, an estimated 250,000 (8% of the population) have been displaced as a result of the war. In 1985, the government embarked on a two-year resettlement programme involving 50,000 people. Under this programme, new settlements were to be established in 135 new communities on land granted by the Agrarian Reform. An infrastructure of housing, education and health services and technical assistance was provided. Some fled the war areas voluntarily; others were moved by the government to enable the army to pursue the war against the Contra without civilian casualties. For many of those coming from isolated farmsteads, the resettlement camps provided their first opportunity to benefit from the revolution. Women in particular gained from the provision of better housing, health services, and clean water. The resettlement camps are easier to defend than scattered households, but they have not been immune to attack. In 1987, for example, La Pradera settlement was attacked and two women teachers were raped and killed.[19]

\* \* \*

*Doña Lesbia is a self-taught potter. She lives in a tiny one-roomed corrugated house with her husband and children in the war-zone town of Matiguas. Behind the house is a minute garden crammed with fruits, vegetables and herbs which Lesbia tends with the same care she gives to her own children. But the garden cannot provide enough food for the whole family which is why Lesbia has turned to pottery. By selling her small clay animals and homemade honeybread, the family can scrape together a subsistence income.*

*Although Lesbia's household exudes a sense of permanence and security, in reality she and her family have been in Matiguas only a year. Before that they farmed in the Bull-Bull region. Local attacks by the Contras, or 'bad people' as Lesbia calls them, drove them to Matiguas. Despite the obvious trauma this move must have caused the family, Lesbia thinks they have been very lucky. On arrival in Matiguas, the town council not only gave them the fertile piece of land on which they now live but also materials with which to build a modest shelter. Lesbia feels much happier in Matiguas, partly because they are surrounded by other displaced people who have had the same experience.[20]*

\* \* \*

## Women's involvement in the Contra

Women have had a very low profile within the US-backed counter-revolutionary forces. The vast majority of Contras killed and arrested are men; in 1987, a total of 212 women only were in prison in Nicaragua. The majority in the 25–45 age group who had been sentenced for counter-revolutionary activities had been mainly involved in economic sabotage, such as puncturing government transport vehicle tyres or disrupting assembly lines. The conservative ideology of the Contra, their close ties with the Catholic Church and emphasis on the traditional family would preclude them from seeing women as a group to be mobilized. Militarily, the image has been of a macho, mercenary army, with leaders sporting such nicknames as 'Death' and 'Suicide'.

Nevertheless, a few women have participated in the Contra — as fighters, collaborators, and support workers in the camps. Some became Contra supporters through conviction, others were drawn in by family connections. Clemen Araica, for example, was married to a colonel in the National Guard. After the victory she was involved in organizing the Legion of the 15th September (one of the first Contra groups to amass in Honduras) and established a group in the Industrial Quimica de Nicaragua Distillery. She later moved to Honduras where she had direct contact with the general staff of the FDN (main Contra group). We know only one women member of the FDN National Directorate, Señora Salazar, widow of Jorge Salazar, who was vice-chair of the right-wing business pressure group COSEP.

Kidnapped *campesinos*, mainly the poorest and most isolated, have been a major source of 'recruits' into the Contra ranks. Although a significant number of women have been kidnapped (863 up to 1987)[21] they were probably taken for sexual abuse and to work in the camp's kitchens or as secretaries, rather than sent into combat. The accounts of people who later escaped describe how the men were separated from the women before being taken off for military training. Veronica Gonzales, who was kidnapped with her family and, she estimated, about 1,800 others, described what happened when she arrived in Honduras: 'The MISURA (Atlantic Coast Contra group) ordered the men to leave their women and march to Rus Rus military base for training to prepare them to fight against Nicaragua.'[22] World Relief, an American church organization that runs a refugee camp in Honduras, described how members of MISURA went around the camp taking away young men from the age of 15 upwards. They also took young girls, but according to World Relief, not for military training.[23] One woman who witnessed ambushes and kidnappings by the Contra and was herself at one point held by them, claims that kidnapped women are forced to work as cooks in the camps. Pedro Espinoza Sanches, a key Contra member organizing internal sabotage between 1981 and his arrest in 1984, testified that he recruited women teachers and students for the Contra camps.[24]

Despite the very few women fighters amongst the Contra, there are some accounts of women receiving military training in Contra camps. A Honduran woman who joined one of the camps to be with her Nicaraguan lover, says, 'The training was the same for men and women. Age made no difference: 12- and 14-year-old youths were trained alongside 40-, 50-year-old men. We had to do physical training so that we'd be able to make it through the long foot-marches with back-packs for all supplies. In spite of everything, my training was very short; it only lasted a month'.[25] She entered Nicaragua with a Contra combat unit but soon decided to defect with some *campesinos* who had been kidnapped; she was then arrested. Emerson Uriel Navarrete Medrano, who had been a member of State Security under Somoza, describes marching from Honduras to Chontales with a number of women in the unit, carrying the same arms and kit as the men. According to Uriel, the women were stronger than the men and when the men were exhausted, the women would take their rucksacks and carry them on their heads in addition to their own equipment. Maria Eugenia Quintana, a crèche worker in the war zone, kidnapped by the Contra and forced to march with them for three days, reports that there were women with the Contra forces who abused and jeered at her.[26]

Amongst the Contra there are stories of dramatic incidents involving Contra women in combat. On a march into the interior of Nicaragua a *campesina* woman who had fought with the Contra for three years turned around, saw men in uniform beside her and, mistaking them for Sandinistas, shot three fellow Contras. Another story involves a young *campesino* who was kidnapped and taken with a band of Contras to attack Ocotal. He had never been in battle before and was very frightened. In terror, he sheltered against the side of a house where he was mocked by a woman fighter who grabbed his gun, as her own was jammed, and was disgusted to find no shots had been fired.[27]

In addition to the military fronts on the northern and southern frontiers and in some of the central mountainous regions, the Contra developed an 'Internal Front' among the urban populations of the Pacific Coast. Links were formed with some parts of the internal opposition parties, in order to undermine the revolution on a political and ideological level. While it is important not to forget that Nicaragua has a pluralist political system with legitimate parties opposing the Sandinistas and elected to seats in the National Assembly, it is also true that some right-wing figures have ties or sympathies with the counter-revolution.

Dr Miriam Arguello is Secretary-General of one of the fragments of the Nicaraguan Conservative Party. Pedro Espinoza Sanches was once in contact with her for help in recruiting people to send to the military training camps. Probably the best-known woman on the right is Violeta Chamorro, widow of Pedro Joaquín Chamorro, editor of the newspaper *La Prensa* and an outspoken critic of Somoza (but not a Sandinista). His murder in 1978 by Somocista forces led to massive riots. Violeta Chamorro was given a seat in the government Junta set up after the victory, reflecting the Sandinistas' efforts to maintain an alliance with the bourgeoisie. She was probably selected more for her late husband's reputation rather than in her own right. In April 1980 she resigned from the Junta and since then has presided over *La Prensa*'s development into the voice of the counter-revolution.

## Mothers of 22 January

The only major mobilization of women by Contra sympathizers has been through a group of mothers of jailed Somocista National Guard members and Contra prisoners. Their role has been to agitate for the release of all 'political prisoners'. The Mothers of 22 January group was set up by Enrique Bolanos, a Conservative party leader in Managua, and is backed by the US embassy, who produce their literature. In 1987 a budget of US$20,000 is thought to have been allocated to the Mothers from CIA funds. In July-August 1988, a group of the mothers toured parts of the US accompanied by a State Department representative. Presented as mothers of political prisoners campaigning on human rights issues, their function is clearly to parallel the pro-Sandinista Mothers of Heroes and Martyrs, perhaps in the hope of neutralizing some of their emotional impact. The '22 January' group has also tried to capture some of the legitimacy won by the Mothers of the Plaza de Mayo in Argentina by copying the Argentine mothers' custom of tying white handkerchiefs around their heads. The Argentine women have, however, repudiated them.

Many members of the group are poor women from the northern areas where traditionally the National Guard found recruits. In an interview with a women's study tour from Britain in 1987, most of the women from the 22nd January group denied that Somoza's National Guard had ever carried out any massacres, claiming that their relatives were in prison because they had been members of the National Guard or were accused of supporting the Contra. It is particularly ironic that the group's own title commemorates a massacre on 22 January 1967 when the National Guard machine-gunned a demonstration of 60,000 people opposed to Somoza, causing some 600 casualties.

To some extent, the Mothers of 22nd January provide the Contra with a useful focus for opposition attacks on the government's human rights record, but they have never really been a force in their own right. The group was artificially created and has failed to take root or broaden its political horizons.

## Conclusion

The military aggression and economic collapse precipitated by the Contra war have profoundly affected women's lives; but women have not been passive victims of this war. They have shouldered responsibility for many areas of civilian life and production while the men have been fighting. They have also been directly involved in military defence, although in much smaller numbers than men. Women's role in the military has ebbed and flowed according to the intensity of the war and has usually been more in the rearguard than men's. Probably few women would want to fight in the frontline, but to accept only the rearguard activities could be seen to contradict demands for equality with men. This contradiction is more apparent in Nicaragua than in some other countries at war because the revolution has promoted women's full participation in all areas of life. On the other hand, those women trying to assert themselves in military defence can at least appeal to revolutionary ideology when their position is under threat.

Turning to the opponents in Nicaragua's war, very few women are known to have fought with the Contra forces but some work as secretaries and cooks in Contra camps. Only a handful of women are prominent in the internal political opposition. The Mothers of 22 January group which has campaigned for the release of Somocista National Guardsmen is a pale shadow of the Mothers' groups organized in pro-Sandinista, anti-Contra activities. In sum, Nicaraguan women are far more prominent in the defence of the revolution than they are in the counter-revolution.

## Notes

1. Hermione Harris, in Isaksson (ed.), 1988.
2. Randall, 1981, p. 142.
3. Black, 1981, p. 225.
4. Deighton et al, 1983, p. 131.
5. *Pensamientos Propios*, April 1987.
6. Black, 1981, p. 229.
7. Deighton et al, 1983, p. 60.
8. 'Unidad de comunicación alternativa de la mujer', Santiago, Chile, March 1983.
9. 'The Woman Combatant: Present', AMNLAE factsheet.
10. Beth Woroniuk, 'Women's Oppression and the Revolution — The Nicaraguan Debate', CUSO, December 1987, p. 14.
11. *Barricada*, 6 May 1986.
12. *Barricada*, 14 June 1989.
13. *Barricada*, 11 June 1988.
14. *El Nuevo Diario*, 9 October 1988, and *Barricada*, 7 October 1988.
15. *Barricada*, 11 June 1988.
16. *Barricada*, 16 August 1988.
17. *Barricada Internacional*, 8 October 1987.
18. *Barricada*, 16 August 1988.
19. Eich & Rincon, 1984, p. 144.
20. Displaced potter, interviewed by Helen Collinson, Matiguas, August 1985.
21. *Barricada*, 16 August 1988.
22. Angel & Macintosh, 1987, p. 54.
23. Gillian Brown, 'Miskito Revindication', in Harris & Vilas (eds), 1985, p. 188.
24. Eichs & Rincon, 1984, p. 144.
25. Ibid., p. 60.
26. Ibid., p. 99.
27. Ibid.

# 12. Women in The Media

Nicaraguan women hoping to see a fair and positive image of themselves reflected in the national communications media start off with some powerful advantages. The very first Provisional Media Law, introduced in 1979 to set the standards for revolutionary media, explicitly bans the commercial exploitation of women's bodies in the press, in television and film. AMNLAE's 1987 'Platform of Struggle' commits the women's movement to:

> Contribute to the elimination of myths, beliefs, prejudices and schemes that reproduce and mainpulate a subordinate image of women, transforming . . . the mass media and all the ideological instruments of society.

## Comics and censors

Clearly, laws and written policies are worth little more than the paper they are written on if there is not the political will to implement them. This was put dramatically to the test in March 1988, when the satirical weekly *Semana Comica* reproduced from a US soft porn magazine a picture of a woman shaving her pubic hair, with the caption, 'Women Get Ready! It looks like this International Women's Day will be well celebrated . . . In the photo, one activist gets ready'.

As AMNLAE saw it, this was in direct contravention of the Media Law against exploitation of women's bodies, and Lea Guido led an angry delegation of women to the MINT's Media Office on 4 March 1988 to demand action against *Semana Comica*.

For two reasons the situation was especially delicate: firstly, the Sandinista government was particularly sensitive about any form of censorship, after the vicious international criticism it received in 1986 for finally cracking down on the US-financed pro-Contra Managua daily *La Prensa*. Having already been accused of muzzling the 'free press', the government would lay itself open to further accusations of sins against democracy by taking action against *Semana Comica*. Secondly,

*Semana Comica* itself held a trump card: it is not only very popular, but also satirical — often very funny indeed. By attacking it AMNLAE women exposed themselves to a classic counter-attack, familiar to allegedly 'humourless feminists' the world over: they can't take a joke against themselves.

*Semana Comica* exists on the fringes of the Sandinista media, specializing in risky, usually acute, and always irreverent commentary on the national scene. In a country where freedom to criticize the state is still relatively new (under Somoza, the premises of newspapers and radio stations that opposed him were bombed) it plays a useful role. The editor, Roger Sanchez, is also well-known for his sharp anti-sexist cartoons. Conversely, the paper also has a reputation for trivializing and stereotyping women, especially in the regular 'Erotic Humour' feature and spoof sexologist's advice column, both written by Roger Sanchez, which lean heavily on the 'whores/nymphomaniacs/frigid bitches' school of humour. The masthead is a good indication of the paper's brand of editorial lightheartedness: 'LA SEMANA COMICA — A WEEKLY PAPER OF HUMOUR, MARXISM, SEX AND VIOLENCE'.

In this delicate context, the response to AMNLAE's complaint was encouraging. *Semana Comica* was shut down, and forbidden to publish for the next five weeks. Lissette Torres of the MINT Media Office also ordered *El Nuevo Diario* off the streets for three days, as punishment for reproducing the offending picture in its coverage of the story of the complaint against *Semana Comica*. AMNLAE was triumphant.

Their pleasure was not shared by everyone. *El Nuevo Diario* carried editorials about the sanctity of the free press and journalistic autonomy (without addressing the question of degrading women):

> *Semana Comica* did indeed violate the laws of ethics and good taste, or aesthetics. But we defend the right of *El Nuevo Diario* to inform. This paper did the right thing, and would have done wrong if it had left out the photograph that provoked the legal action, because that would not have been OBJECTIVE.[1]

The journalists' trade union, the UPN, made representations to the government in defence of *Semana Comica*, eventually succeeding in quietly reducing the specified suspension period for both publications.

Roger Sanchez and the *Semana Comica* staff first issued an apology, reprinted in the other papers:

> In no way did we intend to debase or offend the values of Nicaraguan women . . . We are grateful for the opportune and objective vigilance shown by some of the media alerting us to the danger of defamations like the one under discussion, above all in reference to the heroic women of Nicaragua. Finally we make public our apology and our shame.

This tone, however, was not struck again. When *Semana Comica* reappeared it was apparently quite unrepentant, and made the most of the opportunity to ridicule censorship in general and 'bitter and frustrated' feminists in particular. Pictures of naked women, with elaborate captions to justify their status as jokes, soon continued to be published. The Media Office took up the challenge, and in August 1988 the paper was again suspended, this time indefinitely.

Public debate raged. In an interview with *Barricada* Lea Guido commented:

> We believe that yes, political humour should exist; and erotic humour too, but it must struggle against the prejudices that use women as sexual objects . . . Subordinated images wound women, and don't contribute to the emancipation of women or men . . . We don't want *Semana Comica* to disappear, only to critically analyse the image of women it presents.

In his own defence, Roger Sanchez said:

> It's comical . . . If you look at a naked woman you can see it as something natural and pleasurable, but if you're a disturbed or repressed person you see aberrations and perversity.[2]

The Sandinista Youth appealed for the re-opening of *Semana Comica* on the grounds that, 'they have committed errors, but they have also opened important spaces for ideological struggle'.[3] Gioconda Belli, famous for her erotic poetry, declared herself against censorship but opposed to the 'commercialization' of women's bodies. Her practical suggestion was:

> If men can accept, as they expect us to accept, suggestive photos of the most attractive parts of the male body, without feeling shy or feeling that they are being treated as things by women who enjoy looking at their pictures, then we would have to admit that they are truly liberated and we are indeed the moralists. (Her suggestion was never taken up.)[4]

The final episode in this story may disappoint some feminists. To the satisfaction of its fans, *Semana Comica* soon reopened and 'Humour Erotica's' exposure of pornographic images of women under the guise of political humour continued unabated. As a result, the firm stand taken by the government a few months earlier was all but cancelled out and the extent of official commitment to the Media Law was brought into question.

War — and the masculine, militaristic culture it generates (even in a progressive revolutionary country) — may partly account for the sometimes lax enforcement of the Media Law. It could be argued that a situation in which men are mobilized and women, in most cases, are not, provides a classic context for the increased desire for, and consumption of pornography (and possibly prostitution). The recent striking proliferation of beauty contests can also be seen as symptomatic of a male reaction to the stress and austerity of an eight-year war.

In September 1988, *Juventud Sandinista* (Sandinista Youth), an organization that prides itself on progressive attitudes to women, organized a beauty contest and for weeks the media were dominated by images of pretty girls wearing smiles and swimsuits. Any small voice that spoke out against this event as an exploitation of women was scornfully rebuked in *Barricada's* cultural supplement 'Ventana':

> In buses, parks, schools and workplaces, everyone's discussing 'Why did the jury pick Maris Ines rather than Ana Sofia?' Miss Juventud is undeniably the most popular event of the year. This brings a frown to the faces of dogmatic and orthodox elements who refused to support this festive and youthful activity, hiding behind trite phrases learned by rote — 'Beauty contests are meat markets', 'they promote consumerism and depersonalisation'. These types forget that Miss Juventud is organized in revolutionary Nicaragua, where the concept of beauty acquires a new dimension.[5]

Since then large pictures of lines of young women in bathing suits have become commonplace in the press. To our knowledge, AMNLAE has made no official comment on the increasing prominence of beauty contests either as social events or as objects of media attention. Even Auxiliadora Marenco, a prominent psychologist renowned for her radical views on women's liberation, was reported as delighted that her daughter had won one such contest; her much publicized pride in this seemed to some to contradict and undermine the message of her column in *Barricada*, which for years has argued that women are active subjects not passive objects.

## Cinema and television

### Foreign bodies
The possibility of creating positive images of women in the media is also impeded by the fact that at least 70% of Nicaraguan television and more than 90% of films are foreign. The country lacks the resources to develop local production which is remotely able to compete against the flood of sophisticated foreign material. INCINE and SSTV (the state cinema and television authorities) do make an effort to select the most appropriate material and to cut the most offensive scenes from individual shows; but they are fighting a losing battle. Very little TV or film commercially produced in Brazil, Mexico, the USA or Spain (Nicaragua's main suppliers) measures up to the standards of Sandinista policy on the representation of women. Spain provides variety shows complete

with go-go dancers; chart-topping Latin American soap operas, while not pornographic, promote stereotypes of dependent, clinging women and *femmes fatales*.

Nicaragua's own screen productions sometimes show real flair for screening more realistic images of women, for example, INCINE's 1987 feature film *Mujeres de la Frontera* (Women of the Frontier), which depicted strong, independent and resourceful women confronting age-old stereotypes and the sexism of their husbands and other menfolk.

But the situation is not always so potentially encouraging. Auxiliadora Marenco, who directed a progressive and popular sex education series on TV called *Sexo y Juventud* (Sex and Youth), recounts some of the difficulties she faced:

> They didn't like us, they were scared by what we were doing, so we kept finding that there weren't enough technicians or any tapes to record our programme . . . I remember in the episode on birth, we persuaded the hospital to let us in and film a birth, and spent a long time with the mother-to-be, getting her confidence, till in the end there we all were and we had a real relationship going . . . I was so excited to see how it would come out on screen . . . but then of course I had to submit it to the SSTV committee, three men of course, well, we got to the part about the actual birth, and one of them fainted! They said it was too explicit, filming as we did from between the woman's legs — in the end we had to go back to the hospital and film all over again, this time from the side.

Here, a woman-centred image of birth, an important service in a country where sex education is still minimal and few books are available, fell foul of a system orginally designed to protect women from abuse of their bodies in the media. Auxiliadora Marenco's series was later suspended altogether in the wake of a scandal about her radical treatment of homosexuality.

## Ways ahead?

One of the limitations of Marenco's work was the lack of women trained and working as *technicians* in television; the majority of Nicaraguan journalists (including press, radio, and TV) are, however, women. A revealing glimpse of the attitudes of some of these women, who as journalists are admirably placed to present a revolutionary image of women, was given at a workshop in November 1987. Organized jointly by AMNLAE and Michelle Casellon, Education Officer of the journalists' union, UPN, the workshop (focusing on the representation of women and ways of implementing the spirit of the FSLN'S *Proclama* of that year) was open to both sexes, but no men turned up.

The workshop posed the question: 'What do we want when we

demand more positive images of ourselves in the media?' The well-known government poster showing a young combatant with a big smile, an AK47 rifle slung over one shoulder, and a baby at her breast was viewed with some criticism. 'Are women only valued,' the women asked, 'because they can have babies and can fight? Is the combination of mother and soldier an image that demands too much sacrifice from women?'

The participants complained about the lack of childcare facilities at work. Almost universally condemned was the practice of *Barricada* and *El Nuevo Diario* printing pictures of bikini-clad girls at the beach at the start of each summer season.

## Conclusion

In the wake of a long war and acute economic crisis, there are clear signs that some of the early advances made to eliminate negative images of women (symbolized by the Provisional Media Law) are in danger of being lost. But for those of us in countries like Britain, still fighting the daily exposure of female flesh on page 3 of the *Sun* and the like, the Sandinista experiment is still worth watching closely.

## Notes

1. *El Nuevo Diario*, 8 March 1988.
2. *Barricada*, 13 August 1988.
3. *Juventud Sandinista*, open letter, 9 August 1988.
4. *Barricada*, 19 August 1988.
5. *Ventana*, 3 December 1988.

# 13. The Caribbean Story

> The women's movement is a reflection of the process of peace, of repatriation and reunification of the family — thus for the women of the six ethnic groups, peace becomes the point of departure of their demands as women.[1]

The spread of rainforest and rivers stretching east from Nicaragua's central mountain range to the Caribbean sea is known as the Atlantic Coast region (now divided into the North and South Atlantic Autonomous regions). The 'Coast' covers almost 50% of the country's landmass, but less than 10% of the national population live there. Within the coastal community, there are several different ethnic groups: indigenous Indians, Afro-Caribbean Creoles and mestizos of Spanish descent. This chapter focuses particularly on the indigenous Indian communities.

**Table 8.1**

**Ethnic groups on the Atlantic Coast**

|  | Population | % of total | Language | Origin |
|---|---|---|---|---|
| Mestizos | 182,377 | 64.5 | Spanish | country's inland |
| Miskitos* | 54,000 | 20.0 | Miskito | pre-hispanic, European & African descent |
| Creoles | 25,723 | 9.1 | English | Afro-Caribbean |
| Sumu | 4,851 | 1.7 | Sumu | pre-hispanic |
| Caribs | 1,487 | 0.5 | English/Garifuna | Afro-Caribbean/Indian from St Vincent |
| Rama | 649 | 0.2 | Rama | pre-hispanic |

* Figures for Miskito population in 1982 affected particularly by displacement, kidnappings and people fleeing the region.

Source: *Demografia Costeña*, CIDCA, 1982.

Atlantic Coast communities have traditionally been isolated from the more populous Pacific Coast. Apart from the cultural and linguistic differences, they are separated by many miles of impenetrable forest and wildernesss. Only when the Sandinistas came to power was a road built linking the country's two coasts. Even today, no road or even water transport links the two main Atlantic towns, Bluefields in the south and Puerto Cabezas to the north. 'We don't have reliable communication. In my zone [Puerto Cabezas] there are no telephones or television,' comments National Assembly representative Dorothea Wilson.[2]

## Colonial adventurism

The history of the Atlantic Coast is very different from that of the Pacific Coast. Colonial history began in the former in the 17th century with the arrival of British traders and pirates on its shores. The indigenous Sumu population, preferring to maintain their culture and independence, retreated from involvement with the British, and dwindled over the years. Another Indian group, who later became Miskitos, allied themselves with the British, who then used them as labour to Spanish settlers on the Pacific side, spurring them on with reports of the atrocities committed against the indigenous people there. The other main group on the Atlantic Coast were English-speaking Creoles, descendants of African people brought to the Caribbean as slaves by the British and also used as labour on the Atlantic Coast (they still speak English today). Rivalries developed between the Miskitos and the Creoles, because Creoles were employed by the British in certain higher status jobs as administrators and servants. Miskitos were treated as inferior within this hierarchy, while the Sumu and Rama were even more marginalized, Meanwhile, on the Pacific Coast the *mestizo* population under Spanish rule was encouraged to despise the Indians and Blacks scattered along the inaccessible Caribbean.

In 1849, Protestant Moravian Church missionaries arrived on the Coast, first from Germany, later from the USA. Spreading the Christian gospel among the various ethnic groups, the Moravians also developed the first written forms of the Miskito and Sumu languages in order to translate the Bible and hymn book. Mission schools and health-care facilities increased their influence on the population, until the Moravians became virtually the Coast's regional government.

It was not until 1894 that the Atlantic Coast was incorporated into the Nicaraguan Republic; and even then the promise of unity was not welcomed by the Coast people (*costeños*), who saw the move as further evidence of Spanish expansionism.

At the end of the 19th century, British interests declined, and US transnational companies moved into the Atlantic Coast and began to strip the region of its natural resources of rubber, timber, bananas and gold, shipping the profits to the US. They also introduced wage-labour, especially in the mines, to people used only to subsistence agriculture. Company stores stocked US-made consumer goods, which local people had never seen before. These benefits, though meagre, gave the illusion of improved conditions under the US economic bleeding of the area.

Indeed, some still remember these as the 'good old days', since the Contra war and economic crisis have drastically reduced standards of living. From the 1930s, the Somozas left the US companies in peace to exploit the Coast's resources. Atlantic people experienced very few of the brutalities the Somoza dictatorship imposed on the Pacific. 'Somoza may have neglected us,' said a Miskito leader in 1979, 'but at least he left us alone.'[3]

## Women in traditional *costeño* communities

There has been little research on relations between women and men in the traditional Indian and Creole way of life. It is, however, important to recognize that the *costeño* cultures are quite distinct from the Spanish-influenced, Roman Catholic-dominated culture on the Pacific Coast. Many women look back to a time when the traditional values were paramount, and the sexes respected one another as equals.

Dr Myrna Cunningham, a Miskito woman Government Delegate to the northern region of the Atlantic Coast, points out that a Miskito and Sumu tradition of matrilocality existed before the arrival of Christianity.[4]

A displaced Sumu Indian, Dionisia Frank López, recalling the old village life says:

We used to live well along the Río Coco. We fished and found all we needed. The men hunted deer, wild pig and birds; we grew rice, beans, cassava root, bananas, oranges, coconut and sugar cane as well . . . The women plaited palm leaves to make the roofs, we made blankets from tuno bark, baskets from reeds, and clay pots. The mothers with small babies would stay at home. The others helped the men fish and plant rice and maize, while their children cared for the smaller ones; then at midday the women would return to cook . . . There used to be none of this fighting and drinking.[5]

The equality that used to exist between the sexes is also asserted by Dorothea Wilson:

The indigenous woman has always been the head of the family, always present in the leaders' meetings . . . There was an equitable division of labour, valued as equally important: women cultivated the land while men hunted and gathered firewood . . . It is the contact with capitalism that undermined the values of the man-woman relationship in indigenous society.[6]

She gives the example of the *Sukia*, traditional Elder of the Miskito villages. A *Sukia* could be male or female, and took responsibility for both healing and spiritual guidance. Dorothea argues that the coming of the Moravian Church, which trained men to be pastors and women to be nurses, together with the arrival of US mining companies giving waged work only to men, combined to destroy the old sexual order and put women in a subordinate role.

Nevertheless, according to Mildred Levy, a Black nurse in Puerto Cabezas, women still play a central role in subsistence production and in keeping the indigenous communities together:

> In the Miskito communities it's the women who keep Miskito traditions alive. They do most of the plantation work — the men only fell the trees. It's important that a woman has children so that they can help do the work. A woman has to obey her man and doesn't take any big decision as she is considered a lesser person. Yet when the men go to work, as they did to the gold mines, the women are left with most of the farming.[7]

*Costeña* women were also involved in the resistance against the Somoza regime. Dorothea (herself a miner's daughter) continues:

> It was indigenous women, prostitutes, who helped Sandino when he was here: they hid arms from the North Americans to help Sandino expel them from the Coast. Many Atlantic women belonged to AMPRONAC [anti-Somoza women's association], denouncing the killings of women in our region. There is also a tradition of churchwomen organized in Basic Christian Communities who struggled for housing, health and social services for single women.[8]

## The Sandinista revolution arrives on the Coast

The Sandinista government now acknowledges, in all humility, that the revolution's first impact on the Coast was far from ideal. To quote Myrna Cunningham again:

> After the Revolution . . . there were the first contacts. The Atlantic Coast people didn't feel they had won anything because they hadn't been involved in the fighting; it was like a change without knowing why. People from the new government didn't know how to speak Miskito and knew neither the culture nor the ways of thinking of the Indian people, so the Atlantic Coast people were very suspicious of those who came from Managua . . . Medical attention and schools were really needed, and people thought they would get everything from the revolutionary government, and wanted it all in a very short period. They became suspicious when things didn't come as quick as they wanted.[9]

The mutual suspicion between *costeños* and the new government deepened as the Contra attacks began. Not only were even fewer resources available for the promised development projects, but also the isolated communities of the Coast were militarily vulnerable. In 1982, one incident that caused resentment was the forcible relocation of nearly 10,000 Miskitos from their tribal lands on the Río Coco to the new, more easily-defended settlement of Tasba Pri.

## Indigenous people in the counter-revolution

Amid this crisis of confidence between the two parts of Nicaragua, some of the Miskito leadership began to revive long-cherished thoughts of independence from the Pacific Coast. After the Sandinista Triumph, an indigenous people's organization, MISURASATA, was set up, initially to represent the Coast in the new government. But through the leadership of Brooklyn Rivera (previously of Somoza's State Security) and Steadman Fagoth, it soon became the vehicle for organized opposition. Both leaders used their position to advance their own ambitions and inflame anti-Sandinista feelings, especially among the Miskitos. When the FSLN realized, too late, what was happening, they had the MISURASATA leaders arrested. Hazel Lau, now National Assembly Representative and one of the few women in the original MISURASATA group, recalls her arrest in 1981:

> Before Fagoth could escape we were all arrested and accused of acts against the State of Emergency . . . Straight away the Atlantic Coast people rose up in indignation. Thousands gathered in the churches to demand our release. This was given after 14 days and all charges were dropped . . . Fagoth was the only remaining prisoner.[10]

When he was released in May 1981, Fagoth crossed into Honduras and declared war on the Sandinistas, calling on Miskito men to follow him and join his armed faction, MISURA. A number of MISURASATA people went over to the other side, including Brooklyn Rivera.

Although the reasons for Miskito discontent came from within the faltering progress of the Nicaraguan revolution, outside factors soon pushed the crisis towards the brink of war. Just as the British and Spanish colonial powers had manipulated the ethnic divisions between indigenous people for their own ends, so the USA was quick to exploit the desire for local autonomy on the Atlantic Coast in its efforts to undermine the Sandinista revolution. As Mary Bushey, executive member of the pro-Sandinista indigenous group, MISATAN, says: 'The CIA got interested in MISURASATA when they had started becoming a fledging government in the Region. Some of the leaders were conscious pawns of the CIA. Others did not realize.'[11] Thus the Contra war came to the Atlantic Coast in an infinitely more divisive and complex form than on the Pacific fronts.

US propaganda has represented the conflict in Nicaragua as a civil war between godless Sandinistas and a spontaneous Nicaraguan resistance. For most of Nicaragua, this is not true: the major Contra force, the FDN, was largely created by the CIA out of the ruins of Somoza's National Guard. But on the Atlantic Coast the conflict has taken on some of the characteristics of a real civil war, with a large proportion of the indigenous population taking up arms against the government, and families' and communities' loyalties completely divided. In 1981 Myrna Cunningham was kidnapped and raped by the Contra, a particularly horrific experience because it was carried out not by some anonymous foreign mercenaries or Somocista National Guard but by members of her own tribe — virtually members of her family in Miskito terms. She describes these events as follows:

> I was kidnapped on December 28th 1981, as I was leaving the hospital in Bilwaskarmas with the administrator, a nurse and a driver. Around 500 metres from the gate we were attacked by 15-20 armed men; most were Miskito although one was later recognized as an ex-National Guardsman. They tied us up and beat us; when it got dark, the nurse and I were taken into a hut. They started praying and singing religious songs, and raped us.
>
> Then we crossed the river into Honduras and walked for an hour to a camp. Some of the Miskito tried to tell us why they attacked the hospital: they said it was run by communists, that anyone who worked with the Nicaraguan government was a communist . . . We were told we would be executed, but on Nicaraguan soil, so we crossed back into Nicaragua. On the way, we were raped again, and they made us bathe in a river to remove any evidence. When we got back to Bilwaskarmas, some village elders recognized us and asked them not to kill us. They let us go free but told us to stop working there because they would continue their attacks.[12]

## A man's war

As in traditional Indian society, when the men had gone out to hunt and later to work in the mines while the women had grown subsistence crops at home, so too in the Contra war it was the men who went off to fight the Sandinistas and the women who stayed behind in the communities. This phenomenon, together with the traditional prominence of women in the indigenous cultures, probably accounts for the large number of women in top leadership positions on the Atlantic Coast. The North Atlantic Region is represented in the National Assembly by Dorothea Wilson and Hazel Lau, while Dr Myrna Cunningham is the Government Delegate. Alta Hooker is the Regional Head of the Health Ministry, and the Director of Puerto Cabezas Hospital is Dr Isabel Ramírez. Government institutions on the Coast are run almost entirely by women.

## Autonomy for the Atlantic Coast

Faced with an armed uprising of indigenous people who had sided with Nicaragua's enemies in order to claim their Indian rights, the Sandinista government responded with a bold and unprecedented step. If *costeño* people wanted autonomous control over their own government, land and resources, then the revolution would recognize the legitimacy of their claim, and without waiting for the war to end, would grant the first ever regional autonomy for indigenous people in Latin America. To this end, in 1983, an amnesty was declared for all indigenous people who gave up their arms and rejoined civilian life — with no penalties or punishment. At the same time, the government adopted a much greater sensitivity towards the various cultures on the Atlantic Coast. Trilingual education in English, Miskito, and Spanish, for example, was intro- duced. Under Somoza, only Spanish was spoken in schools.

In 1984, a massive exercise in consultative democracy began, as people put forward their demands in special, village by village meetings, thus shaping the autonomy process from the roots. The process came to fruition in 1987, when a multiethnic Assembly passed the final, painstakingly negotiated draft of the Autonomy Statute (ratified by the National Assembly in September 1987). This guarantees autonomous local control over the use of waters, forests and communal lands; education in ethnic languages; free elections to the Regional Council, with representation of all the ethnic communities; preservation of indigenous cultural heritage; control of local distribution, trade and taxes.

### Women in the Peace and Autonomy Commissions

The women of the Coast are not forgotten in the Autonomy Statute. One article specifically calls on the new autonomous government 'to promote the integration, development and participation of women in all aspects of political, social, cultural and economic life of the Region'. Indeed, the Autonomy process has given a unique shape to the development of women's organization on the Atlantic Coast.

Yet *costeña* women did not wait for the implementation of any law to become involved in the peace and autonomy process. As early as 1985, Miskito women acting as 'popular promoters' in the Autonomy consul- tation had suggested setting up 'Dialogue for Peace Commissions'. Their idea was to establish committees of trusted local people to take responsibility for keeping communications open with armed Indians who had left their communities and joined Contra groups. It was envisaged that the Commissions would encourage insurgents to aban- don their arms, by explaining the amnesty terms and the Autonomy proposals. The genius of the women's idea was that the Commissions, formed within the indigenous communities, would be able to make use of the most reliable intelligence information — direct contact through the Indian fighters' families.

When relatives indicated an interest in taking up amnesty, or pro-peace commanders in discussing ceasefires [explains Atlantic Coast researcher, Jane Freeland] the Dialogue Commissions would seek informal support through a Miskito minister such as Hazel Lau. In this way, an unbroken chain was established between personal contacts and official channels.[13]

By May 1986, the women's work was so successful that the informal local committees were officially constitued into fully elected 'Peace and Autonomy Commissions'. Within a year, 96 of the 120 Miskito communities in the Northern Atlantic region had elected their own Peace and Autonomy Commissions, 70% of whose members were women. Since then women have crossed the border into Honduras and visited Contra camps to talk their menfolk into coming home and testing the government's autonomy proposals. Susana Morley, a *costeña* woman, describes one such expedition:

> One example is Compañero Juan Salgado, who's now in the Indigenous Militias for Peace. His wife went off up into the mountain with her children, to tell him to come home because the children missed him. As a woman, she told him to come back and reintegrate into society.[14]

The work of the Commissions is very dangerous. In 1987 an entire Commission from one of the coastal communities was kidnapped by the fifth Battalion of the Honduran army and held prisoner for three months.

As time went on, the Commissions began to take on a wider local role (in keeping with their place in the development of Autonomy), organizing health and education campaigns, similar to those of the locally based Sandinista Defence Committees on the Pacific Coast. After the signing of the Esquipulas Peace Plan in 1987, the amnesty was extended and the number of men returning from Contra camps increased rapidly. Myrna Cunningham describes the scope of their work:

> Autonomy created something like a bridge of confidence between the people and the government; it helped us stop the war. The Peace and Autonomy Commissions are made up of the natural leaders from the community elected freely by the people. The Commissions have three special kinds of work to do. The first is to find the armed fighters and convince them to enter into a dialogue and sign ceasefire agreements . . . In the struggle for peace, these talks are very complex, because there's no special leader amongst these armed fighters. They're all chiefs — anyone that has 10 men under him is a chief — so we signed over 20 ceasefire agreements. And you have to have meetings every week, because signing the casefire agreement is just the initial step. It doesn't mean much, because they don't give up their arms . . . They sign a paper accepting that they're part of

the Nicaraguan army, the Popular Army. Then you have to meet them, sometimes every day. You have to explain everything to them, you have eternal talks. Sometimes when they are back in the community, fighting groups come in and tell them, 'don't listen to the government, take these dollars'. So they go to the Commissions and say, 'the war group is telling us this. Is it true?'. . . This all drains energy from everyone, but it's advancing.

The Commissions also have to explain the Autonomy process to their communities. This involves organizing training courses and meetings to discuss the law and how each article will be applied. The third task of the Commissions is to guarantee that [everything] to do with production, health, and education is being done. The Commission members don't get any salary, they are voluntary workers . . . Every two months, they inform the government of any problems their community is having and what they have been doing. We have over 1,600 members of the Peace and Autonomy Commissions, in the different communities . . . they're a local communal form of government.[15]

*Costeña* women also participate actively in defence, as highlighted in December 1987 when the Contra launched their biggest attack ever on the North Atlantic mining town of Bonanza. The women's battalion of the local Popular Militia played an important role in repelling the Contra on this occasion. A considerable number of women have also had experience in the Reserves of the Sandinista Army. According to one woman soldier, they have sometimes been mobilized to the frontier (which has hardly ever happened to women reservists on the Pacific Coast).[16]

## *Costeña* Women's Movement for Peace

It was as a result of the invaluable and risky work of bringing about peace by personally confronting the men who were fighting the war and offering them a practical alternative, that the Atlantic Coast Women's Movement sprang up in the North Atlantic Region. The importance of the Peace Movement in creating the conditions for the Women's Movement may be reflected in the fact that women's organization has not developed to the same extent in the southern region of the Atlantic Coast, where the indigenous people did not take up arms. Susana Morley, a Miskito woman from the Río Coco, training teachers in Puerto Cabezas, takes up the story:

In whatever task, we women have been in the majority. Since the evacuation [from the Río Coco] in 1982, the women in the resettlement camps have seen the need to organize themselves, but there was no possibility because there have been so many military attacks . . . When we went back to the Río Coco in 1985, many of us who are working indigenous women, at some time or another have thought to have a strong women's organization . . . so we could do things for the children, for society, for our homes. But with the family partly here, partly in Honduras, it was all impossible, there were so many attacks . . . We had no houses, we were in the rain, muddy, looking for a way to make a humble roof to cover the women and children . . . It undermined any good ideas we had, we were struggling to live, to survive, you couldn't even think. There was just fear and terror.

But with the movement of dialogue for peace, when the women went up into the mountains looking for their husbands and sons, to make them give up their arms and reintegrate into the new society, to become new men in the struggle for indigenous rights, for the interests of our own children, which is the fundamental happiness of our homes, in all this we saw with pride that women really are important. As time passed, indigenous women learned more, and started to think that we could do anything, just as well as the men, or maybe better than the men in a way, because I believe we are strong. We'd do anything, even if it means clinging on by our fingernails . . . The Peace Commissions were begun by women, by the relatives of armed insurgents. We've done everything to get the Miskito *compañeros* to disarm, because we feel the need for it in our own women's flesh and blood.

So when we came to 1987 we saw the idea of a women's organization with much more solid determination. We said to the Regional government . . . 'We need a unifying women's organization for the North Atlantic Region.' Compañera Dorothea Wilson was at the head of this work. She brought some of us to the Pacific Coast so we could identify with the courage of the women there. Some of us from the Río Coco, Puerto Cabezas, and the outlying coast went to Managua for the 8th of March, International Women's Day.[17]

Susana Morley was involved in organizing the inaugural meeting of Costeña Women for Peace, held in Puerto Cabezas in September 1987, only weeks after the Autonomy Statute became law. Over 100 women met for two days with delegations from the Río Coco, the mining communities, Tasba Pri resettlement camp, and the *barrios* of Puerto Cabezas itself.

When I was mobilizing women for the meeting in Puerto Cabezas . . . they got enthusiastic. Other times we've called meetings and they've said they're tired of meetings . . . but now the women want to unite . . . I feel very happy as a woman to be part of this organization, and I'd like to say that we women make everything possible with our work. Sometimes I see that we get downhearted, 'Look, *compañera*,' I say, 'we have to keep struggling as indigenous women. If we don't do everything, we won't do anything.' I give them support, look for ways to solve our problems, put proposals to the government. That's how the Costeña Women's Movement for Peace came about.[18]

Out of the inaugural meeting, the 'Nidia White' North Atlantic Coast Women's Movement was born. The women's priority was peace. Their first annual report read:

From every sector the unifying desire is for a real and lasting peace, the reunification of the family and repatriation . . . The constant concern is to maintain dialogue and make efforts to convince our relatives to lay down their arms.[19]

The women also demanded training: indigenous language classes, health education, courses in women's and indigenous rights, and personal development. Susana Morley stresses the economic basis of these demands:

The most fundamental thing is training for women. We need education . . . so that women are not left and forgotten but grow in knowledge and go on learning . . . because here in the North Atlantic there are no factories, nowhere for women to work, that's why there's so much prostitution. The women on the Río Coco farm, but with the tension of the war they tend to stay in the house with the children, maybe longing to work. One *compañera* from Cuwitun said to me 'I'm an old woman but I like this movement. In my day you couldn't do this sort of thing, but I'm still strong and I want to work.' The profound feeling of women here is that they want to have an educational base and a way of earning their own living.[20]

One hundred *costeña* women met at the second Regional Women's Assembly in Yulu in May 1988. Here the movement adopted a formal structure, led by a group of seven women, with a total of 23 responsible for organizing the zones of Puerto Cabezas, the Río Coco, and the mining communities.

By the end of the first year, the 'Nidia White' movement had set up branches in the *barrios* of Puerto Cabezas, and some of the communities in the Río Coco and Bonanza. They had organized civil defence workshops, mini-literacy crusades for Sumu and Miskito women, workshops for community midwives in the Río Coco, and medical assistance and therapy for prostitutes in the mining areas, with a view to reintegration into the community. They had pushed for women's participation in communal activities, such as school building, family allotments, street cleaning, and church building. They had held discussions on disarming the Contra, the Autonomy Law and the role of women's organizations.

Their plans for 1989 included setting up a women's centre in Puerto Cabezas and the recruitment of more women for technical jobs in the gold and silver mines. The groundwork for the latter had already been laid by the Cristina Rugama Organization of Patriotic Women in Bonanza, who had succeeded in persuading the mines' management to take on 31 women out of a mining workforce of 826.[21]

The significance of women's organization on the Coast is outlined by Dorothea Wilson, previously the Atlantic Coast representative on AMNLAE's National Executive and more recently a central catalyst in the birth of the new *costeña* women's movement:

> The forceful presence of women in the Peace Commissions is not just due to the circumstance that only women and old people remained in the communities when the Commissions were organized. It reflects women's decision-making power, and the faith men place in them . . . Giving women jobs normally reserved for men, in self-defence co-operatives and in the mines, is a return to the traditional indigenous division of labour. This will be the policy of the Nidia White women's movement, which was given life in the struggle for peace. The women's movement is a reflection of the process of peace, of repatriation and reunification of the family. Thus for the women of the six ethnic groups, peace becomes the point of departure for their demands as women. Just as Autonomy had its enemies in imperialism and the Contra, so the women's movement will also have enemies, who take sexist positions.[22]

Susana Morley can testify that the women's movement faces local opposition — in her case from her own husband:

> I have to teach my students and work on this women's meeting and get my children's food and clothes for them to wear to school, so after working all day I come home at night and he says, 'Where the hell have you been? Who do you think you are? Do you think you have balls?' I say, 'Listen, this is the indigenous women's struggle and I am thinking about the welfare of the children, the future; you think you're equal but you go out and drink rum and come home to sleep without even asking what I've been doing. You don't worry about what happens to the children, no, I'm in this women's movement, but I think about everything, the children, getting food to eat . . . So you're wearing the trousers? I'll wear them if you like.' There are other *compañeras* who are widows and don't have this kind of problem, but other women with husbands have told me they have the same experience.[23]

## Women of the South Atlantic Coast

The organized role of women on the Atlantic Coast has been most prominent in the northern region. But in the southern region, which includes Bluefields, and where a higher percentage of the population are Creoles, there are now early indications of women's organization, particularly around training and issues relating to women's economic situation. A fledgling Women's Movement of the South Atlantic Autonomous Region, with close links to Sandinista bodies, is hoping to set up some sewing collectives. Around 100 women have participated in this new movement. While their aim may sound very modest, it must be placed within the context of Hurricane Joan which flattened the entire south Atlantic Coast region in September 1988. Under these circumstances, sheer survival followed by reconstruction have inevitably taken priority. On the other hand, it may have been the collective efforts of the South Atlantic peoples to rebuild their communities that provided the impetus for the new women's movement.

## Conclusion

The existence of an active women's movement in the North Atlantic Autonomous Region does not mean that the obstacles facing women will disappear overnight, any more than the Autonomy process is an instant solution to the Coast's problems of chronic underdevelopment. But the women's organization does provide a framework in which their problems can be addressed by indigenous women themselves — just as Autonomy offers a structure for Nicaragua's ethnic minorities to take on their own self-government within the Nicaraguan revolution. Hurricane Joan, hitting Nicaragua's Atlantic Coast, virtually destroyed the town of Bluefields and once again tragically set back the development of the Coast. Paradoxically, however, even natural disaster held some seeds of optimism: the success of the evacuation and rebuilding operations brought with it a renewed faith in the values of communal co-operation.

## Notes

1. Dorothea Wilson, interview in *Documentos sobre la mujer*, CIRA, April–September 1988.
2. Dorothea Wilson, interview in *Amanecer*, July–August 1988.
3. Freeland, 1988, p. 31.
4. Myrna Cunningham, interviewed by Helen Collinson and Jean Somers, October 1988, unpublished.
5. Dionisia Frank López, in Angel & Macintosh, 1987, p. 32.
6. Dorothea Wilson, interview in *Documentos sobre la mujer*, op. cit.
7. Mildred Levy, in Angel & Macintosh, 1987, p. 48.
8. Dorothea Wilson, interview in *Documentos sobre la mujer*, op cit.
9. Myrna Cunningham, quoted in *Nicaraguan Perspectives*, Nicaragua Information Center, California, Summer 1984.
10. Hazel Lau, in Angel & Macintosh, 1987, p. 52.

11. Mary Bushey, quoted in Alison Rooper & Hazel Smith, 'From Nationalism to Autonomy: the ethnic question in the Nicaraguan revolution', in *Race & Class*, Vol. XXVII, No. 4, 1986.

12. Myrna Cunningham, quoted in *Nicaraguan Perspectives*, op. cit.

13. Freeland, 1988, p. 75.

14. Susana Morley, interviewed by MIREN (Mujeres Internacionalistas Residentes en Nicaragua), September 1987, unpublished.

15. Myrna Cunningham, interview with Helen Collinson and Jean Somers, op. cit.

16. Gloria María Altamirano, of the Organización de Mujeres Patrióticas Cristina Rugama, interviewed by MIREN, September 1987, unpublished.

17. Susana Morley, op. cit.

18. Ibid.

19. Nidia White North Atlantic Women's Movement Annual Report, 1987–88.

20. Susana Morley, op. cit.

21. Nidia White Report, op. cit.

22. Dorothea Wilson, interview in *Documentos de la mujer*, op. cit.

23. Susana Morley, op. cit.

# Conclusion

## 1990 elections

On 25 February 1990, Nicaragua goes to the polls in the second general election since the 1979 Triumph. Because our study was completed before this date, the results of the election were not known at the time of writing. But despite widespread predictions that the FSLN would gain a sound victory over the US-backed UNO coalition, it was clear to the authors of this study that support among women for the Sandinistas was far from unanimous.

Undoubtedly, there is disillusionment in some quarters with the FSLN's ability to restore peace and economic security. After eight years of Contra war and economic blockade, material standards of living for the majority of the population have dropped well below pre-1979 levels, by as much as 90%, according to some sources.[1] Even such basic services as free health care and education, introduced by the Revolution, have been seriously eroded. Women have been particularly affected by these setbacks as it is they who are primarily responsible for housekeeping, childrearing, and for the general well-being of their families. Some women on the fringes of the revolutionary process may have come to associate the FSLN with the war and economic hardship of the past eight years. Many will be sorely tempted by promises from Washington that if UNO wins the elections, the US trade embargo will be lifted and millions of dollars will start flowing into the country. Hunger and exhaustion may thus drive some previous FSLN voters towards the opposing camp.

Despite the involvement of various Contra leaders in the UNO campaign, the coalition's presidential candidate, Violeta Chamorro, may be an acceptable option for a large number of Nicaraguans who no longer agree with the Sandinistas' policies but who would never support a return to the repressive Somocista system of the past. Chamorro's husband — the famous newspaper editor, Pedro Joaquín Chamorro — was killed by Somoza's National Guard; as a result, Violeta can identify with the thousands of Nicaraguan women who lost loved ones in the struggle against the hated dictator. UNO has also made much of

Chamorro's image as the traditional Nicaraguan mother — motherhood, as we have shown in our study, has deep-seated social and emotional meaning in Nicaragua. Just as she has apparently secured peace between the politically diverse members of her own family, declares UNO, so will she unite the national 'family' of war-torn Nicaragua.

## Leadership

Leaving aside Violeta Chamorro, relatively few women candidates are standing in the 1990 general election. Only 19% of the candidates expected to win seats in the National Assembly are women and only 11% of those standing as 'reserve' candidates are women.[2] These figures are much higher than the corresponding proportion of women MPs in the British House of Commons, but in Nicaragua, they have been regarded as disappointing (by AMNLAE) in view of women's massive participation in grassroots political activities. They signify a reduction since the previous Nicaraguan elections in 1984.

These figures should come as no surprise. The number of women who are national leaders in the trade unions is equally small. Very few state-farm managements include women and few agricultural co-operatives have elected women presidents. These facts reflect the age-old obstacles that still prevent women in Nicaragua from putting themselves forward as potential leaders, amongst which a lack of confidence, childcare problems and the attitudes of *machista* husbands figure highly.

Amongst Sandinistas, it is widely held that the 'new man' of revolutionary Nicaragua is equally capable of furthering women's interests as are the women themselves, and that the elimination of the oppression of women is the responsibility of society as a whole. Consequently, the task of influencing male politicians and telling them what women's demands are takes precedence over getting women elected to the National Assembly or appointed to leadership positions in government or trade unions. For example, the *Proclama* of 1987 — the FSLN's official declaration of the need to fight against the specific oppression of women — followed a long campaign by women active in the FSLN, AMNLAE, and by the trade union women's sections, not to displace the male leaders of the FSLN, but to change the consciousness of these leaders.

As one Sandinista woman once pointed out, the last ten years in Britain have shown that women in power do not always further women's interests.[3] Similarly, it is questionable whether Violeta Chamorro, with her emphasis on traditional family 'morals', will really encourage greater equality between men and women. Indeed, the Contra leaders connected with UNO are renowned for their overbearing *machismo* and for their violent acts against women during the war.

## Women and popular democracy

A more meaningful indication of women's participation in politics is their involvement in various revolutionary activities and mass organizations. Here, their presence has been dynamic and startling, especially in view of the time they have had to devote to ensuring their families' sheer survival. Women have made up the majority of activists in the health and literacy brigades, and in the local Sandinista Defence Committees; on the Atlantic Coast, they have been the driving force behind the peace and autonomy process; throughout the war, Mothers of Heroes and Martyrs, and more recently, the Mothers of the Kidnapped, have been a focal point for the non-military struggle against the Contra; and up and down the country AMNLAE has mobilized thousands of women in the revolutionary process. At the height of the Contra war, women predominated in the workforce, forming the backbone of the economic defence of the Revolution. Their increased involvement in the economy also led to a massive expansion of their role in the trade unions; all the major Sandinista trade unions can now boast vocal women's sections.

The impact of this participation on government policy has been considerable, as witnessed by the 1987 FSLN *Proclama* on women's emancipation. Active pressure from below has led to an official recognition of the unique oppression afflicting women, and to the creation of a space specifically for them within the mainstream revolutionary movement. Fora such as the trade union women's assemblies, the AMNLAE Face the People meetings, the women's open meetings in 1985, and the Fundamental Forces meetings in 1989, the various workshops and assemblies organized by the trade union women's sections, have all enabled women confidently to assert their influence on the political process.

## The cult of the beauty contest

Nicaraguan women activists agree that a major revolutionary gain over the past ten years has been the Sandinista government's institution of a whole range of laws aiming to protect women's rights; but putting these laws into practice has often been problematic. Sandinista policies have been successful in those instances in which the government has acted on popular pressure from below. Policies implemented from above without consultation have invariably floundered, as in the case of some legislation introduced in the early years of the revolution. Still reeling from the decadence of the Somoza regime, the FSLN leaders moved quickly after the Triumph to outlaw prostitution and the objectification of women's bodies in advertising. Yet unless the attitudes that prompted Nicaraguan men to indulge in these practices were changed, such laws were worth little more than the paper they were written on. 'There has never been an attempt to fully challenge the idea that women should be judged on the basis of their physical appearance,' comments one British worker in Managua.[4] In the initial enthusiasm for the revolution, most progressive Nicaraguan men willingly accepted that such amusements as pornographic magazines and beauty contests were 'bourgeois' and should be eschewed. But, as the years of war and economic hardship dragged on, they sought distractions to relieve the strain and despair of the national situation.

Prostitution therefore increased slightly, the popularity of the 'Erotic Humour' section of *Semana Comica* rose and, above all, there was an explosion of the beauty contest cult. Recent articles in the press have dismissed the self-censorship of the revolution's early years as too austere and at odds with 'human nature'. Since then, argues one journalist, Nicaraguan society has come to realize that to acknowledge 'beauty' in women's bodies is a respectable cultural pursuit.[5]

Sandinista leaders seem to have taken a similar position, making great efforts to satisfy popular appetite by incorporating beauty contests into the FSLN's routine activities, including the election campaign. In October 1989, one of the main attractions at the inauguration of a new FSLN campaign office in Managua was a catwalk appearance by the local 'beauty queen' wearing a skimpy swimsuit.[6] Even some Sandinista women have succumbed to the 'beauty' fever: in September 1989, a competition was organized to elect a 'queen' of AMNLAE.[7] Daniel Ortega adopted a new image, described in Nicaragua as the 'spurred gamecock' — in November 1989, for example, photographs appeared in the pro-Sandinista press of the President embracing a group of contestants for Miss Sandinista Youth '89.[8] Not all Sandinista women have responded positiviely to these events. AMNLAE activist Berta Ines Cabrales, replying to claims that the new casanova Ortega was likely to win more female votes than in previous elections, commented, 'We'll get women's votes, not because of Daniel's physical image but because of the rights they've won during the past ten years.'[9]

It could be argued that beauty contests in themselves are quite innocuous compared to the hard porn widely available in Europe or the USA. But in Nicaragua, the official, government objectification of women's bodies may be encouraging the growth of a more sinister, more misogynous form of objectification. Despite the ban on the commercialization of women's bodies in advertising, one security company has chosen a graphic image of a scantily clad woman in chains to promote its new range of locks; pornographic films are now screened in some Managua cinemas. Ironically, the emergence of these phenomena coincided with a series of disturbing articles in an outraged Sandinista press, about the rape of a Nicaraguan woman by 100 men in a Honduran Contra camp.[10]

# Women and ideological liberation

As this study has demonstrated, Nicaraguan women's liberation — at least on the ideological front — is in a constant state of flux. Retreats in one area are invariably offset by advances in others. The dearth of women political leaders, for example, needs to be offset against women's active participation in the Revolution's mass organizations. Also, the slight increase in prostitution in Managua was accompanied by a recognition that, basically, general social attitudes, and not the prostitutes themselves, were responsible.

Meanwhile, the recurrence of the objectification of women's bodies coincided more positively with a major national debate, in the late 1980s, on rape, domestic violence and child abuse, resulting in an AMNLAE campaign to tighten the law on these issues. More liberal and open attitudes towards sex have also developed; women's sexual pleasure, sex education and reproductive rights are now routinely discussed in the Nicaraguan media and within the various mass organizations; the FSLN has promised to fight in the National Assembly for the decriminalization of abortion; and, at various trade union meetings in the late 1980s, women frequently demanded improved availability of contraception. Meanwhile, the first issue of a new youth supplement to *Barricada*, in November 1989, focused on sexual relationships, largely from a woman's point of view.[11] Homosexuality is also more openly discussed; for example, in an electoral poll in October 1989, voters were asked if they thought that homosexuals should have the same political, employment, and civil rights as everyone else; 71% replied in the affirmative.[12]

Increased sexism in the media likewise needs to be balanced with the constant growth of a feminist consciousness at the grassroots. The mushrooming of AMNLAE women's centres in several Managua *barrios* and in other Nicaraguan towns during 1989, for example, has provided a new space for women to discuss common problems and formulate strategies. These centres have also encouraged a decentralization of AMNLAE's bureaucratic structure, thus improving the movement's accessibility to working-class women. Outside AMNLAE, there has been a rising incidence of women taking their own action independently of official structures; in some *barrios* in Managua, housewives have started to organize their own workshops and support networks around issues such as domestic violence. Another indication of the growing confidence of the Nicaraguan women's movement is AMNLAE's official acceptance of the word 'feminism'. In September 1989, Doris Tijerino, acting General Secretary of AMNLAE, declared:

> In Nicaragua there has been, there is, and there will be, a Sandinista feminism, a feminism which says to women that we are equal human beings, we have equal rights and work and education opportunities.[13]

Until recently AMNLAE would not have dared to use the term 'feminist', in fear of being accused of creating divisions between men and women or of aping Western feminists.

At the time of writing, it is difficult to assess exactly the kind of feminism AMNLAE intends to adopt or how meaningful AMNLAE's future role will be, either in Nicaragua as a whole, or, more specifically, in the Nicaraguan women's movement. During the election campaign, AMNLAE's sole priority was to mobilize women in support of the FSLN; all other national work was suspended. AMNLAE's focus on FSLN objectives could be criticized as a diversion from its focus on women's issues; conversely, this preoccupation was clearly in the interest of the majority of Nicaraguan women, whose future emancipation depends, to some extent, on an FSLN victory. A return to the right-wing, US-dominated character of past regimes would jeopardize almost all the legal, ideological and social advances women have made since 1979.

## The impact of war on women's liberation

We have been particularly impressed by the contradictory nature of Nicaraguan women's advances over the past ten years, as we have demonstrated. The effects of the US-backed Contra war are a classic example of this. Women have suffered from the erosion of social programmes caused by the diversion of resources to the war effort, and it was they who had benefited most from the new health, education, and housing programmes of the early 1980s. Women have also lost loved ones in the fighting and borne the brunt of caring for family members wounded or mutilated in Contra attacks. The daily struggle to survive the war-induced shortages of basic goods and foodstuffs likewise fell on women's shoulders; while the increasing dependence of the economy on women's production in the mid-1980s, necessitated by men's conscription, merely added to women's daily burden.

Nevertheless, the war may also have contributed to an acceleration in women's emancipation. For example, in common with other wars, elsewhere in the world, women's increased participation in full-time employment has enabled them to move into jobs and areas of the economy previously barred to them. As a result, rural women in particular have played a more visible and self-confident role in the economy and have achieved greater economic and emotional independence from male partners.

Additionally, the public recognition that 'women now feed the nation' seems to have led to their specific demands being seen as an official priority, as witnessed by the FSLN *Proclama* of 1987. Moreover, the concern to solve women's specific problems in order to increase production in a war economy forced trade unions to create space for women in order to discuss their problems. And thus rural women, many of whom had previously remained isolated from each other and from the revolutionary process, were encouraged not only to involve themselves in revolutionary activities but to share and assess their personal experiences with other women.

Finally, it may be that the inability of the war-battered Revolution to meet women's material demands shifted the national agenda of women's oppression towards more fundamental ideological issues. For example, a lack of resources has made childcare provision for all women workers impossible; similarly, attempts to socialize some domestic tasks through communal laundries and corn mills have been uneven and piecemeal. Thus, solutions to relieve women of their domestic burden, to enable them to work outside the home, had to be found within the family. Housework and childcare, it was argued, must be shared between all the family, including men. But because of most men's lingering sexist attitudes, some obstacles to an equitable division of household tasks also had to be explored along the way. The end result was a thorough analysis of relations inside the family, leading to discussions on such issues as domestic violence, rape, paternal irresponsibility, child abuse, and reproductive rights.

The key question is whether an end to the war will arrest these ideological discussions and reverse women's newly found role in the workforce. In post-war situations elsewhere, the return of the men from the front and the desire to recreate pre-war 'normality' have forced women back into the home and the family sphere. To some extent, this has also been the case in Nicaragua; with regard to employment, it is clear that as the Contra war abated over eighteen months prior to the general election, more women than men lost their jobs. But the Revolution has created a more positive vision for the future than did the aftermath of the Second World War. It has enabled Nicaraguan women to build a space in which to assert their demands and influence the political process. To find a government anywhere in the world more willing than the Sandinista government to listen to women's demands would be virtually impossible. Through their political participation in the Revolution, women have also developed the self-confidence to defend their position and have learned how to organize themselves, as women, within the wider movement for social change. Anyone who tries to turn back this tide will meet with a force which, in the words of Nicaraguan poet, Gioconda Belli, continues to grow:

> beat by beat
> stronger
> stronger
> stronger.[14]

# Notes

1. Figure quoted in *Weekend Guardian*, 10 February 1990.
2. *La Crónica*, 8–14 November 1989. 'Reserve' deputies (*suplentes*) act as assistants to the principal deputies and will deputize for them in the National Assembly if necessary.
3. Heliette Ehlers speaking in London, May 1987.
4. Veronica Campanile, interviewed by Helen Collinson and Elaine Ginsburg, January 1990 (unpublished).
5. *El Nuevo Diario*, 16 September 1989.
6. *El Nuevo Diario*, 10 October 1989.
7. *El Nuevo Diario*, 29 September 1989.
8. *El Nuevo Diario*, 25 November 1989.
9. Berta Ines Cabrales, quoted in *Barricada Internacional*, 20 January 1990.
10. *Barricada*, 28–31 August 1989.
11. *Gente*, 29 November 1989.
12. *Barricada Internacional*, 20 January 1990.
13. *Barricada*, 11 September 1989
14. From a poem by Gioconda Belli.

# Bibliography

## Books and pamphlets

Amanecida Collective (1987) *Revolutionary Forgiveness: Feminist Reflections on Nicaragua*, New York, Orbis.

AMNLAE (1988) *Platform of Struggle*, Managua.

Angel, Adriana & Macintosh, Fiona (1987) *The Tiger's Milk: Women of Nicaragua*, London, Virago.

Aria, Pilar (1980) *Nicaragua Revolución: Relatos de Combatientes Del Frente Sandinista*, Mexico City, Siglo XXI SA.

ATC (1985) *Revolución y Mujeres del Campo: El Impacto de la Reforma Agraria Sandinista sobre la Subordinación de la Mujer Rural'*, Managua.

Benjamin, Medea (ed. and translated) (1987) *Don't be afraid Gringo: A Honduran Woman Speaks from the Heart. The Story of Elvia Elvarado*, San Francisco, Institute for Food and Development Policy.

Black, George (1981) *The Triumph of the People*, London, Zed Press.

CIERA (1984) *La Mujer en las Cooperativas Agropecuarias en Nicaragua*, Managua.

CIIR (1988) *Right to Survive: Human Rights in Nicaragua*, London.

Cabestrero, Teofilo (1983) *Revolutionaries for the Gospel* New York, Orbis. (English Translation 1986.)

Close, David (1988) *Politics, Economics and Society*, London, Pinter Publishers.

Deighton, Jane *et al* (1983) *Sweet Ramparts: Women in Revolutionary Nicaragua*, London, War on Want and Nicaragua Solidarity Campaign.

Eich, Dieter and Rincon, Carlos (1984) *The Contras: Interviews with Anti-Sandinistas*, San Francisco, Synthesis Publications.

Freeland, Jane (1988) *A Special Place in History*, London, Nicaragua Solidarity Campaign.

Harris, Hermione (1988), 'Women and War; The Case of Nicaragua', in *Women and the Military System*, Eva Isaksson (ed) London, Harvester/Wheatsheaf.

Haslam, David (1987) *Faith in the Struggle*, London, Epworth Press.

INIES, *Cuadernos de Investigación*, Managua.

Kovel, Joel (1988) *In Nicaragua*, London, Free Association Books.

Massey, Doreen (1987) *Contemporary Issues in Science — Nicaragua*, London, Open University Press.

Melrose, Diana (1985) *Nicaragua: The Threat of a Good Example*, Oxford, Oxfam.

Molyneux, Maxine (1985), 'Women', in (ed) Thomas Walker, *Nicaragua: The First 5 Years*

Pérez, Paola and Siu, Ivonne (1986) *Cambios y Desafios: La Mujer en la Economía Nicaragüense*, Managua, OGM.

*Race and Class* (1986) XXVII, 41, London, Institute of Race Relations.

Randall, Margaret (1981) *Sandino's Daughters*, London, Zed Press.

Robinson, William I. and Norsworthy, Kent (1987) *David and Goliath: Washington's War against Nicaragua*, London, Zed Books.

Rooper, Alison (1987), *Fragile Victory: A Nicaraguan Community at War*, London, Weidenfeld.

Sola, Roser & Trayner Ma Pau (1988) *Ser Madre en Nicaragua: Testimonios de una Historia no Escrita*, Barcelona, Editorial Nueva Nicaragua/Icaria.

*Third World Quarterly* vol. 5, no. 4, London, Third World Foundation.

UNAG, (1987) *La participación de la mujer en la producción*, Managua.

Warner, Marina (1985) *Alone of All Her Sex: Cult of the Virgin Mary*, London, Picador.

'Women's Study Tour Report 1987', (1988) London, Nicaragua Solidarity Campaign.

Woroniuk, Beth (1987) *Women's Oppression and the Revolution — The Nicaraguan Debate*, Ottawa, CUSO Occasional Paper. (December)

World University Service (1988) *Less Arms, More Education*, London, WUS.

## Newspapers/magazines

Amanecer (Nicaragua)

ANN: Women in Central America Bulletin

Barricada/Barricada Internacional (Nicaragua — FSLN newspaper)

Central American Historical Update (UK)

Central American Monitor (UK)

CEPAD newsletter (Nicaragua)

Cuadernos de Investigación (Nicaragua — INIES)

Encuentro

El Nuevo Diario (Nicaragua — pro-Sandinista newspaper)

Envío (Nicaragua)

Intercontinental Press (USA)

International Socialist Review (USA)

The Militant (USA)

Nicaragua Today (UK)
Pensamientos Propios (Nicaragua)
Revolución y Desarrollo (Nicaragua — MIDINRA)
Somos (Nicaragua — AMNLAE)
Tayacan (Nicaragua)
Ventana (Nicaragua — Barricada)

# Index